Dead Reckoning:

A Reminiscence of Life

During the Golden Age of Aviation

By

Captain Sture Vivien Sigfred Sr.

and

Eugene M. McAvoy

ISBN: 1-4033-8735-4 (E-book)
ISBN: 1-4033-8736-2 (Paperback)
ISBN: 1-4033-8737-0 (Dustjacket)

Library of Congress Control Number: 2002095288

This book is printed on acid free paper.

Printed in the United States of America
Bloomington, IN

1stBooks - rev. 7/21/03

This book is dedicated to my wife,
Mildred Sigfred.
"Thank you, Mom, for everything."

Sture V. Sigfred Sr.
1900-1998

Dead reckoning is the method of determining a position by keeping an account, or reckoning, of the course and distance from a previous known position called the *point of departure*. Some dead reckoning is ordinarily required whether or not other methods [of navigation] are used.

P.V.H. Weems
Air Navigation
1931

Contents

Acknowledgments

Though the admission rings of cliché, it does bear repeating that no endeavor of this magnitude is ever completed by an individual, or even two – as were required for most of this project. So I wish to thank several people for support and assistance without which this book would never have been finished. Mr. Larry E. Horne for expending the time and patience to show me how a plane works and for his explanation and blessedly calm demonstration of control surfaces. Dr. Michael Pearson, Director of the Creative Writing Program at Old Dominion University, for passing on to a novice the opportunity to tell this story. Don and Maxine Allert for the hours they spent uncovering the history of the Sigfrid family, without which much of the information in this book might have been incorrect. Pan Am Check Flight Engineer Paul Ryden for his deciphering of many of the nuances of Sture's stories and for his forthright criticism. Temple West for continuing editorial and artistic advice. Janet Peery for teaching me and continually reminding me of what truly makes a story. The countless authors of books about the history of aviation whose works helped fill the voids in my research, most notably Ralph O'Neill for *A Dream of Eagles* and Robert Daley for *An American Saga: Juan Trippe and His Pan Am Empire*. Dr. Sture Sigfred Jr. for patience, understanding and support, and for showing me what the relationship between a father and son can really be. Marc Neidlinger for emotional, spiritual, and economic support. I am in his debt for this and much more. Of course, Captain Sture Vivien Sigfred for sharing his stories with me in the still hours of dusk – both literal and figurative; for repeatedly and patiently explaining what I could not understand; and for demonstrating dignity, humility and a greatness of spirit that had little to do with professional achievement. And finally, Mildred Sigfred, for remembering Sture's stories when it was too late for me to reclaim them; for poring over books and logs and letters to provide me with the smallest and yet most significant of details; for early morning coffees and late afternoon meals; for giving me the time to get it right; for helping me to get it right; and most of all, for a dear friendship I never suspected I could earn. Without her, this book would have been impossible. More importantly, without her, the life this book examines – the life of a man whose greatness must be measured and remembered by the small steps that allowed more famous men to make great leaps – would not have been as rich as, in the end, all of us realized it was.

Introduction

On the eastern bank of the Eastern Branch of the Elizabeth River, a red brick condominium rises incongruously beside the chipped, clay cobblestones of Bute Street. Though strikingly modern amidst more stately and historic neighbors, the building recalls an architect's subtle attempt to merge the old with the new, a tendency apparent throughout this neighborhood, one of the oldest in Norfolk, Virginia. The exclusive complex of homes sits on land that years ago sheltered harbor-pilots from the elements between their trips into and out of Hampton Roads, once the busiest port in the world. Long before that, it was the site of a Chesapeian Indian village, already in ruins when colonists ventured south from Jamestown to exploit its strategic location. The *Pilothouse*, as the building is now called, is a quiet and comfortable home to the successful, the aging, and the elite.

In the summer of 1995, I first met Sture and his wife Mildred Sigfred here, shortly after they had moved into the building. A quiet and friendly couple, they seemed the quintessence of grandparents: warm, wise, tolerant, and surprisingly playful – though they had no grandchildren of their own. Beset by age and Sture's declining health, they had recently relocated from their estate on the banks of the Ware River near Gloucester, to their new home around the corner from their son, Dr. Sture Sigfred, Jr. The same concern for Sture Sr.'s declining health that had prompted him to leave the home he loved so much

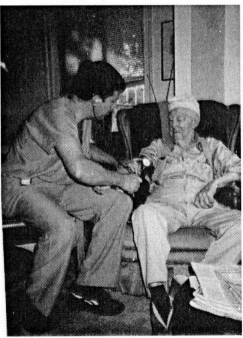

Dr. Sture "Butch" Sigfred Jr. and his father Sture Sr. Norfolk, VA. 1997.
Sigfred collection.

beside the Ware had also compelled him to begin a process he had often considered and had occasionally started, but never completed.

"You ought to write a book about your life," neighbors and friends had told him for the better part of half a century. Sture had simply nodded, vowing to do so when time allowed. But always other matters interfered. There was, it seemed for so long, time enough to tackle the project in the future. Yet, as the need for medication and the number of visits to his doctor grew, the first of half of 1995 convinced him that his time was running out. And the time had come, at last, to tell his stories. With all of the enthusiasm, attention and determination with which he attacked other challenges in his life, he pulled out old journals, sorted through aging files and photos, and scrawled new notes.

This was history. He had to get the facts right.

The task was not so difficult as he had imagined. For his entire life, he had kept meticulous records, and his home was no less than a museum of aviation, a chronicle of a life that had paralleled the growth of aviation in the United States. In the foyer rested a large teakwood desk he brought back from a flight to the Orient in the forties. On the desk stood a scale model of the Boeing B-314 *Yankee Clipper*, one of the Clipper Ships he had flown as a pilot with Pan Am. On the wall above his desk hung several black and white photos that traced many of the most significant events of his life, a life that had spanned, as he was fond of reminding visitors, almost a century: his Flight Orders from 1920; the flagship from the Navy's historic flight up the Mississippi River in 1922; an air approach to Sugarloaf Mountain in Rio de Janeiro in 1930; Sture and Mildred standing beside their Stinson in Parkers Prairie, Minnesota, in 1940; Sture relaxing in Giza during the Cairo Conference in 1944. On the wall opposite the desk hung more photos, new prints and antique lithographs of Martin M-130's, Boeing B-314's and DC-4's; a plaque bearing Sture's captain's wings from Pan American World Airways and the Air Transport Command, and other mementoes of his life in aviation.

In his study, in the center of a bookcase lining an entire wall rested a shelf containing stacks of flight logs and pilot's licenses dating back to 1920, letters and certificates, and more documents from the Golden Age of Aviation. Inside the closet were dozens of manila envelopes, neatly stacked and labeled with the years and names of locations describing their contents. Boxes of letters and photos that Mildred and Sture had not yet organized towered beside the envelopes.

On the afternoon of our first meeting, as he would for the better part of the next three years, Sture sat in a recliner in his living room, peering toward the river, as though trying to see in its current all he had known as one of the pioneers of aviation in the United States. He was a tall man, almost six feet, who, despite his ninety-five years, his friends often joked didn't look a day over seventy. Though he moved more slowly than the vibrant man who smiled from reels of aging sixteen-millimeter films stashed in the study, he still moved with focus and purpose. Asserting the single-mindedness and strength – some say stubbornness – that allowed him with only an eighth grade education to become the nineteenth most senior pilot for Pan American World Airways, he offered the chair beside him, anxious to speak.

A beige cardigan hung loosely from his shoulders, and wide suspenders held his pants up. Wisps of white hair poked at odd angles from beneath his cap. With lively eyes and a quick smile, he leaned back in his chair, adjusted his hearing aid, and without prompting, launched into a story of his first days of flight.

Hours passed, it seemed, before he took a breath. Some of the stories he had clearly memorized through repetition. Others he told for the first time, a shadow passing across his face as he remembered one friend or another who had recently passed away. In the ninety-fifth year of a life that seemed many lifetimes, Sture had already outlived most of his contemporaries. He had watched most of his coworkers from the Navy, the National Advisory Committee for Aeronautics, the New York-Rio-Buenos Aires Line, and Pan Am, diminish and die with each passing year. The more famous among them had left behind street and building names and the accumulated lore of history by which to remember them; the others had left only their families and friends and, of course, their stories. Sture was determined to leave something more to show for his time. Through longevity alone, he had ascended to the dubious position of the oldest living Pan American pilot, the last of a dying breed, and he discovered the need to speak for those with whom he had shared much of his life. For it occurred to him that he too had finally begun to succumb to mortality. So far, the struggle had proven successful.

Like Pan Am, the airline that had once adopted and finally rejected him, he kept bouncing back. But time was running out.

With long, graceful fingers, Sture punctuated his sentences. The gleam in his eyes, undimmed by cataracts that obscured his sight, recalled the young Swede who refused to let his lack of formal education keep him from achieving his dream. With a mixture of bemusement and chagrin, he shared the story of how, as a young sailor afraid to embarrass either himself or his nurse, he had lied about a scheduled surgery and ended up having his tonsils removed rather than being circumcised. Proudly he explained his design of a hoist to remove an engine from the wing of a seaplane. Resignedly he recounted being terminated from Pan Am, the company with which he developed a love-hate relationship not unlike the kind many share with their families. Yet the lines in his face and the timbre of his voice, sometimes little more than a whisper, revealed his reticence to share the names of those who had harmed him over the years, and suggested a man who had finally resolved old conflicts and resentments. He had no axe to grind; time alone had reaped a purer justice than he could ever have wished for. He was simply a man who could finally and truly appreciate having lived his dream.

In the fading light of evening, as the years of Captain Sture Sigfred's life unfolded in his stories, it became clear that he spoke, not merely to create a book, but also to relive that life, one among the many that had been necessary to shape what he called history. Yet more compellingly, he also revealed, through the stories that he embellished and those he edited, the two threads that defined his life. His story was one of having spent half of his life realizing his dream and the other half reconciling himself to its loss.

In the distance, a deep boom floated across the Elizabeth River, and the *Pilothouse* shuddered in a wave of sound. Every evening at 9:00 PM, a canon is fired at the Norfolk Naval Shipyard in Portsmouth, across the river from Sture's home. For more than 200 years, it has announced to southeastern Virginia that, in good years and bad, despite war and recession, death and plague, all is well. As though agreeing, Sture turned toward the sound of the canon, its echo waning as he squinted into shadows. Not yet finished for the evening, he grinned and raised a finger. "Did I ever tell you about my longest flight?"

I no longer hear that canon without thinking of Sture and his idea of history. In many ways, I have come to believe – as did Sture – that memory itself is history. Just as flawed, yet just as valid as the tomes we commonly accept as fact, memory is simply another way of recording of events, admittedly subjective but eerily true, and no less true for its singularity. What is history if not the search for truth, whether individual or communal, a reckoning of position among the various points we occupy over the course of time? And where can truth better reside than in the human heart?

This book, then, is a history of sorts, a reckoning of shifting positions in a single life that spanned almost a century. Where it disagrees with other recorded versions of events rapidly slipping from our collective memory, we have so noted. But we have not altered the personal truths herein, for Sture's memory and understanding of an era grown gray are most important for our purposes here. Conversations, while admittedly reconstructions, remain true to the essence of their original content. But all other claims within this book, unless specifically noted, are documented and supported with original logs, orders, legal documents and correspondence. To the extent practical, we have tried to remain true to the objectivity of history – an oxymoron, it seems to me, at best. Still, this remains, a *personal* history. For that we offer no apology.

Though the man is no longer with us, Captain Sture Vivien Sigfred's stories are as true today as they were when he lived and, finally, recalled them. Greater knowledge and refined understandings offered by time cannot change this. Truth, the emotional and visceral meaning behind experience is subjective, perhaps even skewed, and based more on individual understanding than on observation. This reminiscence, then, above all else, is one man's understanding of a brief flight through history. It is Sture's understanding of the Golden Age of Aviation.

Eugene M. McAvoy, July 2002

Part 1: Departures

Pan Am pilots and crewmembers in the first Pan Am uniform.
Miami, early 1930s. Sigfred collection.

Eugene M. McAvoy and Sture V. Sigfred Sr.

Basic Training
1918

In a belch of steam, Sture Sigfred stepped down from his train on January 8, 1919 in North Chicago, Illinois. A brisk and biting breeze sent his hat flying from his head, and his breath formed crystals of ice on his upper lip. As he chased his hat across the platform, the breeze from Lake Michigan blew even colder and harsher than the wind he had known before leaving Minneapolis. And the snow in North Chicago, he saw with more than a bit of surprise, was deeper and more tightly packed than that in Minneapolis or back home in Parkers Prairie. Though he was not quite sure exactly what he had expected from his new life in the Navy, he was sure that the cold, gray line of barracks in the distance that merged with an oppressively low sky was not it. Hurriedly, he retrieved his hat and ran to the end of the platform. There, a Petty Officer, replete in his dress blues, gathered new recruits for their march to the Naval Training Station just a mile from the depot. The young man, though formal, seemed friendly enough and nodded politely as he scanned Sture's orders.

Sture at the Great Lakes Naval Training Center, 1919.

Sigfred collection.

"Farm boy, huh? Well, at least you'll be able to carry your own pack." He glanced dismissively along the line of fresh-scrubbed faces that gathered before him. "More than I can say for some of these city boys." He nodded for Sture to join the line.

When all of the new recruits had gathered around the petty officer, he pointed toward the southeast. For the next few months, he explained, the wooden barracks they could see in the distance would be their home. The Navy would be their loving parent, and the hard-packed snow that lined their path would eventually melt, revealing a landscape that, like the *real* men inside them, would emerge strong and confident and full of the promise of the future. Almost cordially, he invited the young men to follow him.

Lake Adley in Parkers Prairie, Minnesota, beside which stood the first house John August Sigfred owned, Approximately 1908, Sigfred collection.

No sooner had the rag tag group descended the steps in front of the station and escaped the hearing of most in the depot than the petty officer began to shout. Calling them sissies, pansies and mama's boys, he demanded that they form columns and march double-time to the gates of the training center. As he called an impossibly complicated cadence, the young men stepped on each other's feet, cursed under their breath, and trudged clumsily the mile to the base. Silently, Sture wondered what he had gotten himself into. Home, he realized, was very far away.

For most of Sture's life, home had been Parkers Prairie Township in Minnesota, and as the snow swirled and recruits stumbled about him, he began to miss it more than he thought he could. At the northeast corner of Lake Adley, on a narrow plain in central Minnesota, Parkers Prairie sat at the junction of two major trails forged by pioneers early in the nineteenth century. A thriving village of six-hundred and seventy-seven in 1900, when Sture was born, the town boasted several grocery and dry-goods stores, a flour mill, a creamery, a harness shop, a shoe store and a drug store. Within a few years of Sture's birth, it had become a major stop on the railroad between St. Paul and the Canadian border, though not the hub of commerce its leaders had wished. On Main Street, horse-drawn carriages and an occasional motorcar rattled through puddles and over mounds of earth formed by the paths of westbound travelers. On the wooden sidewalks of the township, in front of the Prairie Hotel and the Johnson Brothers and Saunders General Store, young boys scurried between porch rails while their fathers sauntered between the businesses and entertainments along the walk. Women in groups of two or three held their skirts or adjusted their hats against the continuous breeze that coursed through the valley. Fanning themselves in an August heat or huddling inside bulky overcoats against a January chill, they greeted passersby with a reserved nod or smile. Their voices rose above the village din in the languages and accents of their homelands: Germany, Sweden, England, Scotland and Ireland. And despite the differences in their speech, their accents and intonations, all understood the smiles and nods that greeted them.

Just outside the township, forests of oak, birch, and popple surrounded the village and lined the banks of Lake Adley. During the winter, uncleared flatlands hibernated beneath several feet of snow and rippled outward from the lakeshore. During the spring and summer, wild roses peeked from waist-high prairie grass, and wheat swayed golden on acres of rich, dark pasture. The scent of raspberries wafted thick on afternoon breezes. To the west, the Leaf Mountains rose in a cool, blue haze from the valley floor, and to the east, miles of lakes and streams sparkled on the green carpet of the plain.

The Sigfrid family, approximately 1906. Standing left to right: Helen, John Edward, Anton, and Ebba. Sitting left to right: John August, Sture, Alpha, Berger, and Sophia. Sigfred collection.

5

On the outskirts of the township, on Wednesday, August 29, 1900, Sture Vivien Sigfred was born. While his father, John August Sigfrid, tended the wheat and potato fields that paid the rent on the old Sandstedt house where they had lived since he started his family, his mother Sophia drooped to the oak floor of her kitchen. Her friend Helen Weiberg helped her into the bedroom, and within an hour Sophia gave birth to her sixth child, Sture. The next morning, before the rest of the house stirred, she hurried about her kitchen with the child at her breast, cooking another in an endless string of breakfasts and scouring her wooden counters.

Like most of their contemporaries, John August and Sophia came from a long line of hardy Europeans. Originally from Sweden, John August had lived in the United States since 1888. After working odd jobs throughout central Minnesota for more than a year and saving every extra penny of his $1.00 per day earnings, he returned in 1890 to Furuby Hovmantrop SmΔlland, where he had been born in 1865, to claim his bride, Sophia Lindstrom, four years his junior. With Sophia in tow, he returned to Minnesota, and the couple started their family. Their first child Helen arrived on April 26, 1893, and was followed on July 30, 1894 by Ebba, whom the family nicknamed Teddy. On October 10, 1895, the couple had their first son Carl Anton, whom they called Tony, and on April 27, 1897, their second son John Edward. On January 12, 1899, their third daughter Alpha Augusta arrived.

Though more children meant that the couple would eventually have more help with the farming and household chores, a rapidly growing family also meant more mouths to feed and less room in which the others could grow. Working tirelessly to provide for his family, John August set his sights on what he believed was proof of the American dream: owning his own home.

By the time Sture was three years old, his father had accomplished his goal. In 1903, shortly after the arrival of the Soo Railroad in Parkers Prairie, he purchased forty acres of farmland southeast of the township and built the house that would shelter his family as he believed they deserved to be sheltered. For the first time since he had married Sophia, the money he earned and the harvests he reaped belonged only to him. His purchase of the home had come none too soon, for even after Sture's birth, the family continued to grow. Sture's

The Sigfrid family in front of the house beside Lake Adley, approximately 1908. Left to right: Aaron, Berger, Sture, Alpha, Anton, John Edward, Ebba, Helen, Sophia and John August. Sigfred collection.

brother Berger was born on April 2, 1902; his brother Jacob, who did not live through his first day, on January 25, 1904, and his brother Aaron Werner on July 1, 1905.

Shaped in an "L," the house seemed a mansion to Sture. Though it lacked inside plumbing and electricity, still a luxury reserved for the very rich, the home was equipped with a wood burning stove and registers that conducted heat along the floors of both stories of the house. With a living room and dining room adjacent to the parents' bedroom in the main downstairs section, and a kitchen to the side, the family area proved large enough for the couple and their eight children to gather for meals and regular prayers. It was large enough, also, for Sture's brother Edward to occasionally strap bars of soap to his feet after a weekly scrub in the communal washtub and to sail across its floors on makeshift skates.

A single room occupied the entirety of the second floor, but Edward, in deference to his sisters' concerns for privacy, partitioned the room into smaller sections with sheets of compo-board. Ebba and Helen shared one enclosure, while Alpha had a smaller cubicle to herself. The remainder of the floor served as a loft bedroom for the boys. Tony and Edward shared one bed. Sture and Berger shared another. And the youngest of the children, Aaron, slept on a cot. Largely as a result of their sleeping arrangements, the children would joke for years that, while growing up, they had been packed like sardines into a can.

Like most of the children in Parkers Prairie, Sture divided his youth between hunting, farming and, when possible, learning. Throughout the year, he trapped and hunted and helped his father and older brothers tend to the few heads of cattle, horses, and hogs that comprised their livestock. After feeding the livestock, he milked the cows and worked in the fields. From the time the lakes thawed until they again froze over, he fished. And in the summer and early fall, between harvests, he picked potatoes on neighboring farms for two cents a bushel, often picking up to one hundred bushels a day. Rising before the sun and working well into the night, he developed a love of work and sense of duty that he would never relinquish. Work, quite simply, shaped him, and duty defined him. From the time he first began helping his neighbors, a significant portion of his earnings, from the few cents he earned at odd jobs in Parkers Prairie to his salary as a pilot with Pan Am, went directly to his parents.

Proud and fond of his work, he realized that he would have to become more efficient if he were to have enough time for his studies or to earn enough money for his inevitable journey beyond the fields of Parkers Prairie. And with the mind of a born mechanic, he discovered that mechanization held the key to greater efficiency. Never one to shun hard work, he continually sought new ways of performing his chores and often tried to apply what he learned in school to the tasks of running a farm. By the time he was eight, he had rigged dozens of timesaving contraptions around the farm, and in 1910, with only the castoff parts of plows and tools in the shed, he constructed a bean thresher that the family continued to use well into the 1920s. His efforts helped him refine a process that he would consider for the rest of his life to be his own scientific method. From school or work, he learned theory. At home, he applied that theory to the practicalities of life, and when he returned to school or work, he shared his discoveries so that his classmates and coworkers could reap the benefits of his efforts. During the quiet moments he spent with his tools and materials, he fancied himself a younger version of his hero, Thomas Alva Edison.

In 1907, two years after the citizens of Parkers Prairie approved a bond to build a new schoolhouse approximately one half-mile north of the wooden church that had served as the community school since 1879, Sture began his education. Each October, when the ground froze solid, he attended morning and afternoon classes, but his education was necessarily tempered with hard work. Every morning, after tending to his chores, he delivered milk to several homes along his route to school. And in the afternoons, before he could begin to think of studying, he returned to the fields.

Parkers Prairie school, like many of its time, was a large, red brick building just south of the business district. The schoolhouse stood two stories tall and housed four classrooms on each floor - a separate classroom for each grade - and a library in the center. Though the school lacked indoor plumbing until 1914, modern steam radiators kept the chill off the rooms during the height of winter, and large windows in each classroom provided sufficient light and cooling during the warmer months. The floors were laid throughout with hardwood maple, and all of the walls were delicately plastered. Atop the building, eight redwood columns supported a redwood cupola. One

Miss Taareton and the students at the Parkers Prairie School. Approximately 1910.
Sture is in the center of the front row.
Sigfred collection.

of the tallest structures in the village, the school rivaled the height of the four grain-elevators that hovered over the Soo railroad tracks several blocks to the east. It towered over the community and, even at the turn of the century, symbolized the importance that the Midwestern immigrants placed on education. The citizens of Parkers Prairie were justifiably proud of their state-of-the-art school.

Sture took quickly to education. On his first day in class, his teacher Miss Taareton passed to each child a sheet of orange paper, a cup of dye and a toothpick. At the back of the classroom, Sture took his share of supplies and rendered a drawing of such detail that Miss Taareton promoted him to the front of the class. Though he had to fit his education around delivering milk and farming and hunting, he remained at the head of his class the entire time he was in school. In 1911, the only year he was able to attend classes from the beginning through the end of the term, he passed both the fifth and the sixth grades. Along with his friends Vanche Hall and Minny Zinter, he sat in two different classrooms during the same term and prepared to march into a third.

John August in the buggy he used to deliver the mail. Approximately 1905. Sigfred collection.

Math and reading were among his favorite subjects, but his passion was geography. In the classrooms where he spent much of his youth, but not enough to suit him, he often found his mind drifting to the distant lands he studied. If a book contained a map, he could push no further than to trace its lines with his finger and, in his mind, to cross its rivers and mountains in amazement and appreciation. Merely the name of an exotic locale, almost any place outside Parkers Prairie, could send him into a reverie from which he had to be shaken. The eighth grade especially, his last complete year in school, cemented the love for geography that would last his entire life. While studying the Bay of Bengal that bathed Sri Lanka, India, Burma and Malaysia, he appreciated for the first time in his short life the vastness of the larger world outside Parkers Prairie. The shallow, brackish waters of the bay into which flowed the Ganges, Irrawaddy, and Brahmaputra Rivers represented for him a world in which the old and new, the ancient and the unexplored, merged into one. Imagining himself navigating the sacred waters of the bay, he realized that the world still offered a challenge for pioneers. He grew determined to become one of those pioneers.

The years between 1903 and 1917 were good for the Sigfrids. In 1903, on the heels of the railroad's arrival in Parkers Prairie, mail began to arrive by train rather than by stagecoach, and in 1905, the Postal Service established the Rural Free Delivery system. Winfred Hawkinson, son of the postmaster John A. Hawkinson, owned a farm that John August had worked during his years as a sharecropper. Impressed with John August's intelligence, and willingness to work, Winfred developed a close friendship with the young immigrant. When news of the RFD program

John August on the motorcycle he bought to deliver the mail. Approximately 1909. Sigfred collection.

arrived, he decided that John August would be a perfect candidate for mail carrier and convinced his Swedish friend to take the qualification examination. In the weeks preceding implementation of the program, he coached John August in test taking and what few English skills he would need to pass the mail carrier test. On the day of the examination, to be sure his friend would pass, he provided John August with an interpreter and tacked a crib-note to the floor near John August's desk. With Sture watching, John August, pored over the exam, his eyes occasionally falling but refusing to focus on the notes. Though he was satisfied that he had done his best, and more than a bit proud that he had not cheated, he feared that his lack of facility with the English language would result in his failure of the exam. He was jubilant when he learned that he had passed the test to become one of the first six mail carriers in Otter Tail County.

Beginning first with a horse and buggy, John August delivered the mail along a forty-mile route from early morning until early afternoon. In the late afternoons and evenings, he continued to farm. In 1908, perhaps having learned from his son the value of technology, he bought a bicycle to shorten his delivery days. So successful was his first encounter with mechanization that in 1909 he bought a motorcycle, and in 1914, enthralled with the motorized contraptions working their way off assembly lines to the east, he bought the family's first automobile, an Alter. Each step up the ladder of technology shortened the time he had to spend delivering the mail and lengthened the time he could farm. And though his day was long, he never complained. For him, the American Dream was real: a home of his own, a hardworking wife, and eight healthy children. In Sweden he had dared not hope for this much. In America, he worked for more.

In the long absences of her husband's work, Sophia ran her home with what she called Swedish efficiency. With a confounding mixture of sternness and warmth, she sewed her children's clothes by hand, tended the illnesses that seemed continually to strike them, and taught them to care for themselves and to remain loyal to each other. Her no-pampering approach to their health served the family well. In 1908, while playing Hide-And-Seek, her oldest son Tony sat in the barn loft counting, while his brother John Edward hid outside the barn. After Edward had scurried safely away from home base, Tony rose from the hay to search for his brother and slid from the loft. On his way toward the hard-packed floor, he fell from the hay bed and broke his arm. Unperturbed by his brother's pain, Edward ran from his hiding place, turned his brother onto his stomach, and snapped his broken arm back into place. When his pain subsided, Tony thanked his brother for helping, tagged him, and informed him that he was "It." Later in the day, Dr. Leibold, one of the township's few physicians, examined Tony's broken arm and placed it in a cast, remarking that the set Edward had performed was "quite satisfactory."

Parkers Prairie Post Office, 1921. Left to right: Magnus Larson, Route 1; Herman Larson, Route 2; R.W. Zinter, Route 3; John Fridgen, Postmaster; Carl Carlson, Assistant Postmaster; John August Sigfrid, Route 4; John Edward "Ed" Sigfrid, Route 5; Tony Sigfrid, Route 6. Sigfred collection.

Sophia looked on as Sture and the rest of her children learned from their backbreaking work the often-necessary cruelties and always-wonderful joys of life, the paradoxes that made their simple lives rich and meaningful. Rising with her husband well before sunrise and keeping him company well past sunset, she was stoic and realistic about the realities of life on the prairie. A woman of her times, she could not imagine a life beyond the demands of family and community and was satisfied with her place in both. Though her work was hard and her day was long, she was thankful for the blessings of her home, her husband, and her children in a land where, she believed, hard work met with just rewards. And hard work, she stressed more than anything else, establishing early in her children's lives a reserve that often bordered on coldness and forever stymied the affections of her son Sture.

In the Otter Tail valley, Sophia's life flowed simply between the fixed points of her home, the church where her husband was a deacon, and the ever-present railroad that became the center of Parkers Prairie economic and social life after 1903. She ensured that her children's lives flowed between the same fixed points, making certain that they attended and were confirmed in the Swedish Lutheran Church, and encouraging them to attend school as often as the needs of farming would allow. With a quiet, sometimes harsh, strength, she raised her children to be strong in the face of adversity and always hardworking.

All was not, however, work and prayer for the Sigfrids. What little time that was not occupied with work around the farm, they spent picnicking in the woods around Lake Adley, attending movies in an upstairs room at Old City Hall, or occasionally driving twenty miles south to Alexandria, where they seeped themselves in the emerging American culture. The melodies of *Red Wing* or *Silver Bells* sprang from their lips on long sleigh rides at the peak of winter as they coasted along the frozen surface of Lake Adley. The latest headlines from Minneapolis or the local *Independent* peppered their discussions on treks to Alexandria to see the circus or to shop in department stores more numerous and larger than Parkers Prairie's.

One of Sture's favorite leisure activities was attending the motion picture. A sense of awe overcame him whenever he journeyed to the theater. There, in the darkness of Old City Hall in 1910, as a young man read subtitles to the audience, a gas projector provided Sture with his first flickering pictures of an airplane. Sandwiched between an old time western and a feature with an "actress named Tallulah – but not Bankhead," the newsreel flashed an image of a feeble biplane coursing through the sky. The sight thrilled Sture, filled him with a longing he could neither explain nor describe. He felt pulled toward the image of the plane chugging across the cloudless sky, called to the heavens for a reason that defied reason. He became, in a moment, obsessed, and continued to attend the dime motion pictures as often as he could afford, as much for the newsreels as for the features, as much for the dream as for the reality. Until he left Parkers Prairie, he often lost himself in the darkness of the theatre, staring enraptured at a screen across which a plane would fly, dreaming of a sky across which he could write his name.

Still, more than school or play, more than the motion pictures, or reading, or tending the livestock, Sture loved to hunt and to trap. Rabbits and partridges abounded in the woods and fields around

Parkers Prairie and helped to defray the costs of feeding his large family. So Sture hunted for food and trapped for money, and he spent a significant portion of his youth in the bogs and marshes of central Minnesota. Hiking several miles to the east of his home, past the tamarack telephone poles and gaslights of downtown Parkers Prairie, he scouted the shores of Lakes Augusta and Rainy and relished the solitude and peace of the forest. From the age of eight, he trapped alone in the woods and swamps and sloughs surrounding his home. As his skills as a woodsman developed, he generated a substantial income by selling the hides of the muskrats he trapped.

Sture's first command, a bathtub, rescued from the dump and turned into a rowboat. 1913. Sigfred collection.

But the income did not come without a cost. Long after his evening chores were complete, when darkness shrouded the countryside and the only light that penetrated the forest was a soft yellow moon over the lakes of Otter Tail County, Sture would set out with a burlap bag thrown over his shoulder, a kerosene lantern, and single-barrel Harrington Richardson shotgun at his side. Lest the muskrats he trapped in the morning gnaw off their legs and escape, he traipsed every evening into the woods to gather, kill and skin the screeching animals. Then, as wolves howled in the moonlight and waves lapped the shore, he tossed the pelts into his burlap bag and hiked back to Parkers Prairie where he sold the pelts to businessmen at the railroad station. He received between thirty-five cents and a dollar and thirty-five cents per pelt, depending upon the type of pelt and the season's supply. Most of the money he gave to his father to help with family expenses, but a small portion he kept aside, readying himself for the day he would venture into the world.

The pace of Sture's life quickened in 1914. Faced with his father's illness and an operation in Rochester, and the marriage of his sister Helen, he was forced to take a more central role in the family. Four months into the school year, he quit the ninth grade and substituted for his father along the roads and trails of mail delivery route #4. Still dressed in knickers, his day began before dawn with the regular feeding of livestock, followed by a trip into town to pick up the mail, and long hours delivering the mail to the homes of his friends sprinkled across the county, most of whom were still in school. After a meager lunch, he worked the fields until early evening, and after dinner, traipsed into the woods to hunt and trap. On rare restful weekends, he fished in Lake Adley, but even this recreation, like every moment of his waking life, was spent helping his father and supporting his family.

In 1916, he finally donned the clothing of the man he had much earlier become. After his confirmation on May 16, he tossed his knickers to his younger brother and stepped into the long pants he had longed so often to wear, the trousers that symbolized for him and the community the manhood into which he had grown. Feeling and finally looking the part of a confident young man, he also shouldered his responsibilities with a newfound sense of purpose, scarcely heeding the growing tension in Parkers Prairie. For a while, lost in the endless tasks of helping his father provide for the family, he ignored the news of turmoil in Europe and the beckoning of life outside Parkers Prairie. And though talk around the railroad turned to submarines and the *Lusitania*, the *Arabic* and the *Sussex*, Sture, like most of his neighbors, trusted that President Woodrow Wilson would keep the United States out of the fray.

But in March of 1917, with pelts in hand, Sture listened in horror as the conversations at the depot grew increasingly grave. Explaining that the pelts he sold would be used for fur collars on the coats of fighting men in Europe, the businessmen gave him ever-larger sums for his bounty. With his money safely stowed in his pockets, he lingered at the edges of groups of angry men and listened as they passed along rumors of Germany's guarantee that Mexico could win the states of Texas, New Mexico and Arizona if they joined in war against the United States. Flushed with anger, he listened as the men spoke of places he had read about, states on the frontier populated by pioneers in buckskin jackets and coonskin hats. When he heard that the southwestern states might be threatened by an enemy from a country near the land of his ancestors, he reeled in confusion, the state of world politics forcing itself into his thoughts.

Still, despite rumors growing louder and more frequent, despite young men scarcely older than himself lining up at the post office and

The Sigfrid family, approximately 1908. Standing left to right: Berger, Tony, Ebba, Helen, John Edward, and Alpha. Sitting left to right: Sture, John August, Aaron. Sigfred collection.

boarding one of the four trains that left Parkers Prairie each day for Alexandria and Minneapolis, young men leaving their homes and families to enlist in the Army, the war remained unreal to him. For almost six months, the thought of death and dying seemed but a haze on the edges of his understanding.

In the summer of 1917, however, his older brother Tony received his draft notice. The war became all too real. The peace of his evenings in the woods grew troubled. His bedtime prayers became filled with thanks that Edward held a government job and would remain safe to care for the family. His dreams became haunted by the ghosts of Tony's fellow soldiers. As the summer dragged past autumn and into winter, cold with the news of the dying in Europe, as winter thawed into mud thick with the blood of men no older than himself, as the roads that were ice in the morning became mud in the afternoon,

Sture grew fascinated with the war in Europe and obsessed with his duty to his brother, his family, and his country. The finger he traced along yellowing maps now pointed to Europe, to countries whose borders were aflame, to forests littered with bodies, to sands colored red with blood.

Though his family was against it, Sture knew that the time was drawing close for him to don the uniform of one of his nation's fighting forces. The time for building icehouses and chicken coops with Edward, the time for fixing up rooms that remained unfinished had passed. The world encroached upon the village of Parkers Prairie, making it seem ever smaller, and as the summer of 1917 finally relinquished its hold on the valley, he understood that life called for more important pursuits.

In late 1917, without his parents' knowledge, he hopped a train to Minneapolis and tried to join the Army. But before his train arrived in the city, his parents heard of his plans and sent telegrams to the Army, Navy and Marine recruiters, warning them that Sture was too young to join the service. After Sture discovered that his plans had been thwarted, John August drove to Minneapolis and retrieved his son. Sture sullenly returned to Parkers Prairie, but he continued to plan for his departure. Late in the night, after his parents had read Tony's letters to the family, as his mother lay in bed worrying for her son and his father jumped at the short-long-short ring of the telephone, afraid that it would bring news of his eldest son, Sture counted his nickels and dimes and dollars. Even as he helped his father build a new home in 1918 and seemed to conspire in plans for a future in Parkers Prairie, every penny he earned took him closer to the outside world and the adventures of which he had always dreamed.

Adventure he tried to remember as he forced himself to face the demands of an increasingly constricted life in Parkers Prairie. Finally, on December 17, 1918, exactly fifteen years after the Wright Brothers' first flight in Kittyhawk, North Carolina – though he did not at the time realize the significance of the date – confident that his family would flourish without him, old enough that his parents could not prevent his enlistment, and despite word that the recent Armistice had reduced the nation's need for soldiers, Sture boarded a train for Minneapolis, intent on enlisting in one of the branches of the military. Because he was underweight, neither the Army, the Navy, nor the

Marines accepted his enlistment. Disappointed but not unhopeful, he took a job washing dishes at a restaurant in Minneapolis and gorged himself until he had gained just enough weight to meet the Navy's minimum requirements. In early 1919, he again presented himself to a recruiter in Minneapolis who grudgingly agreed to sign him up. Within days, he was on a train bound for basic training at the Great Lakes Naval Training Station in North Chicago, Illinois, and the adventures of a Navy career.

John August, Sophia and Aaron in front of the house that Sture helped his father build in 1918. Picture taken 1921. Sigfred collection.

For several weeks after his arrival in Great Lakes, Sture thrilled to the sound of reveille each morning. While many of his companions complained of rising so early, he explained that he slept later in the Navy than he had on the farm. As the young men stumbled over the grinder, he reminded them that it was flatter and firmer, easier to march than the furrows of a freshly plowed field. When the recruits shied from the taunts of their drill instructors, he pressed them to understand that the challenges of basic training would make them all men, the finest fighting force in the world. When they complained of having to deal with the Navy's bureaucracy, he reminded them that when the Navy had misspelled his last name as *Sigfred* instead of *Sigfrid*, he had merely adopted the new spelling. What was good enough for the Navy, was good enough for him. And when the young men fell into their hammocks at taps and quickly filled the barracks with their snores, he lay awake, thankful for his chance to find a place in the world.

The months of basic training passed quickly for Sture and the forty-three other men in his company. Without noticing, they began to step more sharply to cadence, to move as a unit. Their complaints diminished as their bodies and minds grew used to the constant striving toward strength. As they became more certain of themselves, more confident of their ability to lead, and more convinced of their eventual success, their gazes began to lift from the tarmac to the fences of the base and finally to the shores of Lake Michigan. Each time a steamship passed through the waters behind their barracks, the men paused and stared, longing to feel the heaving decks beneath their feet, the cold bite of a Gattling gun in their hands, the icy certainty of the difference between enemy and friend.

N-9 similar to that Sture observed during Basic Training, 1919. Sigfred collection.

On an afternoon in early March, while the men practiced formations, Sture heard a loud engine passing overhead. He looked toward the sound and, for the first time in his life, glimpsed in person the tangible reality of an airplane, something still so new that some still referred to it as a flying machine. Passing on its final approach to a landing site on the lake at the north side of the base, the plane flew so close that he glimpsed the number N-9 painted on its hull and caught the reflection of the sun in its propellers. For a few seconds, he stood in awe of its power, of the magic that lifted it in the wind and propelled it through the sky. He lost sight of the airplane when it dipped behind a clump of pines at the edge of the field. Soon even the noise of its engines was lost in the noise of stomping feet and labored breath.

Still he stood, mesmerized, recalling the darkness of Old City Hall and the recognition of purpose that had overcome him with the flitting of a dot across the screen. Only when his drill instructor stood shouting directly in front of him did Sture return his attention to the grinder and to the company of his fellow recruits.

In that moment, he felt changed. The vague sense he had called the future, that he had thought of as simply mysterious and adventurous took shape, became real to the boy who had always been fascinated with machinery and invention. As the drill instructor pounded him with abuse, he smiled. He swore to himself that, no matter what it took, he would someday fly in one of those machines. He would throw his 117 pounds into the cockpit and soar through the air. He had found his future.

Spring had just begun to warm the air when Sture's company graduated from basic training. Forty-four young men stood on the parade ground, accepting the congratulations of their Company Commander who now spoke to them as equals. Sture listened to the commander and wondered how the swells of the ocean would feel, how the salt would taste on his lips, how the sight of an endless sea would seem to a man who had never before abandoned the security of land.

His reverie broke when the commander announced that only forty of the forty-four recruits could be *real* sailors. "The *Delaware*," he explained, the country's first true dreadnought, "has the need for only forty of you fine, young men. So four of you must volunteer for additional

Sture's best friend Matt Kandle and Sture, Great lakes Naval Training Station, 1919.
Sigfred collection.

training here in Great Lakes." The recruits looked at one other, each afraid that after having completed the rigors of Basic Training he might be robbed of his chance to become a real sailor. The columns hesitated as the Company Commander read down the list of available schools.

First he called out, "Radio School."

Sture remained silent.

Beside him Sawyer, a young man who had been his friend since his arrival at Basic Training, jumped from his rank. Sawyer had been known as a "radio nut" throughout his training and had already learned Morse code. "That's for me," he shouted, his face beaming. Without bidding goodbye to Sture or his other friends, he ran for the orders to Radio School, almost snatching them from the commander's hands.

Sture basked in self-restraint. I'll be a real sailor, he thought. Then the commander announced "Aviation Machinist Mate School."

A murmur ran through the crowd, accompanied by a flurry of activity near the left end of the first rank.

"Does he mean airplanes?" Sture asked.

"That's all he could mean," whispered the young man next to him.

Sture thought of his brother in France. He thought of the large guns on the deck of the *Delaware* and the pounding they would give an enemy. He thought of what it means to be a sailor. He knew he could perform as well onboard a ship as any of his peers. He also knew he wanted to be a part of the real Navy. But he could not escape the sound and image of the plane he had seen fly over the base. He could not escape the memory of the planes he had seen at the theatre in Parkers Prairie. If this were to be any man's destiny, he thought, it might as well be his.

As he had as a child, before stepping from the branches of a tree into the unknown but exhilarating descent of a dive into the lake, Sture held his breath and stepped from the rank.

The men behind him nudged each other and snickered.

"Well Mr. Sigfred," the Company Commander grinned, "it looks like you're going to be an a-vee-ate-or. Good luck to you. God knows you'll need it."

Pigeons in the Loft

1918 - 1921

Upon graduating from Aviation Machinist Mate training in February of 1920, Sture received orders to Squadron #3 at the U.S. Naval Air Station in Pensacola, Florida. Matt Kandle, a young man from Chicago whom Sture had met immediately after completing basic training and who quickly became his best friend, received orders to Squadron #2. Though they would not be in the same squadron, they would spend the next several years in the same location, and both looked forward to the demands of their new careers.

Sture with the Model-T that he and Matt Kandle purchased in 1920. This is the first car either of them owned. Pensacola, Florida.
Sigfred collection.

They arrived in Pensacola in early March and quickly pooled their resources to buy a used 1917 Ford Model-T. When free from their duties at the air station, the two Midwestern boys who had never before ventured near the Mason Dixon Line explored the villages of Florida, Alabama and Mississippi that dotted the Gulf Coast. They immersed themselves in the blend of Spanish, French and English cultures the area offered, and sought to see as much of their corner of the world as they could. But as much as they enjoyed their forays into the countryside, as much as they relished their time away from work, they were both intent on becoming the best in their field. Not surprisingly, a friendly rivalry developed. Sture's innate ability in mechanics, though, gave him a natural advantage in aviation. While Matt performed respectably, Sture excelled in the work that came naturally to him and advanced rapidly. By the end of 1920, he was working, though not being paid, as a crew chief for the squadron's fleet of seaplanes, affectionately known to the airmen as flying boats.

F-5L in Pensacola, Florida. 1920. Sigfred collection.

The squadron's fleet at the time consisted of several F-5L and H-16, twin-engine seaplanes. With the exception of NC boats, these were the largest seaplanes in the U.S. fleet. Powered by two Liberty, 380 horsepower engines, the F-5Ls and H-16s cruised at 75 miles per hour at altitudes up to 6000 feet. The engines were water-cooled, with large radiators mounted on their lower wings, forward of the engines, to provide the necessary heat transfer surfaces for cooling the water that cooled the engines. A thirty-gallon flat tank mounted inside the top wing gravity-fed gasoline to each engine. The tanks were filled by windmill plunger pumps and were provided with overflows to a catch tank inside the hull. Though slightly different in appearance, each plane had upper and lower, linen covered wings that spanned 100 feet from tip to tip and ¼ inch plywood hulls. Two, eight-foot wooden propellers mounted forward of the radiators provided the thrust necessary for the planes to develop sufficient lift for continuous flight.

Both planes were capable of flying for up to seven hours, but their oil capacity was only four hours. This necessitated in-flight oil replenishment and offered Sture his first opportunity to distinguish himself in the squadron. While cruising above the Gulf of Mexico and with the copilot maintaining a firm grip on his belt, he regularly ventured five feet out onto the lower wing and, with one hand gripping

H-16 in flight over the Gulf of Mexico, 1920.
Sigfred collection.

the brace wires on the wing, unscrewed the cap on the oil pan with his other hand. He then returned twice to the hull for two one-gallon cans of fresh oil that he poured into the oil tank. When he finished this for the first engine, he repeated it for the second engine on the opposite wing. Few members of the crew liked the fact that the oil had to be replenished in such a dangerous way, and no one rested easily until he was finished. Still, because he was tall and light, offering less wind resistance than many of his coworkers, he was able to perform the task with relative ease and willed himself not to consider the possibility or results of slipping. He quickly earned a solid reputation among the flight crews for the speed with which he could complete the oil replenishment.

As much as he excelled in the air, Sture was even more proficient on the ground. The Liberty engines required overhaul every 75 hours. This significantly affected the squadron's ability to perform its training missions. A good mechanic, next only to the pilot, was often the most important member of the crew, for he more than anyone else maintained the plane in a condition to fly and could repair the planes in the not unlikely event of problems underway. With the skill of a born mechanic, Sture quickly became an expert on the Liberty engines and a favorite of many of the pilots who frequently selected him to accompany them on their regular navigation and training missions. He even persuaded a few of them - against regulations - to teach him how to fly.

While most training flights proceeded without incident, the seaplanes operated so closely to their design safety envelopes that every flight was a precarious undertaking, a balancing act for both pilot and crew. Everything that went onto the plane - everything - had to be accounted for and a balance struck between the weight of the plane and the amount of loaded fuel. Too much fuel might prevent the plane from taking off. Too little might prevent it from returning. So sensitive were the planes to the weight of their cargoes that the crews made a regular practice of relieving themselves before embarking the plane, and the crews carried only what was absolutely essential for a mission. The cockpits were equipped with only the most primitive instrumentation, normally a magnetic compass and a crude drift sight, and most navigation was performed visually. This, compounded with the Liberty engine's propensity for stripping gears, made each flight a dangerous venture of man against machine. No member of the crew allowed himself to forget that he alone might make the difference between a successful flight and a failure.

Sture on the tail of an H-16 during flight. Pensacola, Florida, 1920. Sigfred collection.

Though each minute of a flight was equally dangerous, none was more threatening than the takeoff. The planes, heavy with a full load of fuel, were at their least responsive. They sat low in the water and provided a drag that the engines were barely able to overcome. The pilots were trained to face their planes into the wind and to fully power their engines to generate enough thrust to increase the airflow across the wings. During a good takeoff, the plane quickly rose onto the step at the bow of the hull and experienced less drag from the water. More power from the engines could then generate thrust, resulting in increased speed and airflow across the wings. Wind rushing more quickly over the nozzle shaped wing created a lower pressure above the wing than below, thereby generating lift.

When the engine's thrust exceeded the plane's drag, and the wing's lift exceeded the plane's weight, the plane would lift more or less smoothly into the air.

The full power necessary to drag the plane through the water, however, placed a significant strain on the engines, and, as often as not, resulted in the engines overheating and spitting water through the radiators' overflow. In these cases, the pilots were forced to abort their takeoffs and return to the loading ramp to refill their radiators. The best pilots became known as those who could take off in only one attempt. Every pilot, the best and the worst, knew that successful flight had far less to do with him than others might think. On the water, his best friend was the wind. In the air, his best friend was the mechanic.

And Sture was the best friend of many a pilot. For this reason, Lieutenant Junior Grade Ralph Davison selected him to serve as crew chief in February of 1921 for a routine training flight over the Gulf. Davison, a pudgy, pleasant graduate of the Naval Academy, was the gunnery officer at Pensacola. Balding, with a ruddy complexion, and always ready with a smile, he held extensive influence over the Officers Corps. To be selected by him was both a compliment and an honor. Sture anticipated the flight with excitement.

The flight was scheduled to start early in the morning and to last approximately five hours. The flight plan called for takeoff at the mouth of the harbor, a leisurely cruise at 6000 feet for one hundred miles to the southwest, a turn to the north for ninety-five miles and an approach and landing at the lighthouse entrance to Mobile Bay, fifty miles west of Pensacola. For the most part, the flight proceeded as expected from its flawless takeoff into the wind until its approach to Mobile. But without warning, before Davison started his descent, the starboard engine simply quit working. Davison compensated for the loss of power by accelerating his port engine to full throttle, but the plane rapidly lost altitude. Davison tried to maintain his altitude as long as the engine would allow and managed to fly the plane over Mobile Bay where the water was smoother than in the open Gulf. He knew that the plane would not survive his abuse all the way to Pensacola. So he performed a forced landing in the bay.

On this flight, as on most others, the crew carried not only a full load of gas, but extra oil, and a spare set of gears. They also carried a sea anchor, something akin to a giant canvas umbrella, to cut down their drift and to keep the nose of the plane heading into the wind. Though Sture had never before found it necessary to use any of these supplies, except the oil, he was glad to have them onboard this flight. His investigation of the engine revealed that the drive gears for the right overhead camshaft required

H-16 landing in the Gulf of Mexico, 1920. Sigfred collection.

replacement and that the engine would have to be retimed. Most, if not all, of the spare supplies would be required.

Because he had never performed such extensive repairs at sea, he was equally happy that the crew had stowed their regular cargo of two cages of homing pigeons, extra lunches, and several thermoses of fresh drinking water. He was afraid they might need them if he were not successful with his repairs.

This time, the fates were with him. The sea was calm and the afternoon bright. He replaced the gears and retimed the engines in an hour, and the crew flew back to the base rather than having to be towed. LtJG Davison, realizing that his arrival by air reflected as much on him as it did on Sture, was both pleased and impressed with the young mechanic. Though he had heard many good things about Sture, he never suspected that he or any other man could have accomplished underway repairs so quickly. As he powered up his engines for the short hop to Pensacola, he had the other officers share the best of the sandwiches with Sture and vowed to mention Sture's performance to the Squadron Commander.

He was true to his decision. Soon after disembarking from the plane, he arranged an appointment with his commanding officer. In their meeting, he carefully explained the situation and the speed and skill with which Sture had accomplished the repairs, and respectfully suggested that Mr. Sigfred should become more than just a mechanic. The commanding officer trusted Davison completely and within the week ordered Sture to regular flight duty and approved a 50% increase in his pay. After less than a year in Pensacola, Sture was making $108.00 a month. The increase in pay that accompanied his

H-16 at top and bottom of loading ramp, Pensacola, Florida, 1920.
Sigfred collection.

Flight Orders remained a permanent part of each serviceman's record, and from that point forward, Sture was a regular - and compensated - fixture on navigation flights over the Gulf, often serving as crew chief for long distance, weekend flights to New Orleans, Donaldsonville, and other ports along the Gulf coast.

By the end of 1921, he had amassed three live bombing runs, four gunnery runs, seven search and rescue missions, including the at-sea rescue of an RGL crew after a crash destroyed their plane, and countless test and training runs, navigation exercises, and other exhibition flights. As New Year's Day, 1922, dawned, he had 190 flights and 246 hours and 45 minutes of airtime to his credit. And while his skill continued to improve, his luck did not always hold.

Just over a year after his at-sea repairs to Lieutenant Davison's F-5L, Sture found himself accompanying another training crew on a navigation flight over the Gulf. Numerous flights over the previous year had made him an old salt on such jaunts, and though he soberly faced the potential disaster that each flight offered, he boarded the plane with no special worries for his return. The flight proceeded as expected, and the crew relaxed as the plane approached its southernmost point, approximately 100 miles southwest of Pensacola. The copilot scanned the horizon for the rarity of another craft. The pilot busied himself with the constant battle for power and altitude. The radio officer turned a few dials and sat absorbed in thought as Sture began preparations for his regular underway oil replenishment.

While Sture gathered his supplies and placed them beside the port hatch, the plane began to jolt violently and head into a spin to port. His stomach sank as he looked out the hatch and watched the port engine disintegrate before his eyes. As though in slow motion, the propeller came loose from the plane and, still spinning, smashed into the brass radiator. The propeller splintered and drifted to the glassy surface of the Gulf. The radiator broke loose from its foundation and became tangled in the brace wires of the port wing, dangling like a kite in the wind. The plane began to buffet. The pilot cursed in the

A Liberty engine used for training at the Great Lakes Naval Training Station, 1919. Sigfred collection.

cockpit and tried to regain control of the ship. As the radiator pounded into the engine, four connecting rods and pistons flew from the engine, and the lower half of the crankcase peeled from its base. As he watched helplessly, the debris fell to the sea. Sture was certain that only God could keep the crew from dying.

Silently, and without thought, he began to pray. No sooner had words formed in his mind than he noticed the struts and left wings begin to cave in on themselves. Without securing himself to the hull, he climbed out onto the wing and grasped the radiator, forcing himself to hold it lengthwise in the wind. The buffeting of the ship abated slightly, but the radiator fought against Sture's grasp and threatened to crush his hands against the bulk of the engine bed. The plane nosed into a steep dive. The linen of the wing slid beneath his chest as his body inched its way to the front edge of the wing. Unable to release his hold on the radiator, he wrapped his legs around the brace wires of the wing. He clung to the warm brass radiator as the sea rushed toward him.

At 3000 feet, the pilot steepened his dive and within seconds leveled the lurching and groaning plane over the sea. He pulled back on the throttle and called to the crew to brace themselves. The plane skipped lightly over the water before settling into moderate waves. The pilot cut the good engine, and the plane quickly decelerated and drifted to a stop, bobbing like a cork on the foam. The afternoon was silent but for the lapping of waves against the plywood hull and the pounding of four hearts in the middle of the Gulf of Mexico.

Drenched in oil, Sture let go of the radiator and stretched his aching fingers. Untangling his legs from the brace wires, he looked at the still and cooling engine. Amid the mass of black oil and scorched metal, he clearly saw a broken crankshaft sitting lifeless at the engine's center. He crawled to the hatch and poked his head inside the hull. The crew, as though hypnotized, freed themselves from their seats and kneaded their limbs, scarcely believing they were still alive.

Inside an H-16 cockpit, 1920.
Sigfred collection.

"I guess you'll have to take my wings," Sture called to the pilot. "I don't think I can fix this."

The fresh-faced lieutenant looked at Sture, then at his copilot and radio officer. Without a word, they began to laugh.

The radio officer, a forty-three year old Lieutenant Commander and the senior officer present, was also a medical doctor who had volunteered to learn to fly despite his age. He grasped Sture's hand and pulled him into the plane.

"No one could take those wings away, Sigfred. You kept this plane in the air. There'll be no demotion today."

Within minutes, the radio officer took charge. "I was told I'm too old for flight training, and that's true, but I'm still the senior officer here, and, gentlemen we have work to do. We also seem to have a problem," he announced with gallant understatement. "I suppose a more experienced operator might have gotten a message off before we

31

ditched, but all I could do was watch Sigfred hold that radiator while the trailing antennae fell into the sea. No one knows we're here, and I'm afraid we're on our own. First, we need to get a message to the air station."

The pilot agreed, and Sture stepped toward the back of the hull to retrieve the homing pigeons. When he turned to the other men, cages in hand, the pilot's face fell. Both cages were covered in thick, black goo where oil from the failed engine had blown through the open hatch. Although the oil had cooled and did not threaten to kill the homing pigeons, each was covered with the black and sticky fluid. The radio officer pulled the least soiled pigeon from its cage and wiped it clean with his shirt. Then the copilot, who also served as navigator, composed a message citing his best estimate for their location and slid it into a small aluminum tube wired to the pigeon's foot. He held the pigeon outside the hull, and all four men watched as the pigeon lifted into the air, circled twice around the ship and came to roost on the skid fin of the upper wing. Despite their shouts and jeers, the pigeon refused to move.

The radio officer pulled a second pigeon from the cage while the navigator composed a second message. At the radio officer's suggestion, Sture opened the basket of lunches and removed several slices of bread from the basket.

"We may regret this later, but the bread will absorb more oil than our shirts." Sture and the radio officer carefully bathed the pigeon with bread, and when its breast shone almost white, strapped the second message to its feet. As the men held their breath, the pigeon flapped its wings, lifted into the air and circled halfway around the plane. Gaining its bearings, it flew to the northeast and disappeared from view.

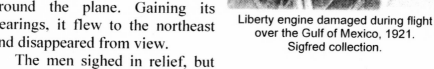

Liberty engine damaged during flight over the Gulf of Mexico, 1921. Sigfred collection.

The men sighed in relief, but dared not smile.

The navigator estimated that it would take two hours for the pigeon to reach the air station and several more for a search party to find the stricken plane. He recommended that the pilot try to make headway toward Mobile using the remaining engine. As the pilot started the engine, Sture rigged a five-quart bucket and trailed it behind the right wing to keep drag on the operating engine so the ship could maintain a straight course. The ship made some progress through the water, but the pilot was forced to operate the engine near idle to prevent waves from breaking over the bow. Soon the engine fouled and began to backfire. Realizing that the engine and standing oil posed a fire hazard, he killed the engine. Sture rigged the sea anchor from the bow cable to keep the ship's nose headed into the wind. When the sea anchor was fully trailed, he moved all of the spare gears to the tail to force the nose higher into the air.

Because the plane was not equipped with a horizontal stabilizer, the crew maintained twenty-pound bags of sand onboard to help adjust the ship's trim in flight. These Sture also placed strategically throughout the hull to keep the nose of the ship out of the water and to compensate for the decreased weight of the port wing. When he finished, the list and trim of the ship were as close to zero as a man could accomplish without delicate instrumentation.

While Sture busied himself stabilizing the ship, the radio officer inspected the hull for damage. He discovered several small leaks, but none was larger than those the ship normally experienced while sitting on the water overnight. He concluded that the hull, at least, was safe. To ensure the plane did not lose buoyancy, however, he regularly pumped water from the hull using a bilge pump installed as part of the ship's standard equipment.

When the radio officer was convinced that the ship was as secure as they could make it, the men turned their thoughts toward rescue. In the event that a hawk or other predator had intercepted the first pigeon, all agreed to release with messages the last two pigeons in the first cage. The copilot recommended that they also release the four pigeons in the second cage, but Sture interrupted.

"With all due respect, sir, if we're not rescued in the next several hours, we may need those pigeons for more important business than delivering messages."

The copilot looked at him without comprehending.

"We have only a few sandwiches left and a long wait ahead of us. I suggest we keep these last four pigeons with us as long as is necessary to ensure our survival."

Finally understanding, the copilot nodded. "Good thinking."

The copilot released the two pigeons and informed the other men that the first pigeon still maintained its watch on the upper wing.

While the copilot watched the two pigeons disappear in the distance, Sture opened the second cage and searched for some grain to feed the remaining pigeons. All he found was a pad of fine message paper and a grease pencil. "At least the loft realized we needed paper for messages," he muttered. "But if a bird starves to death, I doubt he would make an efficient messenger." Once again opening the lunch basket, he pulled several pieces of bread from their wax wrapping and

Radio tower at the Pensacola Air Station, 1921. Sigfred collection.

tore them to pieces to feed the birds.

The sun began to slip toward the west, stretching the plane's shadow increasingly toward the northeast and Pensacola. Low storm clouds moved in from the west.

"Not good," said the pilot. "If the pigeons have made it to the air station with our position, the commander may launch an air search. But it won't get very far with a storm moving in."

"A whole fleet of planes would do us little good right now," the radio officer answered. "Unless they dropped food or an insulated raft right on top of us, we would be hard pressed to retrieve anything. The best they could do for us is to radio our position to a rescue ship, and that, gentlemen, we have already done as best we can."

The sea grew more choppy, and despite the crew's efforts to pump the hull, waves lapped at the hatches on the port and starboard sides. The men listened carefully for the sound of an approaching plane, and the pilot readied himself to shoot a flare. The afternoon was silent except for the continuous lapping of water against the hull and an occasional coo from the pigeons. Around three o'clock, the pilot thought he heard a plane in the distance and fired one of the flares. It blazed as it was supposed to, but its light was lost against the dull gray sea and the waning light.

"Better save the flares for evening. They'll be more easily sighted." The copilot's voice sounded dull and far away.

"You're right," said the radio officer. "If we save them for the evening, we can fire them periodically. That should help a plane or ship locate us. But now, we need to think of ourselves. All of you should wear your life vests. I know they'll get waterlogged, but at least they'll keep us a little warmer when the sun goes down.

"I've also drawn up a watch list. Two of us will keep watch from the cockpit, each on his respective side from dead ahead to 45 degrees left or right. The other two will keep the bilge pump operating and keep watch from the hatches for anything abeam or aft of the ship. After two hours, we'll change positions."

Pensacola Air Station from the air, 1921. Sigfred collection.

He divided the remaining sandwiches equally between the four. The emergency rations, packaged in a metal container with bread and chocolate, he kept stowed until hunger became a more pressing concern. A doctor as well as a radio officer, he knew they could survive for several days without food. The limited supply of fresh water, he realized, was another problem. Rather than alarm the other men, he remained silent about the water and encouraged them to stay out of the setting sun. In just a few more hours, he knew, the sun would be the least of their concerns.

Sture sat in the starboard hatch scanning the horizon. Occasionally, a wave wet the hem of his trousers, but the plane remained fairly high in the water, and the danger of sinking seemed remote, the last concern in a mind filled with more pressing worries. His stomach churned from hunger and the relentless rocking of the plane, but he refused to eat until absolutely necessary. He forced himself to think of sitting in the woods outside Parkers Prairie, remaining perfectly still for hours at a time, waiting silently for the rustle of leaves to announce the presence of a stag that could feed his family for several weeks.

He sat in the hatch, staring at the ocean for hours. When his turn came, he sat in the cockpit and stared at the ocean. And when his turn was over, he returned to his vigil in the hatch. The sun occasionally peeked through the gathering clouds and cast a brilliant yellow beam upon the water. Though it appeared only erratically and each time fell lower in the sky, he was comforted by the beam. He imagined that his family might be watching the same beam of light shining brightly on Lake Adley, and prayed silently that they were not worried. As the sun set over the horizon, long since obscured by thunderheads, he felt strangely at peace, as he had often felt beside the still waters of Lake Adley. It was now a wiser and more mature peace, but still the essential peace of faith.

Algorma, the tug that rescued Sture and his crew, 1921.
Sigfred collection.

The night fell without grace of moon. The sea churned beneath them, but reserved her anger for places further west. The plane bobbed on the waves, but remained afloat, a dull gray message to the men who manned her. Though the message differed for each, all had the common theme of hope. They spoke to each other, in whispers at first. Then their voices gained strength and volume, and they seemed to call to the land beyond their sight as much as to each other. They spoke of dreams and of the past, of a sweetheart's glance in the moonlight, a kiss stolen at the edge of a bee-humming garden –

anything to beat back the monotony and buoy their spirits. They spoke of their heroes and their awe at the endless and quickening march of technology, the march that had landed them on this sea. When they realized that technology had also landed them in this situation, their conversation drifted to faith. And finally, with the understanding that only their strength and determination could save them, they fell silent.

At approximately 10:30 PM, the pilot spotted a flare slightly west of direct north. He hurried to the hatch and fired his own flare in response. The blast startled all of the men and temporarily blinded them. But when their night vision returned, they watched the flare with hope. It climbed in a brilliant, spattering arc above the plane and hung for several minutes in dazzling red, sending streamers of light to the sea below. In the quiet night, sparks sizzled as they landed and were extinguished in the water.

The ship fired another flare to answer theirs. It hung white in the sky for several minutes, then disappeared behind the dark, glimmering mass of the sea. Sture noticed that he could see only the flattest portion of the flare's arc and informed the other men that the vessel was beyond the horizon, more than seven miles from their current position. The radio officer shook him by the shoulders. "They'll be here soon." The night was too dark for Sture to see the officer's face, but he knew the look he would see. He imagined the bright eyes, the white teeth forced into a smile, the skin of the forehead pulled flat, its lines disappearing, in the tension that exhaustion and hope created. He knew the look without seeing it, and imagined that his face, too, bore the same expression.

By midnight, the vessel pulled close enough to shine her searchlight on the stranded seaplane. Then she adjusted the light higher to illuminate the upper wing so the light would not blind the crewmen. From high up on the deck, a light signaled in Morse code that the vessel was the *Algorma*, the tug stationed out of Pensacola Air Station. The men were relieved. They knew the *Algorma* had participated in at-sea rescues before, though never at night and never this far from land. Still, they did not doubt her ability to save them, and before they were in tow, each man's thoughts turned to his first action upon reaching land.

Squadron #3 in front of their barracks, 1921. Sigfred collection.

The tug pulled within seventy-five feet of the plane and fired a thin white line that arced high but fell on top of the wing. Sture shinnied up the brace wires and engine mount of the starboard wing and grabbed the braided silk line. He carried the line down and attached it firmly to the hull. When assured that the ¾ inch line was securely attached, the other three men went hand over hand along the line to the *Algorma* where sweating boatswains pulled them onto the deck.

The *Algorma* then signaled that a heavier line had been attached to the ¾ inch line and that Sture should haul it in. Tugging hand over hand, he hauled the line in until a loop of the thicker line, a hawser, was visible. He grabbed the loop and attached it to the heavy steel bridle permanently fastened to the ship's keel. When he had finished securing the hawser, he hauled in the sea anchor and signaled that the tug could take over.

Before commencing her long trip to land, the *Algorma* signaled for Sture to trail a bucket from the tail to stabilize the plane. When he finished, the *Algorma* let out her towline, and by adjusting its length with a winch as the wind changed speed and direction, she towed the seaplane to land.

When the sun broke over the eastern horizon, Sture noticed in the distance the land and fading lights of Fort Pickins on Santa Rosa Island. The *Algorma* towed the seaplane to the front of squadron 3's hangar, and Sture unhitched the hawser. A landing crew in a smaller boat tied up to the seaplane and pulled it to its ramp. Then they connected a dolly below the ramp to a tractor and hoisted the seaplane onto the apron in front of the hangar.

Sture jumped from the plane onto the hangar floor and watched his crewmates step from a launch that had retrieved them from the tug. Politely ignoring the slaps on the back and congratulations of his squadron, barely hearing their apologies for a search plane having turned back after experiencing engine trouble, he met the other three men beside the plane. Silently, they shook hands with one another. Just as silently, they left the hangar, their ship injured, but still alive, behind them.

H-16 in flight over the Gulf of Mexico, 1921. Sigfred collection.

As was standard procedure for operational accidents, a board of inquiry convened the following day to determine the cause of and lessons learned from the F-5L's mishap. Each of the crewmembers testified, surprised that the board was, indeed, looking for ways to improve their aeronautics program and not for fault among the crew. The board listened attentively to each of the crew's recommendations, including those recommendations that life preservers be made a more brilliant color and the top of the upper wings of seaplanes be painted bright orange so they could be more easily located from the air. Within days the commanding officer ordered most of their recommendations implemented.

NC-2 outside hangar at Pensacola Air Station, 1921. Sigfred collection.

When the board adjourned, Sture returned to the hangar where the damaged Liberty engine had already been removed from its mounts and set beside the port wing. Torn linen dangled from the wing in a slight breeze from the harbor. Kneeling to the engine, he inspected the cold and jagged metal. He ran his fingers across deep ridges in the piston bores and smelled what remained in the engine's recesses of black, viscous fluid. Shards of steel no bigger than grains of sand glinted in the oil. He sat back on his heels and remembered the previous day.

A bright sun bathing the gulf in silver.

A jolt.

Descent.

Without realizing a question lay on his lips, he wondered how, and why, he was alive.

Behind him, a deep voice echoed through the hangar and broke his reverie. "All of the pigeons returned to the loft."

Sture looked over his shoulder to see the radio officer looming tall at the edge of the wing. The officer stared through the open hangar doors to the Gulf, not looking at Sture. Outside the hangar, the afternoon sun bathed the water in a yellow haze, and two F-5Ls bobbed on the surf.

"Even the first pigeon that perched on the wing. Got back about an hour before we did. Evidently figured it could make it back when it sighted land, even with the oily feathers."

With his left hand, the lieutenant commander removed his hat and dragged his palm across short brown hair matted in a ridge where his hat had rested. With his right hand, he wiped his forehead and kneaded the back of his neck. Then he placed his hat squarely back on his head and looked directly at Sture.

"Damnedest thing I ever saw. All the pigeons made it back to the loft."

Flying Submarines

1921 -1922

In late November of 1921, the Personnel Officer at Pensacola Air Station called general quarters. Hundreds of enlisted men gathered in the large green gymnasium that also served as the base movie theater when weather prevented use of the outdoor screen. The Personnel Officer stood at a lectern before the crowd, his lips pursed, his gaze cast down at a sheaf of papers on the panel before him. While the men milled about the gymnasium, gathering and spreading rumors about the officer's speech, he straightened the papers, leafed through them, licking his thumb at every third page, then straightened the pages again. At precisely ten o'clock, he glanced at his pocket watch and

N-9, primary trainer at the Pensacola Air Station, 1921.
Sigfred collection.

cleared his throat. The men grew quiet as they took their seats, and the gymnasium filled with palpable expectation.

"As you may be aware, the aeronautics program has experienced significant scrutiny and growth since our victory in Europe. Against tremendous pressure from the highest levels of government, our military leaders have taken every opportunity to prepare for another war so that there may never again be a war. If there is another war, they have prepared so that we may be better armed and better trained than we, or any other fighting force in the world has ever been. But these preparations have not come without a cost."

He looked up from his papers, directly into the eyes of the men sitting nearest him. Slowly and often referring to his notes, he explained that while the Bureau of Navigation had redoubled its efforts in the area of aviation, most of those efforts had been directed toward the development of carrier-based airplanes. Science and technology would characterize the Navy of the future. Even while the Navy prepared, however, perhaps *because* it prepared for the future, the nation had called for reductions in defense spending. The bottom line, he concluded without emotion, was that the Navy had already reduced its number of men by approximately 75% and its number of ships by approximately 51% since the end of the war, but the Bureau of Navigation demanded further reductions.

"If any one of you is not satisfied with your current situation, this is your chance to change it. All you have to do is to walk down to building #45, the stone office building near the gate, and ask for an

HS-2L, secondary trainer at the Pensacola Air Station, 1921.
Sigfred collection.

application for a Special Order Discharge. Sign it and give it to the yeoman, and you will be a free man tonight."

To hear the words spoken aloud that until then had been only whispers sent a current of surprise through the room. For weeks, Sture, with the other members of his squadron, had listened to and doubted rumors that the Bureau of Navigation had ordered additional reductions in the number of naval personnel and ships. Only a week before, he had read that the nation's shipyards were scrapping at least four 10,000-ton battleships for which the keels had already been laid. Now, the Personnel Officer had essentially verified those rumors and more. Only three years after the end of the war to end all wars, the nation was turning its face away from the world and from the Navy, hiding behind the economy and, in the name of global politics, from the threat of global war.

Though he could not explain why, a sense of emptiness crept through his body. His arms and legs grew heavy with fatigue.

"If you want to be home for Thanksgiving dinner," the Personnel Officer added, "get out today." Again, he straightened the papers in his hands, shoved them into a brown file, and exited the gymnasium without another word.

For several minutes, the room was silent. Then, behind Sture, a stout young man stood and picked his way past the feet of the other men in his row.

"I don't know about you, but turkey and trimmings sounds awfully good to me." He strode quickly from the room, followed by several others. Floyd Thompson,[1] who had won the silver medal for graduating at the head of his class in mechanics school at Great Lakes, joined them.

Paul "Pappy" Gunn, Sture and Roy Lubeck, Pensacola, 1921. Sigfred collection.

Sture watched the men leave, not believing they could so easily go.

---

[1] Though few could anticipate it at the time, the break with the Navy would prove a good move for Floyd Thompson and several others. After leaving the Navy, Thompson completed his Doctorate in Aeronautical Engineering, and served a long and distinguished career with the National Advisory Committee for Aeronautics (NACA) and the National Aeronautics and Space Administration (NASA). He was Director of the Langley Research Center during the early and middle sixties at the height of Projects Mercury and Apollo and served as Chairman of the Apollo 204 Accident Board that investigated the deaths of Lt. Colonels Grissom and White and Lt. Commander Chaffee on the launch pad in January of 1967.

Paul Gunn,[2] on his right, elbowed him in the ribs and winked. "Let 'em go if they want. Just means more flights for us. I'll tell you, $108.00 a month and free room and board is just too good an arrangement to give up. Are you with me?"

Sture looked at his friend. He realized that the life he had grown so quickly to love, that had seemed to offer the fulfillment of his dreams was changing before him. He remembered his brother on the battlefield in France, an image he had created years before of a scared and blood-soaked ground, a gray sky falling toward the earth, the charred branches of a tree reaching toward that lonely sky, and a lone soldier leaning against its trunk. He recalled his father rising from bed in the cold, dark hours of morning, his muffled cough and whispers, and the muted rustling of cloth against his bearded chin. He heard again the slap of reins against a horse's flanks as his father prepared for another day in an endless string of days, delivering strangers' words to strangers' homes. Life, he had already learned, was what he made of it, but life in Parkers Prairie seemed both remote and unpromising. Though he loved his family more than he could imagine, he knew that the last thing he could do was return home. Somehow, to do so would be to give up on a future he could not yet articulate, to buy into the hopelessness and complacence that

---

[2] Paul Irvin "Pappy" Gunn joined the Navy on August 8, 1917 and was discharged on August 7, 1924. He reenlisted on August 8, 1924, after discovering that Congress had passed a rider to the Appropriations Bill allowing enlisted men as well as officers to be trained as pilots. Had Sture waited, he too could have received the flight training he desired. On August 6, 1937, with twenty years of service, Gunn finally retired from the Navy. He went to work as a pilot with the K-T Inter Island Flying Service, and in 1939 became a pilot with Philippine Air Lines where he remained until the start of World War II. Sture often accompanied Gunn on his flights when he had a layover in the Philippines. On December 8, 1941 Gunn was sworn into the Army Air Force by the adjutant general at Fort McKinley in the Philippines. In January of 1942, while Pappy was evacuating President Quezon from the country, the Japanese occupied Manila, and Gunn's wife and children were detained in the University of Santo Tomas where they remained until February of 1945. Fueled by his desire to be safely reunited with his family, Gunn embarked upon one of the most successful aviation careers of World War II. The press, however, to protect Gunn's family, never reported his successes against the Japanese. His exploits became famous after publication in 1959 of his biography *The Saga of Pappy Gunn* by his former commanding officer General George S. Kenney. After the war, he returned to civilian flying and died on October 11, 1957 in an airplane accident.

characterized the nation's determination to shrink from the world around it. Without the Navy and the future it offered, his life, like the various pasts he imagined, seemed dark and shapeless.

"They won't get rid of me this easily," he whispered. "I'm with you."

Two lines of men snaked their way down the paths of the Air Station, one bound for building #45 and the freedoms of civilian life, the other for their barracks. Gunn and Sture lagged behind and lost themselves in a discussion of an air-cooled engine due out soon from Packard. The two men forgot the Personnel Officer's ominous invitation. Their planes, if nothing else, awaited.

Despite Sture's hopes, the realities of international politics forced further reductions in the Navy. Even while the Personnel Officer's words echoed over the shellacked floors of the gym, representatives from the United States, Great Britain, Japan, France and Italy were meeting in Washington, DC. Their reported goal was to pound out the details of a treaty that would halt the post-war naval expansion. On February 6, 1922, the nations signed the Treaty for the Limitation of

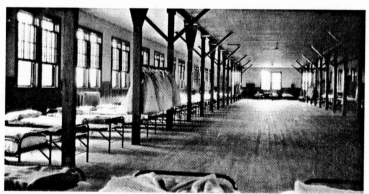

Pensacola Air Station barracks, 1921. Sigfred collection.

Naval Armament. The treaty limited the size of each Navy in relation to the others and established the maximum displacement of all ships at 35,000 tons, the displacement of aircraft carriers at 27,000 tons, and total U.S. aircraft carrier displacement at 135,000 tons. Though U.S. negotiators hoped these limitations would breed efficiencies into naval planning and construction and encourage the development of more promising technologies, the immediate effect was to force drastic reductions throughout the fleet. If ratified, the treaty was to become effective in August 1923. The ratification vote was scheduled for February.

Though forced to plan for the nation's defense with a severely limited fleet, the Chief of Naval Operations was determined not to let the Navy go down without a fight. Acting quickly and quietly outside official channels, he arranged several public relations activities in which the Navy would demonstrate its strength and encourage the nation to withhold its support of the "Five Powers Treaty." One of the most impressive and symbolic, he planned, would be a flight of the

The Fifteenth Regiment in Pensacola, 1920. Sture stands in the back row, fourth from the right. To the left of Sture is Floyd Thompson.
Sigfred collection.

Navy's famous "Flying Boats" down the Mississippi River. He ordered Pensacola's Squadron #3 to lead the flight.

The commanding officer of the Pensacola Air Station named his old favorite, Lieutenant Ralph Davison, as the flight's commander.

Demonstrating the leadership that would carry him to the highest ranks of the Navy, Davison rose to the challenge.[3]

He lost little time preparing for what he expected to be one of the highlights of his career. He arranged for three of the station's largest seaplanes, F-5Ls, to fly from Pensacola to New Orleans and up the Mississippi River to Hannibal, Missouri, hometown of Admiral Koontz, the Chief of Naval Operations. Laden with handbills urging voters to write their congressmen and ask them to vote against ratification of the "Five Powers Treaty," the planes would fly down the river from Hannibal and drop the leaflets over every town, large and small. The handbills were to be shipped by train to Hannibal where the ships' crews could collect them when they arrived. To add impact to the display, Koontz planned for the flight to set out from Pensacola the day after Navy Day, on October 13, 1922.

#3789, flagship of the flight up the Mississippi. Pensacola, 1922.
Sigfred collection.

Although Squadron #3 had several F-5Ls in its contingent of seaplanes, only two had been recently received from the factory. So Davison ordered that the third plane, the flagship, be borrowed from Squadron #5. To ensure its safe arrival, he dispatched his crew chief

---

[3] Lt. Davison ultimately rose to the rank of Rear Admiral and commanded Task Group 38.4 during its World War II bombardment of the Bonin and Volcano Islands.

to escort the plane from Squadron #5 to the Squadron #3 hangar. Several of the station's older chiefs, veterans of the war, were anxious to serve with Davison and actively sought assignment to his crew. But in a move that surprised everyone, he selected a young 2nd class petty officer as the crew chief of his flagship, #3789. Claiming to remember a flight from two years before in which a wet-behind-the-ears Swede had repaired and re-timed an engine in just over an hour while his plane floated lifelessly in Mobile Bay, Davison selected Sture as the crew chief of his flagship. Though the chiefs were disappointed, they knew Sture and were well aware of his skill. Most accepted the news gracefully.

The men in Squadron #5 were not so graceful. Resenting that their plane, the flagship for the flight, would not be accompanied by a crew chief from their own squadron, they booed Sture's arrival. As he taxied the plane to his own squadron hangar, he listened silently to their jeers. Though he sympathized with the men from squadron #5, he refused to let their anger dampen his excitement.

He had only a week to prepare the plane for flight. Although almost new, she had fifty hours on her engines, and his first duty was to replace both engines with recently overhauled engines so they would not exceed seventy-five hours of run time during the trip or, worse, develop problems several hundred miles from suitable repair and supply facilities. He selected a young sailor from Baton Rouge

One of the planes of the flight up the Mississippi. Pensacola, 1922.
Sigfred collection.

named Pete Felder to assist him. Together, the two worked round the clock to prepare every inch of the ship for perfect flight.

Their primary concern was the plane's engines. The Liberty engines developed during World War I were produced by General Motors, Packard, and Ford. In most respects, they were equal in quality and workmanship, but the welding of the water jackets on the Ford engines was superior to that of the other two, so Sture selected two Ford engines to install on the plane. Because the ships would operate in fresh water where they would have significantly less buoyancy than in salt water, he also decided to replace the plane's propellers. A spray of water from the bow wake would inevitably hit the props during take off, before the plane rose onto its step. This spray damaged the propellers, often so severely that it was necessary for the crew to return to the hangar to change props. Sture knew that the plane's sitting even lower in fresh water would only exacerbate the problem. So with the help of a friend who worked in central supply - better known as the "Storm Cellar" - he located and installed two wooden props covered in Bakelite[4] and tipped with Monel[5]. The Bakelite coating would protect the props from the force of the bow

#3789 preparing for takeoff, Pensacola, 1922. Sigfred collection.

---

[4] Bakelite, a forerunner of Teflon, is a synthetic resin with properties similar to plastic.

[5] Monel is a nickel-copper alloy noted for its superior corrosion resistance, high strength, and high ductility across a wide range of moderate temperatures.

spray, while the Monel tips would resist pitting. Because they were six inches shorter than the normal props, the propellers would also provide higher revolutions per minute. Though this would result in greater wear on the engines, the higher RPM would also provide the plane with more power for thrust and result in better take off performance.

Sture's selections proved effective. During her long distance test flight on October 10, 1922, #3789 not only performed better than most of the other planes in the squadron, she also outperformed her sister ships for the flight up the Big Muddy. In every respect, from reduced take off time and fuel consumption, to increased speed and maneuverability, #3789 was the finest flying boat in Pensacola as the "Flight to Save the Navy" drew near.

On the morning of Friday, October 13, 1922, the bay shone smooth as a mirror. No wind rippled the surface of the silver water. No tide sent waves toward the white sands of the beach. Because of this, each of the three planes slogged awkwardly through the water, attempting flight that refused to come and reminding Sture of the defiant throes of an oil-soaked duck, thrashing in brackish surf. The planes sat, nose high, near the shore of Santa Rosa Island, the shallow water providing little buoyancy to assist their takeoff, the lack of breeze offering little hope of lift.

The flagship carried Lieutenant Davison, a copilot-navigator, a radio officer, Sture, the crew chief and his helper Pete Felder. In addition, a 130-pound Carpenters Mate and a 250-pound Chief Photographer were onboard to participate in the flight. Several aborted takeoffs proved that the combination of poor buoyancy and extra weight would prevent a successful takeoff, so Davison taxied the plane to a dock on the island and ordered the photographer off-loaded. The radio officer sent a message to the Air Station to pick the man up, and Sture called his regrets to the chief standing at the end of the dock.

"I suppose we won't get our history in pictures now."

The photographer cupped his hands in front of his mouth and shouted back to Sture. "You have your own camera, don't you?"

Sture signaled that he did.

"Then you'll have your history." The photographer clapped his hands. Even from several hundred feet away, Sture watched his body jiggle from the force of his claps, ripples of flesh undulating beneath his loose fitting coveralls. The photographer gave the crew a thumbs-up, and the plane turned toward open water and, once again, taxied for takeoff.

Behind the flagship, the two other F-5Ls lined up in single file. Without a headwind to assist them, a tandem takeoff was necessary. With luck, the airflow generated by the wake of the flagship would provide enough extra lift to the second plane to get her airborne, and her airflow would do the same for the third plane.

The planes paused for several minutes as the crews adjusted sandbags toward the back of the hull to provide the greatest nose-up attitude they could achieve. The radio officers performed their final radio checks, and the navigators rolled their maps and stuffed them into waterproof tubes. When all was ready, Lieutenant Davison pushed his throttle wide open, and the plane began to quiver in the cool water. The hull hummed as the propellers gained speed, and the plane inched forward sluggishly. Gradually gaining speed, the plane began to bob nose up, then down and up again. Sture and the Carpenters Mate moved as far back in the hull as they could climb and leaned against the aft bulkhead. Even the pilot and navigator leaned back in their seats as though to give the plane a better attitude. Slowly, the plane trudged forward, her engines roaring and the hull vibrating with the regular beat of the engines' reciprocating motion. The bow wake splashed the windshield of the cockpit, and Sture silently prayed that his Bakelite covered, Monel-tipped props would hold. Eventually, the buffeting of the hull diminished. Sture felt the plane ride higher as airflow across the wings generated the lift necessary to pull the plane onto her step. The nose rode higher, and the spray across the windshield grew thinner. Still, the men pressed their weight back against the bulkheads and their seats, willing the plane into the air. Sture closed his eyes and mouthed the words no one else could hear, but a version of which all were reciting. "Come on. Come on. Get into the air."

Suddenly, the shaking of the hull ceased, and Sture's legs, which had grown used to the vibrating, tingled as though their blood flow had just been restored. The roaring of the engines grew softer, and the nose pointed higher. Davison pulled his control wheel toward him and the angle of the plane grew steeper. The ship was in the air.

Sture, 1922.
Sigfred collection.

At approximately 1000 feet, Davison banked the plane to port and flew a wide loop around the takeoff area. The other two flying boats limped their ways into the sky. Then, when all were airborne, the two sister ships approximately three hundred yards off and behind the flagship's port and starboard wings, the formation flew in a small V to the west and the mouth of the Mississippi River.

The formation ascended to approximately 3000 feet and cruised at sixty knots toward their first destination, 224 miles and just over three hours to the west, Donaldsonville, Louisiana and the South Louisiana State Fair. Beneath them, a clear sky revealed the northern Gulf coast drifting lazily by in a soft arc of green and gold and brilliant blue. As the plane hummed hypnotically, the crew strained to catch a glimpse of the land passing silently below them. Each of the men, in his own way, thanked the sky for her welcome. Though they got off to a precarious start, the small fleet of planes was on its way to the heartland, to history, and to the future of the Navy.

Over the weekend, the fleet made daily flights over the small town of Donaldsonville, twenty-five miles south of Baton Rouge, daringly demonstrating for the crowds of rural southerners the tricks of the Navy flying boats. The planes flew dazzling dives through the air over the town and lightly touched down on the muddy green waters of the Mississippi. When the Fair was over, the three planes flew fifty-five miles east to New Orleans for the 2nd annual American Legion Convention. In New Orleans, they made two flights each day for almost a week, familiarizing themselves with the fresh water and shear air currents of the river. From the air, Sture finally understood how the city had gained one of her many nicknames, the "Crescent City." Facing Lake Ponchartrain to the west and Lake Borgne and the Gulf of Mexico to the east, the city formed an almost perfect arc along the lake and gulf shores. At her back, in a last gentle curve to the east, the Mississippi River stretched languidly before turning and rushing to the south.

Takeoffs from the river's fresh water proved significantly more difficult than the takeoff from Santa Rosa Island, but the crew did all they could to assist the planes. Carrying only necessary supplies, an anchor and sixty feet of heavy rope for mooring in the river at night, they dutifully practiced their tandem takeoffs. After the Fair and the American Legion Convention, the crews had become adept in their techniques, making the difficult and dangerous ascents and descents look easy from the ground.

On Sunday, October 22, 1922, the crew took off for their four-hour flight from New Orleans to Greenville, Mississippi, where an after church crowd of almost one hundred greeted them at the dock. The crew spent the night in Greenville, basking in the interest and good wishes of the Mississippi natives. On Monday morning, they departed early from Greenville on a four-hour flight to Memphis, where they refueled within sight of the downtown business district. Though it was a workday in the bustling port of Memphis, a crowd even larger than that in Greenville met them at the dock. Women held their wide-eyed children in the air; businessmen shook their heads in wonder, and a small group of Negroes at the back of the crowd stared with, what seemed to Sture, more than wonder, almost reverence on their faces. The crew had little time to speak with the crowds, and

Memphis, Tennessee from the air. 1922.
Sigfred collection.

hurriedly refilled their tanks for the flight to Cairo, Illinois. They expected the flight to take less than three hours.

They reached Cairo in mid-afternoon. Circling around the city before descending, they marveled at the sight of the Ohio River flowing powerfully into the even more powerful Mississippi. Sture could not help feeling that he was seeing time in the dark rivers below him and lost himself in remembrance of the books he had read as a child. Pioneers had forged their way across these rivers only a half-century before on countless journeys to the west.

The West. It had long hovered in his mind and memory as an embodiment of courage and spirit, all he thought it meant to be an American. Disappointment seized him as he realized he would never be a pioneer, that time and technology had robbed him of the opportunity. But in a rare moment of understanding, he saw that the little boy who had been born in Parkers Prairie, further west than he now flew, the boy who had headed east to find adventure had, in fact, found destiny. Though he seldom allowed himself such indulgence, he basked in a sense of pride as the flagship, *his* flagship, dove toward the swirling Mississippi and settled gently on its surface, as though a part of the river itself. Perhaps the world still had room for pioneers.

#3789 over St. Louis, 1922. Sigfred collection.

The next morning, the small fleet made its way to St. Louis, Missouri, Lieutenant Davison's hometown. Hundreds of people crowded the river's shore to welcome home their favorite son. When Lieutenant Davison stepped from the plane, whispers of recognition passed from the front of the crowd to the back, followed by a wave of cheers. Young girls waved at the cheerful lieutenant. Businessmen nodded knowingly. Davison waved back, and, like a politician on the stump, shook hands and kissed babies as he passed through the crowd.

While the Lieutenant greeted his hometown, the crews busied themselves with anchoring the planes and tying them securely for the night. Chief Sobola, crew chief for the #3681, stood on the wing of his plane and faced into the wind. "It looks like a cold front is moving in," he shouted to Sture.

Sture nodded and checked the tension of a line tied around his wing strut.

"Are you going to drain your radiator if it gets cold enough to freeze tonight?"

Sture looked into the sky. "I'm going to drain it," he shouted back to the chief, "but not because of the weather. The system needs to be flushed. When I checked the water in Cairo, it looked like creamed coffee, and the engine's been running a little hotter than it should. You probably ought to flush yours too."

"Well," Sobola yelled back, "where in the hell am I going to get fresh water to refill it."

Sture looked at the chief and laughed. "How about here? In this river?" He shrugged and pointed toward the gray water.

Sobola looked around him and laughed, a deep, loud laugh that skipped across the water. "Well," he shouted, "I guess I spent too many years at sea. Just a salty old dog."

Sobola jumped from the wing of his plane to the dock. Bending to one knee, he dipped his hand into the river and brought it to his lips. "Sure enough," he called. "Fresh as water from a well."

Though every town along the Mississippi had greeted the crew with admiration and jubilation, St. Louis offered the largest, most boisterous welcome so far. As the men stood surrounded by well-wishers, a thin, distinguished man stepped up to Lieutenant Davison.

Bridge between St. Louis and East St. Louis, 1922. Sigfred collection.

"My son is in the Navy," he stated quietly. "He is, in fact, like you, an aviator stationed in Pensacola. Since he can't be with us, well, I would be honored if my wife and I could welcome you and your crew as we would like to welcome him."

Knowing all to well the ache of separation from one's family that military life offered, Lieutenant Davison thanked the man for his invitation and explained that he would have to get permission from his family. Like the man, he suggested, they too missed their son and he did not want to disappoint them. After greeting his own family and spending a suitable amount of time catching up, Lieutenant Davison asked for their indulgence to allow him to accept the man's invitation. Acknowledging that they had to share their young aviator with the public, his family agreed. The man flushed with pride as he ushered the crew through the crowd and escorted them to his home.

He was true to his promise of providing a welcome fit for his own son. Mr. Snitzer, as he introduced himself, and his wife treated the men to a lavish dinner and forced them to tell and retell of their adventures in the air. Though they had heard a few stories from their son, they admitted that this was too little to satisfy their curiosity, and like most of the country, they hungered for information about the exploits of the men who dared to challenge gravity and to regularly face death. With admiration that bordered on worship, they sat enraptured as each of the men contributed his perspective about aviation. As the night faded into morning, Lieutenant Davison apologized for having to leave and thanked Mr. Snitzer for his hospitality. Snitzer shook hands with each of the crewmembers, and his wife offered her hand for their kisses. Then the men stepped into the darkness, suddenly quiet without their stories. When they turned the corner, Sture looked back to see the couple standing in their doorway, silhouetted against the stark yellow light of their hall. He waved to the couple before disappearing around the corner.

The following morning, the crew attempted to make their flight to Hannibal, but shortly after takeoff, the flagship's right engine quit running, and Lieutenant Davison was forced to land the plane in the river just north of the city. The other two ships followed.

Troubleshooting revealed that the ignition battery was dead. Not normally prone to failure, the batteries were small and light, so, anticipating the possibility that it might fail, the crew had carried an extra in their supplies just to be safe. Though repairs and a test flight went quickly, the crew decided to remain in St. Louis for one more evening to catch up on the rest they had lost the night before. They were again treated to festivities, but the night ended earlier than the previous, and the crew rose early the next morning to make their way to Hannibal.

The Bar Building in downtown St. Louis, 1922. Sigfred collection.

They arrived in Hannibal shortly after noon; the levee beside the river was crowded with people. The local newspaper had published several reports that three seaplanes were to arrive shortly after Navy Day, and the town had waited expectantly for several days for the three dots to appear on the horizon. A crowd even larger than in St. Louis had ventured to the river to welcome them, and as word spread that the planes had arrived, the crowd continued to grow. Fortunately, the river ran relatively shallow in autumn, and there was plenty of room for crowds to gather on the levee.

Because the river ran shallow, however, its current was also especially swift, and Davison made the approach to the levee slowly and carefully. Sture tied a coil of rope to one of the wing struts, and as Davison taxied the plane near the levee, he jumped from the wing and quickly tried to locate a place to moor. The levee was paved with cobblestones similar to those in the street and featured large iron rings several feet apart for tying up boats. The crowd was so thick that he had trouble finding a ring, and the plane began to drift with the current. Sture planted his feet on the stones and pulled with all his strength to keep the plane from drifting downstream. A large man in coveralls stepped from the crowd and directed several people away from the levee's edge. He then pointed to a ring and helped Sture lash the plane.

As the two men struggled with the rope, a voice boomed from the crowd. "Sir, you'll have to move your ship farther upstream. Three airplanes are landing here today, and this is where we plan to moor them."

Sture finished tying his knot, then stood and looked at the heavyset man who had obviously arrived after the planes' landing.

The man in the coveralls who had helped Sture tie up the plane looked at the heavyset man and spat into the river. "Well what in Sam heel do you think these are?"

The larger man looked at the crowd, then at the three airplanes floating on the current. Speaking slowly, as though to a child, he answered, "Why, these are submarines. Haven't you ever seen a

#3681 on the Mississippi River. This is the plane that was damaged while landing in Hannibal. Sigfred collection.

submarine?"

The crowd roared with delight, and the man reddened.

Removing his hat, Sture stepped toward him and offered his hand. "I'm Aviation Machinist Mate Second Class Sture Sigfred, sir. I'm attached to the Naval Air Station Pensacola, and I assure you, as strange as they may appear, these are, in fact, airplanes. Seaplanes, to be more precise. We are here at the Chief of Naval Operations' orders and are happy to be guests in your city." He had heard Lieutenant Davison's speech all the way up the river and, to save the man some embarrassment, decided that he should give it rather than wait for the lieutenant.

The large man took Sture's hand and pumped it up and down for several seconds. "Well, we're darned glad to have you," the man replied. Then he bent to Sture's ear and whispered, "Seaplanes? Well, I'll be damned."

During their exchange, Sture noticed that the second plane had tied up next to his. But when the man let go of his hand, the third plane, #3681, had still not tied up. He looked across the river and saw the plane near the center, drifting south, her engines silent. A thick wire was coiled around her starboard propeller and one of the wing struts, and the radiator had been pulled loose from its foundation. A quick scan of the river and adjacent shoreline revealed that one of the telephone wires that spanned the river about 2000 yards downstream was missing. As he was later to confirm, Sture suspected that the plane had flown into the wire and would be out of commission until the crew could have spare parts shipped from Pensacola.

Pete Peterson, who assisted Sture in repairing the #3681, on the levee in Hannibal. 1922. Sigfred collection.

Working quickly with the crew chief from the second plane, Sture cleared a path along the levee and called to the third plane to heave a line to shore. After three attempts, Sture caught the line. Gesturing for others to help him, the other crew chief and several of the men who had come to see the planes grabbed the line and heaved against the current to pull her in. Struggling to maintain a foothold, the group inched the plane toward the cobblestone levee, while another group wrapped the slack in the line around a cleat near the iron ring to which still a third group had tied the plane.

When all of the men were sure that the plane was secure, they wiped their hands against coveralls and trousers, and Lieutenant Davison stepped from #3789 and shook his head. The mayor greeted him and welcomed him to Hannibal. Then looking down the levee at the stricken plane and gesturing to the group of men that had helped secure the plane, he smiled. "I'm sure it's clear by now, we'll do whatever we can to make your stay here enjoyable."

The crowd gathered around the crews of the three planes and moved en masse from the levee toward the street. The large man who had earlier thought the planes were submarines draped his arm over Sture's shoulder. "Well, sir, you can keep your machinery. It looks to me like it still comes down to muscle."

Sture looked up at the man and nodded. "Yes sir. Sometimes it still comes down to muscle." Under his breath, he added, "and sometimes to muscle and brains."

Because of the mishap with the #3681, the crew had little time to socialize in Hannibal. They swiftly let out the anchors on all three planes then checked into the Mark Twain Hotel. After taking warm baths and changing into clean uniforms, they met for a summit.

"The first thing we need to do is determine what parts we need and send a message to Pensacola to have them shipped." The pilot of the damaged plane, Lieutenant Crinkley, took charge. "Sobola, you'll need to take care of that."

"Yes sir," the crew chief answered.

"It will take a few days for the parts to get here, so we'll also have to make arrangements to stay on in Hannibal until they arrive. I'll take care of that."

Lieutenant Davison spoke quietly. "When you get the chance, Lieutenant, I'll also need a report on the accident."

"Understood," answered Crinkley.

Sobola looked at Crinkley and Davison and started to speak. Unable to find the right words for his request, he turned to Sture and sighed. Finally, as though steeling his courage, he inhaled and spoke quickly. "Sigfred, I know it's a lot to ask, but we've been away from Pensacola for almost two weeks now. Between that and the time we took to get ready for this trip, I haven't seen my wife and son in almost a month, and, well, I miss them. I'd be very appreciative if you and I could trade places and I could return to the air station with the other planes while you repair #3681."

Sture, who considered his own plane a part of himself and not something he could easily leave, thought for a moment before he answered. "Well, chief. I suppose that's all right with me, but I need to talk with Lieutenant Davison before I let you know." He turned to the Davison. "Sir, could I speak to you outside?"

"Certainly." Davison instructed the men to continue their conversation, and he and Sture stepped into the hall.

As soon as the door shut behind them, Davison began to laugh.

"What do you want me to do, sir? I mean #3789 is my ship. I got her ready, and I know every inch of her as well as I know my own hand. And, well sir, honestly, I don't want to hand her over to someone else."

Davison stifled his laughter and placed a hand on Sture's shoulder. He spoke quietly, his voice still broken by laughter. "Take the plane if you want, Sig. Or don't. It's your decision. You can stay on here for a few extra days, take the ship, and maybe see some of the sights of Hannibal. That's fine with me. Just understand that Sobola's afraid the repairs are out of his league. He's not homesick at all. He just thinks he's not up to the job."

"But that's not true, sir. He's here because he's one of the best crew chiefs in the squadron."

"Well, Sig, you know that. I know that, and Crinkley knows that. Heck, everyone knows that except Sobola. But as long as he thinks he's not up to it, he isn't. What was it Henry Ford said? 'Think you can. Think you can't. Either way you're right.' Something like that. Now come on inside. Help the chief save face and take his plane, if you want. But don't worry about us. You've done such a fine job with ours that anyone can maintain her."

Sture thought about the lieutenant's words for several minutes. He had done such a fine job with #3789 that anyone could maintain her. He thought about the long trip back to Pensacola and the perils a solitary plane might meet. Though a repair on the river would be nothing compared to repairs in the Gulf that had long ago become second nature to him, he thought it his duty to take the plane that needed him most.

"I'll swap with him, sir. But I would like to fly with you this afternoon one last time."

"I wouldn't have it any other way. Now let's go back inside and get this problem taken care of."

#3789 in the Mississippi River at Hannibal, just after Sture's last flight in her. 1922. Sigfred collection.

That evening, October 26, 1922, just before the sun set over Hannibal, Missouri, Sture boarded the #3789 for the final time. As Davison flew the plane over several of the small towns around Hannibal, Sture dropped leaflets from an open hatch. When the bag of leaflets was empty, the plane landed on the river and again tied up to the levee. Sture disembarked slowly from the plane that had once belonged to squadron #5 and in less than a week would again belong to them. But for three weeks, she had been his.

With a down-turned gaze and a sadness that surprised even him, he met Sobola at the edge of the levee. "She's yours. Take care of her."

Twilight descended over Hannibal, and a chill filled the air. As the other crewmembers hurried toward the hotel, Sture lagged behind and walked alone back to the Mark Twain Hotel, staring toward the sky and occasionally glancing back to the river where #3789 lay moored for the night.

The next afternoon, the two good planes departed for the south. Sture, his new assistant Pete Peterson, Lieutenant Crinkley, the navigator and the radio officer remained in Hannibal, waiting at the hotel for word from the express office as parts slowly arrived from the east. Peterson, also from the Midwest, and Sture got along well, and the two enjoyed their few days of rest in the hometown of Admiral Koontz and Samuel Langhorne Clemens, better known to them as Mark Twain.

They spent their days performing the routine installations they had grown used to in the hangars of Pensacola as parts filtered in from the Air Station. The only difference here was the need for extra care to prevent dropping the precious parts into the river. To help them, Sture tied string around each of their wrists and secured it to their tools and the parts they were installing. During the evenings, their tools carefully stowed and the plane securely tied to the levee, they explored the streets and alleys of Hannibal and imagined themselves the grown Huck Finn and Tom Sawyer.

On the afternoon of Monday, October 30, they completed their repairs, and Lieutenant Crinkley completed a successful test flight over the river. He planned to leave the next morning, but another cold front brought rain and heavy winds into the city. Partially to wait out the weather and partially to reward the efforts of his young crew chief and helper, he agreed to indulge their whim and remain in Hannibal for Halloween. Perhaps because he was worried about the repercussions of flying into the telephone lines or perhaps because he was simply the senior representative of the Navy in the Chief of Naval Operations' hometown, he was uncharacteristically reserved. But he refused to let his personal concerns interfere with a few days of fun for the two younger men. They behaved well and worked hard, and one more evening in Hannibal would have little effect on their careers or the future of the Navy.

Halloween passed quietly. Sture and Pete sat in front of the hotel, passing out hand-pulled taffy to the children and sharing their sea stories with a few businessmen who ventured into and out of the hotel restaurant. When the sun finally set and gaslights buzzed in the darkness, the two men grew quiet.

"Do you think you'll stay in?" Pete asked.

Sture stared into the flame of a gaslight on the corner. "A year ago I would have said yes. In fact, just over a year ago I did say yes. But they won't let enlisted men be pilots anymore, and I don't see any way with an eighth grade education I can get into college and get a commission. The pilots have been good about teaching me to fly, but unless I can be a pilot, it'll always have to be on the sly. I'll have to steal my time, and I

Pete Peterson and Sture repairing the #3681, Hannibal, 1922. Sigfred collection.

don't want to do that."

"So you're going to get out?"

"I suppose so."

"What will you do?"

"Fly. That's all I want to do. That's all I can think to do."

Sture unwrapped a piece of taffy and tossed it into his mouth. Rather than chew, he allowed the taffy to melt and coat his tongue with a warm, sweet blanket. "I don't know how I'm going to do it, but I know that's what I'm going to do."

He leaned back on the bench in front of the hotel and closed his eyes. The street was vacant, and from the hotel lobby, only the voices of the porter and night clerk drifted into the street. "That's all I know. I'm going to fly."

The two men sat silent late into the night, while on the corner, a gaslight flickered and hummed against the surrounding darkness. Near midnight, the sky cleared, and a soft yellow light reflected sharply on the surface of the still river.

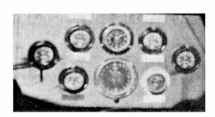

F-5L instrument panel. Sigfred collection.

The next morning, under a bright sun that burned the chill from the air, the crew loaded their belongings and completed their pre-flight checks. With all of their sandbags placed aft and the nose of the ship pointing up, they shoved off from the levee. Facing into a light wind, Lieutenant Crinkley applied full power and the ship began to gain speed. But before she rose onto her step, Sture heard a loud banging and scraping under the hull. The plane lurched

Mississippi River at St. Louis, from the air. 1922. Sigfred collection.

to a stop. Crinkley quickly reduced his engine speed to idle and informed the crew that they had hit a sandbar.

"We're cursed. That's all it can be," Pete called from the back of the plane, admitting a superstition that had hounded seamen for centuries and had already begun to hound airmen.

65

He threw his hands into the air and shook his head with disgust.

"May be," Crinkley answered, "but we'll be skewered if we don't get back to Pensacola soon."

While the lieutenant maintained control of the plane, the navigator, radio officer, Pete and Sture stripped to their skivvies, climbed onto the wing, and jumped into the waist deep water over the sandbar. From the levee, hoots and whistles rose from a crowd of men, and the few women who had come to see the crew off turned away from the river. The four men, trying to ignore the catcalls and laughter from shore, grabbed hold of the struts at the very tip of the wing and pushed downward as Crinkley again applied power to the engines. The weight on the wing and increased power raised the keel clear of the sandbar and the plane broke free, leaving the four men stranded in the cold water. Crinkley taxied the plane upstream and turned toward the sandbar, trying to maneuver close enough to pick up his crew. Afraid of grounding again, he stopped far short of the sandbar and turned the nose upstream; signaling for the men to swim to the plane, he applied only enough power to keep her still against the current.

"This is not going to look good on his record," Pete whispered to Sture.

Sture nodded and added, "The only record that has to look good in

Members of Squadron #3 lounging on the beach at
Pensacola, 1922. Sigfred collection.

my mind is his record of landings. If we make it back to Pensacola alive, his record is plenty clear for me."

One by one, the men swam to the plane and climbed onto the aft edge of the wing, taking care to avoid the spinning propellers. Once onboard, they removed their wet underwear and donned their flight suits. As Crinkley, one last time, applied full power, a gust of wind on the bow lifted the plane quickly to the step and into the air. Crinkley climbed as rapidly as he dared and turned to the south as a squall moved in behind him. As he passed over the levee, he saw a few women scurrying for cover while the men stood in the rain and cheered the successful takeoff.

With only the river to guide them, Crinkley kept the plane below the clouds as a storm chased them south. Two-and-a-half hours later, virtually exhausted from fighting the wind and rain, he sighted St. Louis on the horizon and lowered his altitude for the approach.

A thirty-knot west wind greeted him just north of the city and whipped the river into churning waves. Forced to make a cross-river landing, he banked to port and then made a 180-degree turn to starboard, facing the plane into the wind. Holding the control wheel with both hands, he ordered all of the sandbags moved to the front of the hull and pointed the nose toward the seething waters. As the men clutched their seats, he guided the plane low over the eastern bank and reduced his speed, allowing the plane to stall approximately a quarter of the way across the river and to drop onto the waters that churned like the heavy seas of the Gulf. Once on the water, Crinkley applied more power and turned to the north, against the current, and attempted to locate a safe anchorage. Several hundred yards from the shore, Sture dropped the anchor and slowly paid out his line, allowing Crinkley to jockey the plane into a secure position. With its bowline paid out, the plane shifted like a weather vane to 315 degrees, caught between the swift southern current and the brisk west wind. For several minutes, the men sat silent in the plane, bobbing on the waves, as a small launch performed her own battle with the wind and current off the starboard wing. When the crew was certain that the anchor would hold on the muddy river bottom, they stepped, one by one, onto the wing and inched their way toward the launch. Crinkley was the last to emerge from the plane, and as the five-man crew rode the small launch toward the shore and its promising warmth, he turned back as though to assure himself that his plane was at last, truly safe.

Members of Squadron #3 on extra duty for sleeping late, 1922.
Pensacola. Sigfred collection.

The Snitzers met the crew at the head of the dock and drove them to the Belcher Bath Hotel. They waited patiently in the lobby as the men changed their uniforms and calmed their nerves, then drove them to their home for a warm dinner. When the men finished eating, Mr. Snitzer leaned back from the table and looked at Crinkley, still pale and haggard from the difficult flight and landing. With his wife in the kitchen, he pulled his chair next to the lieutenant's.

"You need a drink."

"Really, Mr. Snitzer, that's not necessary," the lieutenant answered.

"Aw, to hell with decorum *and* prohibition. You need a drink."

Informing his wife that they were simply going out for a drive and would return soon, he led the men back to his Model-T and drove them to 205 S. Broadway. "This," he said, as they entered a large, old fashioned bar, "is my place of business. And you, my adopted sons, are welcome to all we have."

Several hours later, slightly tipsy and much calmer, the men struggled back to the Model-T. Snitzer deposited them in front of the Belcher Bath and wished them luck. As he drove toward his home, the men made their way to their rooms and slept more peacefully than they had slept in weeks.

Their takeoff the next morning went smoothly, and with clear skies around them, they arrived in Cairo in just over two hours. During their landing, the plane snagged something under the water that tore one side of a pontoon from its wing. With nothing onboard to repair the pontoon and no desire to wire Pensacola for additional parts, the crew decided to continue the trip without the repairing the pontoon.

Sture with friend, Roy Lubeck, Pensacola, 1921. Sigfred collection.

Sture cautioned Crinkley to be extremely careful with the plane, and Crinkley cautioned Sture and Pete to stand by to jump onto the opposite wing to keep the damaged wing out of the water during takeoffs and landings. The crew refueled and, with nerves on edge, successfully managed another takeoff.

As the plane quickly gained altitude, Pete turned to Sture. "I really don't know if this is worth $1.68 a day."

Two hours and forty minutes later, they landed safely in Memphis and walked away from the plane without a backward glance.

Somewhat bedraggled and almost broke, the crew laid over for an extra day in Memphis, and on the morning of the November 3, performed a twenty-five minute test flight to reassure themselves that the plane was safe enough to return to Pensacola. The following day, they flew two hours and

Matt and Sture joking around in Pensacola, 1922. Sigfred collection.

twenty-five minutes from Memphis to Greenville, two hours and twenty-five minutes from Greenville to Natchez, Mississippi, and two hours and fifteen minutes from Natchez to Donaldsonville. With seven hours and five minutes of airtime behind them, they landed in Donaldsonville and without ado checked into a hotel for a much-needed rest. The following day, they made courtesy calls to some of the people they had met on their way to Hannibal, and on November 6, the last day of their twenty-five day odyssey, made the return leg of their trip from Donaldsonville to Pensacola.

Squadron #3 on work detail, 1922. Sigfred Collection.

Three hours and forty-five minutes after takeoff, they taxied to the Squadron #3 hangar in Pensacola. With a mutual sigh of relief, they killed the engines and turned the plane over to a crew of mechanics who pulled the plane onto the ramp and into the hangar for long

Sture in Reo, 1922. Sigfred collection.

70

overdue repairs. Four days later, Sture was back onboard an F-5L for regular test and navigation flights over the Gulf, but he never again flew in #3681. Unlike his feelings for #3789, which had been returned unharmed to Squadron #5, he never regretted the loss.

The next two months proved routine for the seasoned crew chief. Two test flights, a solo qualification flight for Lieutenants Peterson and Kiefer, and five navigation flights ended his naval career. On the blustery morning of January 6, 1923, he changed into his civilian clothes, packed his uniforms and logbooks into his sea bag, and accepted an honorable discharge from the U.S. Navy. With 257 flights and over 343 hours in the air, he bid goodbye to his friends and promised Matt he would keep in touch.[6] Then walking past the gate of the Pensacola Air Station, he aimed himself toward the railroad station and chased another day.

Sture driving through Alabama, 1921. Sigfred collection.

---

[6] Sture and Matt Kandle remained friends until Matt's death at sixty.

Vagabond

1923 - 1925

After his years beside the Gulf of Mexico, the deep snows and biting winds of Parkers Prairie in the winter of 1923 proved more bitter than Sture had remembered. In what seemed a whiteout of drifting powder and time, a numbing blankness that obscured his future, he stumbled like a somnambulist through his days, clinging to and surviving only on his tenuous hopes for a career in aviation. But the roar of an airborne engine never broke the deafening regularity of Lake Adley's waters. The shadow of wings never darkened the plain.

Sture on his return to Parkers Prairie, 1923. Sigfred collection.

Though he tried, however feebly, he could not shake his obsession with aviation. With enough time in aviation to have developed a love for it and not so much time as to have lost a sense of romanticism, his remained a youthful desire, more passionate than reasonable. Most people aware of the field, armed with the knowledge that each month brought another death to the ranks of those who chose to fly, felt that aviation could never establish itself as a viable form of transportation. And while they admired, often worshipped as heroes, those men and women who pursued careers in aviation, they also wondered at their sanity. Despite this and the warnings from family and friends that he ought to find a more suitable, a more practical career, Sture's one consuming goal remained to soar, full throttle, past a sculpted ceiling of billowing white and into the rose-hued rays of the sky.

After only a few weeks as a civilian, before spring melted the snow from ruts that passed as roads, and plows passed unobstructed along rails leading from the township, Sture once again boarded the local train. Laden with what little he owned, he climbed into the warm hold of the passenger compartment and headed toward Chicago, the Windy City, where each breeze was a headwind that promised quick and easy flight.

Chicago was not what he remembered from his days in the Navy; nor was it what he imagined or hoped. The short-lived, post-war expansion had already played itself out, and the Harding administration's refusal to meddle in free enterprise had resulted in a severe agricultural depression that gripped the Midwest. The effects of the bust spread quickly to Chicago. Crowds of dark-cloaked and unemployed hopefuls crammed the lobbies of businesses that clustered like a frightened mob at the southeast arc of Lake Michigan. Businessmen along the loop, trapped in economic recession, added to the number of unemployed. Those lucky enough to find jobs as laborers in the warehouses and depots that radiated from the city, for the first time in the nation's history created a new class of the underemployed. Despite reductions in immigration, businesses could not keep pace with the number of laborers flocking continually to the city. The "return to normalcy" that had seemed so promising only two years earlier had resulted in increased isolationism, less government involvement in business and trade, and increased corruption. It left the city with little more to offer the optimistic and dreamy young man than had the bleak, snow-packed plains of Parkers Prairie. Combined with a national sense of skepticism over the potential of aviation as an economically viable form of transportation - despite regular transcontinental airmail flights - the economic conditions in Chicago and throughout the country made Sture's hopes for a career in aviation seem less promising with each passing day.

Still, he refused to allow conditions he could not control to affect his attitude. Though his first year in Chicago was a confusion of dashed desires and wandering, almost aimless, employment, he clung to his goal of forging a path into aviation and, somehow, made each job, however unpromising, a firm landing of his foot along that path. Shortly after his arrival in Chicago, he and Matt Kandle, recently discharged from the Navy, served a brief apprenticeship in the dusky business district of the city to learn pattern making. The job, like many in the Chicago of the early twenties, paid less than a livable salary, and Sture was forced to accept a position as a clerk in the Chicago Post Office. After only a few months, he realized that he was unsuited for inside work and saw no future with the Postal Service. He resigned his position and applied for a chauffeur's license.

On January 12, 1924, with Illinois Chauffeur's License number 53681 in his hand, he took his third job in less than a year, driving a taxi. The job provided little satisfaction, but it paid relatively well and offered him the opportunity to explore the city. He saved a substantial sum of money, which he placed in the bank in preparation for the day he would be able to buy his own plane, and sought the one lead that would open the door to his endless sky. Though distracted by his need

Sture's original 1924 Chauffeur's License, Chicago, 1924. Sigfred collection.

to earn a living, he vigilantly scoured the papers and listened in the streets for some promising word that might help him enter aviation. Only one opportunity presented itself in the long, barren months of 1923.

One of the many air mail terminals that sprouted across the country after initiation of the first Washington to New York route in May of 1915 sat in Maywood, Illinois, just outside Chicago. Sture was determined that he would be hired at the terminal. The DH-4, a copy of the British De Havilland, equipped with large Liberty engines rather than Rolls Royce engines, was the major component of the fledgling airmail fleet, and Sture was an expert with the Liberty engine. So with a confidence he had not felt in months, he led the terminal's Maintenance Manager into the engine overhaul hangar, explaining every fact and fancy of American aviation's workhorse. Recounting his story of repairing the Liberty engine while downed in the Gulf of Mexico, his fingers traced the familiar lines and curves of the engine. He grew more animated as he spoke, as though feeling again the adrenaline, the life and death struggle he had felt just a few years before. In reality, a feeling had descended upon him that this, even more than his bobbing in the middle of the Gulf, was a life and death struggle to reenter aviation. His face flushed, and his blood pounded as he demonstrated the behaviors of the Liberty engine.

"You see, this gear," he said to the manager, pointing to the camshaft gear, "has thirty six teeth, and it meshes with the tower shaft gear here with twelve teeth." He held the two gears in either hand and brought them together in front of his chest to demonstrate the meshing of the gears. "It's a reduction ratio of three to one, just as it was when I was in the Navy. Only in the Navy the camshaft gear had forty-eight teeth and the tower shaft gear sixteen. Same principle, same ratio, just a different number of teeth. These gears are heavier than those we used in the F-5L, too. A good thing; those gears never stopped giving us fits."

The manager remained attentive and polite, though his eyes betrayed a preoccupation that hung palpably between the two men. He nodded in agreement with Sture's assessment of the Liberty's performance. He even arched his brows over rheumy eyes when Sture shared a bit of trivia about the engine, some arcane fact gained through experience, that not even the manager understood. But his eyes never lost their preoccupation, a shadow through which occasionally peered the shine of interest. When he had finished talking with Sture, the manager shook his hand heartily, gripped tightly and assured Sture that he would be in touch. But his eyes continued to stare into a distance that Sture could not penetrate.

Believing the words he had heard more than the feeling that overcame him as he left the hangar, Sture allowed himself to feel more hope than he believed he should. He bounded from the hangar, already counting the days until he could start working on the one love of his life.

The manager's call never came.

When Virgil King, a friend of Sture's from the Navy, who had also been bitten by the flying bug, left the service, he and Sture continued to correspond. In early 1924, Virgil wrote that he had made a down payment on a $500.00 Standard OX-5 to the owner of a machine shop in Jamestown, New York. Despite the fact that the plane was not completely paid for, the owner allowed Virgil to store it at his father's home in Chandlers Valley, Pennsylvania, about 20 miles south of Jamestown. Winter was rapidly approaching, and the owner had no place to store the plane, so the arrangement benefited both men. In Chandlers Valley, Virgil's father owned a blacksmith shop and a large shed in which Virgil kept the plane. Virgil, or Slip as his friends called him, had paid one-half down on the plane and was looking for a partner to buy the other half. The opportunity sounded better to Sture than driving a cab, and he agreed to Slip's offer to move to Jamestown where jobs, he was told, were plentiful.

He took the train from Chicago to Jamestown. On the day he arrived, he was hired at the Salisbury Axle Works where Slip worked as a milling machine operator. They had both learned machine work in the Navy during three weeks of intensive training at the Navy Machinist Mate School and took quickly to turning out spindles for the front axles of the Rawlins, a new automobile slightly larger than a Chevy. They stayed with Salisbury Axle Works until the spring of 1924 when they ventured back to Chandlers Valley to stay at Slip's home near their plane.

They poured their lives into the plane, working feverishly, night and day, to prepare her for flight. Within weeks, they finished a complete overhaul of her engines and painted her bright orange. But, despite their best efforts, the plane continued to thwart them. Her weakest part, as they expected, was her engine. There was no record of the hours on the engine. To check it out, they towed the plane to a nearby field, attached her wings, and ran up the engine. Though the engine should have turned the propeller at no less than 1650 RPM, 1400 was the most they could coax from the groaning machinery. Undaunted, they ground the engine's valves and tried again. Though only slightly better than before, 1540 RPM offered more power than they had achieved when they started. The two men congratulated themselves on their mechanical prowess.

One afternoon while they worked on the plane, a car pulled down the road beside the open field. A well-dressed gentleman stepped out of his blue Packard as if he were interested in what they were doing. He offered his hand to the grimy mechanics.

"My name is Packard.[7] You boys seem to be having a little trouble. I have some experience with engines. My company built quite a number of Liberty engines during the war."

Sture nodded, knowing that Packard had indeed turned out hundreds of Liberty engines, as had Ford and General Motors. The Ford, he thought, had proven the most reliable, but he did not want to talk himself out of any assistance the man might provide and kept his opinion to himself.

"I'm familiar with your engines," Sture told the man. "When I was in the Navy and it came time to change the engines, I always insisted on Packards."

"Nice of you to say that," the man answered. "And I hope my new engine, larger than a Liberty by the way, will be as successful. I hope I'm not speaking too prematurely, but we are flirting with a Packard diesel in the near future. If you boys come up to Hammond Port, I have a few OX-5 engines, some with very few hours on them. You can cannibalize eight cylinders and pistons from one of those that seems to have only a few hours on it. Just bring the proper wrenches to remove them. It's my way of helping aviation along." After wishing them luck, Packard shook each of their hands and left.

As time slowly passed, it became obvious that the two men had more work to accomplish and more money to spend to get the plane into flying shape than they had anticipated. To make matters worse, their field was soggy from spring rains that they thought would never end. In addition, it was not long enough to successfully launch the

---

[7] Though he introduced himself only as "Packard," this could only have been James Ward Packard, since his brother William Doud died in 1923. The two brothers from Warren, Ohio, founded the Packard Electric Company in 1890 and developed their first automobile at the New York and Ohio Company, a subsidiary of their Packard Electric Company, in 1899. The success of their motorcars resulted in formation of the Packard Motor Car Company in 1902. Though better known for their automobiles, the Packard companies played a significant role in aviation through the early 1930s. James Ward Packard died in 1928.

plane. As they poured more and more time into the plane, both began to grow disenchanted with their venture. Sture, despite his frustration, maintained a stalwart desire to get the plane flying, but Slip began to talk of another line of work, another, more stable life than aviation could provide. The previous summer, he had worked on the crew that laid the main road through Chandlers Valley, the first concrete ribbon to be built in that part of the county. Before the plane was ready for flight, he received an offer to work as a bulldozer operator on another project to construct new roads through the county. He grudgingly admitted that he was more interested in a local girl and marriage than a career in aviation and asked Sture to help him find someone to buy his share of the plane. Sture agreed. That day, he sent a letter to one of his best friends, Leo Muller, and asked if he would be interested in Virgil's interest in the plane.

Leo Muller, Matt Kandle and Sture in Pensacola, 1921.
Sigfred collection.

Leo had been discharged several months earlier. Between the time of his discharge and receiving Sture's letter, he and Eric Montgomery, another friend from the Navy, had purchased a used Jenny from the Army Air Force at Love Field, Texas. Because it was still winter, they decided to barnstorm in the south, primarily in Eric's home state of Louisiana. After a string of bad weather and worse luck, including two crackups, both Leo and Eric decided to walk away from their endeavor. Leo, though, did not want to walk away from aviation. He answered Sture's letter that had coincidentally arrived just as his partnership with Eric was drawing to an end. Leo traveled immediately to Warren, Pennsylvania, the railroad station closest to Chandlers Valley. Eric reenlisted.

Leo, a good pilot, a hard worker, and a spendthrift, fit right in with Sture. He also fit in with Chandlers Valley, telling Sture that it reminded him of his hometown, Muscoda, Wisconsin. The two set to work on the plane immediately after Leo's arrival. Working slowly and carefully, they removed the cylinders from the engine and painstakingly marked each of them so that their corresponding pistons could be reassembled into the same cylinders in the same positions in the crankcase. Then, after machining each of the parts, they just as carefully reassembled the engine, praying that it would work. Finally, after almost a week of non-stop work, their day of reckoning arrived. After a long warm-up, they applied full power to the engine. To their surprise and delight, the engine turned at 1675 RPM, a gain of 275 RPM and 25 RPM higher than it was rated.

Now only the soggy field held them up.

They attacked the field with as much vigor as they had the engine. First, with shovel and rake, they leveled a twelve-foot strip of rough plowed earth at the east end of the field. The narrow strip bordered a short fence of barbed wire, beyond which ran a shallow creek. Here they would start their takeoff. They had previously determined that if they taxied to the east end of the field, picked the tail up, turned the

Leo, two unidentified friends and Sture with the *Vagabond*.
Chandlers Valley, 1924. Sigfred collection.

plane around and pulled it back to the fence, they could lengthen their takeoff run by the twelve feet they had just leveled. At the west end of the field, where they prepared the plane and filled her gas tanks, a single telephone line hung fifteen feet in the air. This they carefully, and without permission, lowered to the ground. They then located a splice in the wire and threaded a fifty-foot garden hose over it. They also decided to bury it a couple of inches beneath the damp sod in case they were forced to cross over the wire with the tailskid. When they finished their calculations and improvements to the field, they discovered that they had increased the effective length of their makeshift runway to 400 feet.

Now, they told each other, with some sunny days, the runway would be suitable to launch their plane and their business. When the field finally dried, it resembled the top of a pool table, flat, hard and vibrantly green.

Because it had been almost two years since Sture had flown, they decided that Leo should be the first to test the plane. With more hope than confidence, he climbed into the cockpit and glanced at Sture who gave him a thumbs-up. Nodding slightly and knitting his forehead in concentration, Leo gradually applied power to the engine. The engine roared, and the plane chugged across the field. It tossed him on the seat as it traversed the pasture, and he realized the field was not nearly so flat as it looked. Snorting loudly, the plane lifted from the ground

The *Vagabond*, 1924. Sigfred collection.

at midfield and crossed the road with twenty feet of clearance directly over the spot where he and Sture had buried the telephone wire.

Barely concealing his excitement, Sture bounced on the balls of his feet as Leo brought the plane in for its first landing. Before Leo had completely climbed out of the cockpit, Sture jumped in and launched the plane into her second flight. More calmly for their third takeoff than for the first two, both pilots boarded the plane, and Leo graciously agreed to let Sture fly. Even with the weight of two grown men, the plane performed wonderfully. It crossed the buried wire with almost the same clearance it had attained without a passenger.

As Sture passed over the field preparing to land, he glanced at Leo and shouted, "We're in business now." Leo nodded and slowly broke into a smile. They christened the ship *Vagabond*.

Chandlers Valley, Pennsylvania lay midway between Warren, Pennsylvania, and Jamestown, New York, where the two men worked. On the gently sloping terraces of the Allegheny Plateau, the town huddled just off state highway 62, far from a major thoroughfare or crossroad. Both Leo and Sture realized that their location was not the most desirable, but they believed that the novelty of flying would see them through lean times. They expected that aviation would earn its rightful place in the culture, and that they would be able to grow with the industry. The site was a pleasant area of short but extreme winters and summers, sandwiched between long, comfortable springs and autumns. A prevailing westerly breeze from Lake Erie moderated the climate, and forests of white pine and hemlock flourished outside the city. Inhabited predominantly by petroleum workers and dairy farmers, the town sat unobtrusively on the plain. The area offered what were often ideal flying conditions and a thrilling view from the air of the Allegheny River and Lake Erie.

Rising early in the mornings to check out their plane, and working late into the night to prepare for another day's work, Leo and Sture passed a leisurely summer. They worked the linen, wood and aluminum that were the realization of their dream. On busy days, the two men took turns flying tourists over the terraces that led like steps to the Great Lakes. Though rides were rather costly at $5.00 each, the locals thrilled to the rush of wind in their faces and the whistling in their ears. They kept the plane busy enough for the two men to survive on what they made.

Sture in the *Vagabond*, Chandlers Valley, 1924. Sigfred collection.

To give those who did not have $5.00 a chance to fly, Sture assembled a roulette wheel on a three-foot square of heavy plywood. He fashioned the wheel's spindle bearing from the hub of an old bicycle's front wheel. He forged its arrow from a flat piece of steel about 2 ½ feet long and ¾ of an inch wide. He then passed one end of the bearing axle through a hole at the base of the arrow and the other end through the plywood. Finally, he bolted all of the pieces on the opposite side. He held a lottery for rides in the *Vagabond*. For fifty cents per ticket, he sold the *chance of a lifetime* to the local farmers and their sons, until he had raised the normal $5.00 cost of the flight or until the crowd of interested onlookers dwindled. Word spread quickly across the plain about the two barnstormers in Chandlers Valley who looped and spiraled and spun across the Pennsylvania sky. Near the end of June it appeared that their business might actually thrive.

In late June, only two weeks before July 4th, which they expected would be the most lucrative day of their summer, a businessman from Warren presented himself at the field. The *Vagabond* sat in a brilliant afternoon sun. He handed Leo five, crisp one-dollar bills and asked for a ride. Leo obliged, and over the next two weeks, both he and Sture came to know the man well. Mr. Holtberg, a local landowner and half owner of a small factory in Oil City, approximately twenty miles west of Chandlers Valley, was very interested in aviation and the plane. He quickly proved to be one of the plane's most loyal passengers, arriving almost every day for a ride over the Allegheny River. Within only a few days of his appearance at the field, the three men had grown quite familiar. Holtberg had no qualms about letting Sture and Leo use his Model-T. Even more than lending his car, however, Leo and Sture most appreciated that he always paid in cash for his rides.

The *Vagabond*, Chandlers Valley, 1924. Sigfred collection.

One afternoon shortly before the 4th, Holtberg arrived in the field as usual and announced proudly that he had arranged for the local Chandlers Valley reporter to write a story about Sture and Leo and their barnstorming activities. The article, he explained, would appear in the paper in time to provide ample publicity for Independence Day. All the two pilots had to do in return for the favor was to fly him over the city of Warren, twelve miles from Chandlers Valley, at 6:00 pm on the evening of July 3rd. The flight, he assured them, would take only about thirty minutes, and for their efforts he would pay them $20.00. Without debate, they agreed.

At 6:00 sharp on the evening of July 3, 1924, Mr. Holtberg arrived for his flight. He wore a new white scarf tied smartly around his neck. As he normally did, Sture deferred to his more experienced partner and insisted that Leo pilot the plane for their esteemed passenger. As they had rehearsed many times before, the two men prepared the plane at the west end of the field and topped off the gas tanks for what they expected to be a longer than normal flight. Then Sture strapped Mr. Holtberg into his seat, secured his safety belt, and spun the prop to start the engine. The wind blew from the west as it normally did, so Leo taxied downwind to the eastern edge of the field where the creek ran cool and clear. He got out of the plane to lift the tail and face the plane into the wind.

Before Leo could get the plane turned and properly situated, Mr. Holtberg noticed a shiny lever with a black ball for a handgrip. Without asking its function, he grabbed the lever and tried to pull it back. Because the engine was idling, the plane did not respond to Holtberg's manipulation, and Leo noticed nothing awry. Surprised that nothing had happened when he pulled the lever back, Holtberg shoved the lever forward as far as it would go. To his momentary delight, something happened.

From the far end of the field, Sture watched in horror as the plane, at full throttle, inched unguided and gaining speed toward the fence, with Leo dangling from the tail, trying to slow the plane. Before he could move, the plane crashed through the fence and continued toward the creek. At the bank, the plane tilted forward, and the tail rose to a forty-five degree angle, knocking Leo into the dirt. With the tail high, the propeller hit the ground, throwing soil and grass into the air. The engine ground painfully to a stop, and in the silence, Sture was sure an explosion had deafened him. Powerless to save his plane, he stared as the tail, still traveling from its own inertia, went past vertical to 135 degrees. Mr. Holtberg, suspended by his safety belt, dangled upside down over the creek, unable to free himself from the plane. Hot oil gushed from the engine. Afraid a fire would erupt, Sture ran to him, reached up, and unclasped the seatbelt. Holtberg fell head first into the creek.

Regaining his footing in two feet of water, Holtberg stood and shook like a dog. With Sture's helmet sitting half on and half off his head, he presented a shocked and miserable sight. His long white beard dripped mud, and the white scarf around his neck was spotted with oil.

He raised his arms into a shrug and looked imploringly toward Sture. "I thought the lever would raise the seat. I wanted to have maximum exposure when we flew over Warren."

Sture tried to control himself, standing silently and shaking his head.

"I'll pay for the damage, of course," Holtberg said and pulled a billfold from his pocket. He picked out a wet dollar bill and handed it to Sture.

Sture pocketed the dripping bill. "I don't have change right now."

Leo sat on the ground, slightly dazed, with blood dripping from a knot on his head. He explained that he had tried to grab the horizontal stabilizer when he hit his head on the tailskid. Then, looking at his plane, he fell silent.

Before any of the men had fully recovered from the shock of their mishap, several people who had seen the cloud of dirt thrown up when the propeller hit the ground came running from the west end of the field. Seeing Leo sitting in the dirt and bleeding raised their concerns, and one woman began to sob. Mr. Holtberg's son Emery, shaking his head and refusing to look at his father, carried a long rope to the rear of the plane and handed the end to Sture. With his 6'2" frame and two hundred pounds of flesh anchored in the mud, Emery hoisted Sture up so he could secure the rope to the tailskid. With several hands helping, the men pulled the tail of the plane to the ground.

Leo lifted himself to his feet. Walking to the wire fence laying flat on the ground, he dipped his handkerchief in the cool water of the creek and washed the blood from his forehead. He looked at the crowd and smiled. "It wasn't very graceful was it?"

The crowd helped push the plane back to the west end of the field where Sture and Leo removed the cowling to survey the damage. The engine mount was split and broken. Peering over Sture's shoulder, the owner of the local sawmill said he would rip out two identical oak timbers. "But not soon enough to get Mr. H. flying over Warren tonight," he added.

Holtberg looked away.

That evening, Sture and Leo sat late into the night. A gas lamp hissing behind them, they calculated and recalculated the

Airmail pilot Baskey in Fremont, Ohio, to whom Sture and Leo sold the *Vagabond*. 1924. Sigfred collection.

85

costs and returns of their summer. Finally, Sture leaned back in his chair, lifting its two front legs from the pine floor. He wiped his eyes and dragged his hand through his thin, blonde hair. Though disappointed by the freak accident and its implications for his barnstorming career, he remained the pragmatic Swede and spoke without emotion.

"It just doesn't work out," he said. "We're too far from a crossroads to supply enough passengers. The repairs alone will drain all of the money we've earned so far. I just don't see that we can make it. I think we should cut our losses, sell the plane, and start again later when the time is right."

Leo remained silent for a moment, staring into the gaslight. Finally, he turned to Sture and nodded his head. "If that's what we have to do, that's what we have to do."

Sture placed an advertisement for the *Vagabond* in *Aero Digest*. On July 8, 1924, he sold the plane, cash on delivery, to Mr. Baskey, an airmail pilot in Fremont, Ohio. Sture and Leo agreed to deliver the plane to Fremont during the first week of September. Throughout July and August, they divided their time between the machine shop in Jamestown and repairing the plane in Chandlers Valley. On September 3, all repairs complete, they made their bittersweet departure from the western Pennsylvania pasture and flew to Cleveland, Ohio. There, they refueled before making the last leg of the flight to Fremont. For eight days, they remained in Fremont, familiarizing the plane's new owner with the *Vagabond*. When not busy with him, they also flew advertising jaunts for India Tires and Pennzoil over the city that survived geographically and physically on the fringes of the bustling automotive industry. Sture hand-painted the letters for their advertising onto the side of the fuselage and the underside of the wing. He marveled as people on the ground stopped in the streets and pointed toward the sky as he streaked across.

Finally, on September 11, with Mr. Baskey satisfied that he was in command of the plane, they collected their $350.00 and their wages from advertisers. Leo left Fremont and journeyed back to Chandlers Valley where he negotiated to buy the blacksmith shop. For Sture, a familiar haunting overcame him. He bid farewell to his friends and returned to Chicago, the hub of all his travels.

Windy City

1925 - 1926

Grudgingly, Sture returned to the Post Office, but refused to make the same mistake he had made two years before. Rather than working as a clerk, he accepted a position as a temporary driver in the Department of Motor Vehicle Services. His routes changed frequently, and his tenure proved less boring than the last. His nighttime jaunts to branch offices in and around Chicago again offered him the diversion of exploration and the solitude to develop and nurture the only undying dream of his life.

He thought only of flight in the darkness of the Chicago night.

He also returned to driving a taxi and to the long days of shuttling strangers between locations he knew better than their faces. He still deposited much of his money in the bank, after sending a significant portion of his salary to his parents, and prepared for a dream that he was beginning to believe he might never realize. For the first time, he seriously questioned whether or not he would be able to make a career for himself in aviation. Still, what little money he allowed himself for the pleasures of life, he used to purchase his monthly copy of *Aero Digest.* Leafing repeatedly through its pages between fares and before the softly glowing fire of his room, he could get no closer to aviation.

In late February, Chicago began to thaw and to rise from the beneath the cold shell of winter. As the days grew longer and warmer, and the familiar stirring arose within him, Sture resolved once again to improve himself, to actively prepare for the day he knew he would enter aviation. After reading an advertisement in *Aero Digest* for a correspondence course offered by the Western Airplane Corporation, he dropped by its offices on the Loop in downtown Chicago to spend some time with like-minded men.

The office in the Monadnok Building was staffed by a single man in a single room lit by a single electric bulb hanging from the ceiling. The man explained to Sture that the Chicago Flying Club was in its infancy, that its only members were officers in the club, and that none of the officers were pilots. John Hinckley was the instructor under contract to teach the flying course that interested Sture. Six foot four inches tall and a heavy drinker, Hinckley had been a Royal Air Force

Pilot during the war. The remaining members of the club were simply interested in what most were sure would remain a summer festival pastime, a pleasant way to pass the day, like yachting, exploring caves, and climbing mountains.

Sture was surprised that the flying club had no pilots, but the man brushed his comments aside and smiled. "Really no need for pilots when you haven't got a plane."

Sture informed the man that he had flown in the Navy and had flown his own Standard over the Pennsylvania countryside only a year before. The man brightened, and the two sat in stiff backed chairs late into the evening, discussing their shared passion. The man mentioned that the club members planned to apply the $15.00 per man annual dues toward the purchase of a plane. Because the only members were the club's officers, however, the total capital they had raised was only $105.00.

Unidentified friend and Sture outside the Minerva Avenue apartment building, Chicago, 1926. Sigfred collection.

Seeing at long last an opportunity to fly, Sture volunteered his assistance and became a dues-paying member of the club. Within a week, he was signing up fellow cab drivers for membership. Within a month, he was appointed the club's acting secretary.

Each Friday, the club met in a small building beside the Drake Hotel, and each week the line of yellow cabs parked in front of the building grew longer. The Yellow Cab Company, with a long and proud tradition of discouraging union activity, assigned some of its older drivers to ride around the city in roadsters checking for evidence that some upstart might be trying to organize his fellow cabbies. The line of yellow cabs beside the Drake Hotel beckoned like an alarm. During one meeting, a large man entered the room, ready to break the back of a newly discovered union. To his surprise, the men in the room were discussing neither management nor the need for higher wages and shorter hours. Instead, they were discussing flight.

With the shallow breath of excited children, they shared tales of war and flying aces, of the beauty of a shore seen from the cockpit of a roaring Jenny. They spoke of the thrill of power throbbing around them as a plane awkwardly gained speed and lifted like a gangly bird into the air. The man sat at the back of the room and listened as Sture explained the goals of the small but growing club and its progress toward achieving that goal. When the meeting was over, the strikebreaker, with the same shallow breath of the other members,

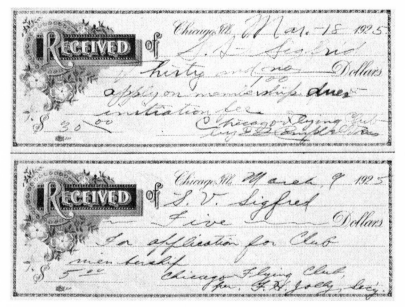

Receipts from the Chicago Flying Club. 1925. Sigfred collection.

joined the club. He passed word of the club to management and to his friends among the older drivers. Within days, what seemed an endless stream of yellow cabs began to flock to the weekly meetings.

For the next several months, the club flourished. New members joined every week. One businessman, Joe Cartier, though he attended all of the meetings and hoped to become engaged in some aspect of aviation, for reasons he refused to discuss never became a member of the club.[8] Still, believing that aviation was as an up-and-coming industry, he eventually purchased a new Jenny from Lambert's in St. Louis. He made arrangements with Mr. Coombs, president of the Chicago Flying Club, for one of the club's pilots to go to St. Louis and fly his plane to Chicago. John Hinckley, at Mr. Coombs' request, agreed to accept delivery of the plane for Mr. Cartier and to fly it back to Chicago. Preferring not to travel alone, Hinckley asked Sture if he would like to go to St. Louis with him and bring the Jenny back. He explained that Cartier had already approved Sture's going. Sture accepted the invitation.

A few weeks later, before Sture and Hinckley went to St. Louis, several members of the Chicago Flying Club tasked Sture with finding a convenient and suitable field for flying and storing the plane they eventually hoped to buy. During his drives, he surveyed various sights and finally recommended a large, level hayfield northwest of the city. Marked by firm ground and an unobstructed approach for several miles, the hayfield proved to be exactly what he had been searching for. Coombs immediately rented the field at Irving Park Road. The site soon became the club's regular landing field,[9] and after the Second World War, as the city grew up around it, the airfield was renamed O'Hare Field to honor the Medal of Honor recipient and son of a local mobster, Edward "Butch" O'Hare.[10]

---

[8] There are few surviving records about the Chicago Flying Club or its members, just a few notes scrawled into Sture's papers and receipts for dues. It has been impossible to date to correctly identify Mr. Cartier who purchased the plane delivered by Charles Lindbergh.

[9] By 1940, the area known originally as Irving Park Field and later as Orchard Field served as the site of a Douglas aircraft assembly plant. In 1945, Orchard Field, already equipped with four runways, was selected as the site of a new airport to service the Chicago area. In 1949, the name was changed to O'Hare Field, and in 1955, the airport officially opened for business.

[10] Lt. Cmdr. Edward "Butch" O'Hare received the U.S. Congressional Medal of Honor for an attack on enemy fighters that was credited with saving the *USS Lexington* on February 20, 1942. He received the Distinguished Flying Cross and the Gold Star for action near Marcus Island on August 31, 1943 and near Wake Island on October 5, 1943. In November 1943, O'Hare led his squadron on the first-ever Navy nighttime fighter attack from an aircraft carrier. His plane was lost, and on November 27, 1944, he was declared dead. The Navy recognized him with the Navy Cross award.

The Friday evening before Sture and Hinckley planned to depart for St. Louis, the Chicago Flying Club held a dance to raise money for purchasing their first plane. Saturday night, they believed, might have drawn a bigger crowd and raised more money, but most of the club's members were taxi drivers. Saturday night was also the busiest night of the week for them. Most of the drivers could earn as much on that single night as they could for the rest of the week. In deference to the drivers, the club agreed to hold the dance on Friday. Hinckley, flushed with the excitement of his imminent journey, was placed in charge of the dance. Caught up in what he considered a celebration, he took most of the money from the advance ticket sales and spent it on bootlegged whiskey that he hid in the room next to the dance hall. Despite warnings from his colleagues, Hinckley got thoroughly inebriated on the evening of the dance. With a young blonde whose name he would not remember, he put on a show in the middle of the dance floor that shocked even the most raucous of the club's members. As Hinckley slurred his speech and stumbled across the floor with the blonde in tow, Mr. Cartier looked on with disgust.

The next day, Sture and Hinckley arrived early in Mr. Coombs' office. Cartier was already there. In clipped tones that barely hid his anger, he informed Sture and Hinckley that he had witnessed Hinckley's performance the night before.

"You acted like a drunkard," he said, his eyes even with Hinckley's, "which I can only presume you are." Cartier, as calmly as he could, explained that he had already made arrangements for Lambert in St. Louis to have a former airmail pilot deliver the plane to Chicago. He would not, he concluded, require Hinckley's services.

Somewhat disappointed and more than a little angry, Sture left Hinckley standing in the office and returned to his apartment.

The following morning, a beautiful Chicago day with a slight breeze coming in from the lake, Cartier's new Jenny arrived. Its pilot was a tall, slim man with dark hair. Strikingly good looking, he was polite to the assembled club members but interested only in the plane. Somewhat reserved, he seemed almost bashful when Cartier offered to take him to dinner.

"I'm not very hungry right now," the man responded, "but if you get me a hot dog while I check the gas and oil, I'll be glad to hop some passengers for you." He nodded toward several dozen people assembled near the plane. "You seem to have quite a crowd here."

When Cartier returned with the hot dog, the man pulled the control stick from its socket in the rear cockpit of the plane and handed it to him. "Never have a control stick in when carrying a passenger," he warned, gesturing with his hot dog. Recalling the incident with Mr. Holtberg in Chandlers Valley, Sture nodded in agreement. With that warning, the man crawled into the front cockpit. Between bites, he indicated that he had enough gas for a couple of flights. A man rushed forward from the crowd and climbed into the aft cockpit. With the passenger safely strapped in, the young man revved the Jenny's engines and taxied down the field, still chewing.

Cartier beamed. "Outstanding pilot, don't you think?"

Sture, still disappointed at having missed his chance to fly from St. Louis to Chicago, stared after the plane. "He seems good enough. What's his name?"

Cartier never removed his eyes from the plane circling overhead in a dizzying array of turns. "I think his name is Lindbergh."[11]

In May, Sture began flying with various members of the Chicago Flying Club. In yet another plane that was only partially his, over a vacant field he had found, he flew across a sky he had claimed as his own. His hopes grew in direct proportion to the greater altitudes he was able to reach on each successive flight. Aviation was finally taking off. Of that, he was sure. He was equally sure that he was taking off with it, and that he would help steer it through good times and bad.

In solo flight, a rare luxury for any pilot, over Lake Michigan, he looked down at the white caps inching their way toward the city. He banked to the southeast and flew over freighters belching black smoke

---

[11] Charles A. Lindbergh, of course, gained fame as the first person to fly solo across the Atlantic Ocean. On the morning of May 20, 1927, he departed in *The Spirit of St. Louis* from Roosevelt Field near New York City, flying northeast along the coast to Nova Scotia and Newfoundland. From St. Johns, Newfoundland, he flew over the Atlantic toward Ireland, and less than 34 hours after his departure, landed at Le Bourget Field outside Paris, France.

into the sky. Pointing the nose of his plane toward the city, he soared high over the skyscrapers that dotted the shoreline and seemed to grow higher each month. After a long leg to the south, he looped back to the north and began his approach to Irving Park Field.

Below him and slightly to his right, small dots of yellow crawled across the black asphalt. Friends, he thought, perhaps some noticing the plane and wondering if Sture were at the stick. Men with their sleeves rolled up over sunburned arms. Men trapped in traffic, in the black smoke that was the city's scent. Men stuck on a ground that had burned and been rebuilt by the strength of men just like those in their cabs. They were merely men, he thought, just like him with one small exception. Sture's journey was just beginning, while the men below him, their daily toil complete, would soon park their cabs and saunter into the shadows of the local speakeasy or a warm dining room. Without realizing it, they had become trapped into their routines and to the ground. But Sture was free. He was flying.

Stewart Rouse didn't call to invite Sture to another of the Chicago Flying Club's weekend outings. He didn't try to persuade him to take him in the club's Jenny over Lake Michigan.[12] Instead, the aspiring artist called simply to let Sture know that one of his paintings adorned the cover of the latest issue of *Aero Digest*.

Sture was as excited as if the painting were his own. Without sharing small talk with the man whose voice trilled on the other end of the line, Sture rushed into the waning afternoon light and jogged to a newsstand at the corner. Handing a quarter to the shopkeeper, he waved the magazine in the air and pointed. "This is my friend," he said. "My friend painted this picture."

The shopkeeper nodded and turned to the next customer.

Handling the magazine carefully so as not to mar it with the oil from his fingers, Sture admired the cover and leafed through its pages. He felt that, somehow, strangely, the magazine with the cover painted by his friend was already a collector's item, something of grave

---

[12] Though he flew the *Vagabond* commercially in 1925, Sture did not obtain his first pilot's license until 1926 while with the Chicago Flying Club. Prior to 1926, the Department of Commerce did not require pilots to be licensed. Though Sture's license has long since been lost or destroyed, other documents in Sture's archive refer to the fact that he had been licensed since 1926.

importance in his life. He held it very much as he had held the family Bible when he was a child.

Near the back cover, where articles announcing the latest innovations in flight surrendered to the din of common advertisements, Sture's gaze fell on an ad placed by the National Advisory Committee for Aeronautics. The Committee was the most important organization in aviation. Charged with supervising and directing "the scientific study of the problems of flight, with a view to their practical solution," the committee was composed of two members from the War Department, two from the Navy Department, one member each from the Smithsonian, the Weather Bureau, and the Bureau of Standards, and five members unaffiliated with the federal government who were acquainted with aeronautics. Since 1917, theirs had been the guiding hand of aeronautics throughout the country, and when Sture saw the announcement, he stopped on the sidewalk to read it.

The Langley Memorial Aeronautical Laboratory near Hampton, Virginia was searching for a junior mechanic with two years aviation experience, and a senior mechanic with four years experience. Feeling somewhat lightheaded, Sture looked up from the pages of the magazine, into the blank faces of people passing him in the street. He then looked back to the magazine and reread the advertisement. Again, feeling lost, he looked into the faces passing him in the street and, finding no recognition, walked briskly toward his apartment, the index finger of his right hand still holding the place of NACA's advertisement in the magazine.

This, he understood and believed more clearly than he had ever believed anything in his life, had to be evidence of divine intervention.

He had been looking for a position in aviation since he had left the Navy. He had been unable to obtain a position in commercial aviation, and his barnstorming days had been tragically numbered. While the flying club had helped satisfy his appetite for flying, it had long been only a wish and a prayer that he would actually find a job in his chosen field. Now, because his friend's picture had appeared on the cover of a magazine, that prayer was chillingly close to being answered; the opportunity to finally break into aviation was at hand. He was sure that he was qualified for either of the positions. Time alone, he believed, could keep him from getting one of the jobs.

Barely avoiding the unfamiliar faces and corpulent bodies of the Chicago streets, he rushed to his apartment and jotted a letter to the address in the ad, asking for an application.

A response arrived from Washington, D.C. within a week. The application and enclosed letter explained that the job he had inquired about was a civil service position. In order to apply for one of the positions, he would have to complete the application and provide a recent photo and the results of a recent physical examination. Hurriedly, he rifled through his papers to find a photo. After finding a suitable picture, he phoned the Yellow Cab Company and asked for a letter detailing the results of his most recent exam. As he waited for his call to be routed through the labyrinth of wires, his toes tapped nervously under the table where he sat. With assurances from the company that he would receive the letter, and stacks of documentation spread neatly before him, he composed a letter to the Committee explaining his desire for one of the positions and detailing his experience with seaplanes and land planes alike. To ensure that the reader of his letter would understand the intensity of his desire, he also advised that, despite having to provide two weeks notice to the Yellow Cab Company, he could be in Hampton by October 20, 1926.

Again, a response arrived within a week. Explaining that time constraints in the hiring process could not justify his immediate departure from Chicago, the letter informed him that he should proceed at his convenience to Hampton, Virginia, where he would be hired at NACA upon his arrival.

Sture's hands shook as he read the letter. He forced himself to sit still at his small oak table beneath a humming electric lamp. The buzz of the bulb rang in his ears, matching only the ring of his surprise at having been selected for employment at NACA. He stared at the letter in his hands and noticed a small arc of blue at the base of his nails, a smudge across the bottom of the letter where it had been folded before the ink had dried. He closed his eyes, leaned back in his chair and felt the late summer wind blow through the open window that overlooked Minerva Avenue. After years of roaming and hoping and grasping at every opportunity to pass his way, he had finally realized his elusive dream. Though prayer had been second nature to him for most of his life, it had sometimes been little more than an exercise, a habit. But now, he prayed, in English, thanking God for this, the chance he needed to make good on his life.

As though it were tangible, he imagined turning the dream in his hands and gazing at the reflection of light upon its surface. Fragile, ethereal and light, it was as real to him as the noise of traffic from the street. He, Sture Vivien Sigfred, with only an eighth grade diploma and a short-lived tour in the Navy, was finally and truly an aviator. Lost in his thoughts, he felt as though the floor buckled and rose beneath him, jolted by currents of air speeding under a wing. The room vibrated with the sound of propellers. The scent of fuel wafted upon the breeze. And he saw again, amid stars shooting across his clenched eyelids, the Gulf of Mexico glistening beneath a crippled plane, the Mississippi River rushing angrily through fields of autumn brown, and a homing pigeon, perched alone on the tail of a seaplane that bobbed at once hopeless and hopeful on the open water. This, he thought, is what it took.

NACA

1926 - 1929

Langley Field, named for Samuel Pierpont Langley, the former secretary of the Smithsonian Institution and founder of the Smithsonian Astrophysical Observatory, nestled on the banks of the Back River on a peninsula formed by the James and York Rivers. Its wetlands drained into the Chesapeake Bay, and even in late October when Sture arrived, its temperature remained pleasantly warm. With the scent of a salt spray floating over the marsh when the tide blew in and egrets curiously watching the goings on at the field, its serene

Administration Building at NACA in the early and mid-1920s.
Sigfred collection.

landscape belied the excitement of forging the future of aviation that characterized the Langley Memorial Laboratory.

Upon arriving in Hampton, Sture checked into the Langley Hotel where many of the bachelors who worked for NACA lived. Tossing his luggage onto the twin-bed in his room, he was anxious to go to the laboratory, but darkness quickly descended on the Virginia peninsula, and he suspected there would be no one to meet him. Torn between the need for sleep and an almost overwhelming desire to explore his new home, he settled for a light dinner at the hotel and turned in early. The following morning, he checked in at the administrative offices at Langley and was sworn into the Civil Service. Within an hour, he was assigned to the laboratory's Free Flight Section located in a large hangar near the center of the site. As he made his way to his workstation, he noticed five airplanes parked quietly in the hangar, most on loan from other government services for wind tunnel and flight-testing. It was the largest number of airplanes he had seen in one location since leaving the Navy.

The first thing he noticed about the laboratory was what seemed to be a sense of disarray that ruled over the hangars and office spaces on the site. He learned rather quickly that the disarray was not due to poor management, as he had initially feared, but to a spirit of creativity and entrepreneurism encouraged throughout the research center. Because few of the employees seemed to be assigned to positions in which they were experts, a sense of creativity was necessary merely to survive the hectic pace that faced the laboratory's staff.

The *Eaglerock*, owned by Dan Cummings, is the first plane
Sture flew after leaving Chicago. 1928. Sigfred collection.

Although the organization grew more formal during his tenure, the NACA that he discovered in 1926 provided a rare opportunity for its employees to exercise their own initiatives, to chase their own dreams. Though regular procedures for authorizing research were developed and strictly adhered to, workers were also encouraged to pursue - on the side and without formal approval - their own ideas, so long as the ideas were not too far-fetched and did not interfere with the conduct of formally approved research. Creativity ruled among slightly more than one hundred workers at the center. For Sture, the environment proved both a challenge and a reward for the painstaking work he had performed and learning he had gained during his Navy and barnstorming careers. Still, while he became one of the most proficient mechanics in his shop and earned the respect of his peers and supervisors alike, he considered the position only temporary. Even with the relative security and generous salary of his position with the government, he refused to relinquish his goal of becoming a pilot.

Sture maintained his residence at the Langley Hotel for more than a year before the itch to move struck him. One afternoon, on his way back to the hotel, he noticed that Hutton's Plumbing Shop, beside the Ford Agency on Armistead Avenue, was building a room in the back of the second story of the building. With time to spare, he stopped to ask the owner what he was building. The owner replied that he was building an apartment. He had read that apartments were the wave of the future in large cities up north, and thought that owning one would be a good way to generate extra income, though he seemed uncertain he would be able to find a renter - apartments were, after all, new to the peninsula.

Sture climbed the stairs outside the plumbing shop to the building's second floor and took a leisurely stroll through the half-finished apartment. He was pleased with what he saw: a large living room, two bedrooms, a bathroom with the largest bathtub he had ever seen, and a kitchen complete with running water and electric stove. A

The NACA flight line, 1928. Sigfred collection.

furnace in the downstairs shop provided heat for the apartment, as the owner noted, free of charge. Sture was no stranger to indoor plumbing and electricity, but even in 1928 it was still rare to find both in the same building. He asked the owner what he planned to charge for the five-room walk-up.

The man hesitated before answering that he had to have thirty dollars a month. Any less than that, he explained, would make building and renting the apartment not worth his while. Sture jumped at the opportunity, and before the plaster on the walls was dry, began moving into his new home, the first apartment in the city of Hampton.

One of Sture's closest friends, Johnny Haynes, a World War I veteran and mechanic in the cowling and layout section at NACA, moved in with Sture shortly after he rented the apartment. The two men, with no flair for fashion but a great taste for comfort, furnished the apartment with an eclectic collection of other people's castoffs: a leather sofa, a Victorian lounge, and an ice box with a special cable that could be easily disconnected to allow the two men to lower their monthly electric bill when the luxury of cool beverages was not necessary.

News of the apartment spread quickly through the area, and within weeks the apartment hummed with the voices of their friends from

Widely distributed photo of the cowling team at NACA, 1928. Sture stands at the far left. Sigfred collection.

100

Langley and a small group of locals. While the aviators considered themselves brash and daring, they paled in comparison to the peninsula natives, most of whom made their livings from the sea as fishermen, river pilots or workers at the shipyard in Newport News. They reminded Sture of the hunters and fishermen back home, ruddy-faced and somewhat coarse. As he had been wherever he lived, he was at ease in their company, and the motley collection of aviators and oystermen were often heard late into the night arguing the latest theory proved or disproved at the laboratory. Fortunately, there were no neighbors to complain.

In 1928, the National Advisory Committee for Aeronautics included among its members Orville Wright, Chief of the Naval Bureau of Aeronautics Admiral Moffett, and Ed Warner, the Undersecretary of the Navy for Aviation. The committee was the most powerful aviation organization in the country, and these three men were the most powerful men in the organization. To the benefit of NACA, they understood that their real power lay in the quality, depth and practicality of research at the laboratory. They were as devoted to its work as they were to their own families. Among the men on whose reputations the committee's rested was an engineer named Fred Weike who originated the engine-cowling project that thrust the laboratory into the international spotlight in 1928. Weike had begun the cowling project several years before. It had become clear to all in aviation that military and civilian craft would have to be equipped with radio transmitters and receivers. Without them, navigation would be forever limited to daylight flights and would remain a pursuit on the fringes of danger. While the radios did much to enhance the safety and efficiency of air transportation, they inevitably picked up noise or arcing in the engine sparkplugs, dramatically reducing their effectiveness. United Airlines had recently tried with limited success to shield each spark plug with a small metal cover. Weike believed it was possible to shield the whole engine in much the same way by covering it with a large metal cowl. Long after he had informally adopted the project, it officially became his in 1926.

At the time, the Navy's Bureau of Aeronautics had requested that NACA investigate the potential of using cowlings as a method to improve the performance of air-cooled engines. Up until that point, the engines had provided more drag and wasted more power than their water-cooled counterparts used by the Army. The project proved one of the more promising at the laboratory, and men from all divisions

First wind tunnel at NACA, early 1920s. Sigfred collection.

clamored to join in the research.

One of those men, Ernest Johnson, the hangar foreman, was an expert welder and a master draftsman. He had mastered welding as an apprentice in shipyards throughout Great Britain and the United States, and had in the process become proficient at drafting. As one of Weike's trusted assistants, he tried to teach each man in the hangar the process of triangulation so the hangar would be able to keep the job of drafting and constructing the cowls. Most of the men in the hangar, however, were unable to grasp what was at the time a difficult concept. Finally, after having unsuccessfully tested each man in the section, he returned to Sture who had been one of the first men tested.

"Well Sig," he said, "you came the closest to getting it. I'll try to explain it one more time. I hope you get it, because I want to keep this job."

He was careful and precise with his explanations and spoke quite slowly as Sture observed his every move. Finally, with a smile on his face, Sture understood what Johnson had been trying to teach him.

"I see," he said to the older man. "It's not that complicated. Just needs less math and more common sense." Sture jabbed Johnson on the shoulder and quickly reached for his tools.

Sture set up his drafting operation in a loft between the shop and the hangar, where he could easily spread his maroon drafting paper and supplies on a fifteen by five foot drafting table. He used a needle-sharp scribe to etch bright pink lines on the drafting paper, and manhandled the six-foot by one-hundred foot rolls installed at the left end of his table. Though stiff, the paper was thin enough to roll, and Sture found himself quickly going through roll after shimmering roll as he hunched over the dimly lit table.

N-9 training plane at NACA. First Navy plane equipped with the cowling. 1928 Sigfred collection.

He started with drawings for the cowling of the Wright Whirlwind 235 HP engine. As his skills developed and the scope of research expanded, he developed drawings for several other power plant cowlings, including the Pratt & Whitney Wasp and the Pratt & Whitney Hornet 650 HP engines.

When he completed his drawings, he forwarded them to the Pattern Shop whose pattern makers he often referred to as his carpenters, since most of them were former master woodworkers and carpenters. The Pattern Shop constructed frame-like structures from the drawings, with coordinates evenly spaced at four-inch intervals. The structures resembled wooden birdcages to which the pattern makers attached $^1/_{16}$th inch thick aluminum sheets. To prevent the aluminum from crystallizing and becoming work-hardened, they heated the sheets with an acetylene torch until black char marks appeared when touched with a thin stick of white pine. The sheets were then hand-hammered and fitted into place on the wooden frames. During his many years in shipyards, Johnson had become intimate with the behavior of metals, and under his guidance, the process of developing the cowls progressed swiftly.

Sture first created original drawings for cowls that covered the area between the back of the engine to the front of the windshield of the fuselage. He designated these as #1, or first generation, drawings. The drawings and their corresponding cowlings, like the research project itself, grew, until they covered the entire front section of the airplane, reaching the top of the windshield and forming a cabin cruiser-like cover. These, Sture designated as cowling #10 drawings.

Laboratory work on the cowling project continued for well over a year before tests in the propeller research tunnel demonstrated the effectiveness of the metal shrouds. In late 1928, NACA installed its cowling on a Curtiss AT-5A advance trainer that the Army Air Corps had provided for testing. The cowling effectively silenced radio interference from the sparkplugs. More importantly, as the Navy had hoped, when the plane was placed into the recently built wind tunnel and tested in free flight, it also flew eighteen miles per hour faster than it had previously flown at the same power. The improved efficiency equated to adding approximately eighty-three additional

Sture touring eastern Pennsylvania while employed at NACA. 1928.
Sigfred collection.

horsepower to the engine without increasing its weight. This was a tremendous breakthrough, not only for the hangar section, but for NACA as well.

When Weike published the results of his research in November of 1928, airlines throughout the world took notice. The cowling essentially increased the range of an airplane while decreasing its fuel consumption. Most experts in the industry considered the breakthrough a turning point in establishing an efficient and cost-effective basis for cargo and passenger air transportation using newly designed axial-radial engines.

In the fall of 1928, at the height of excitement over NACA's cowling research, another, more palpable excitement spread through the apartment on Armistead Avenue. The Virginia Military Institute homecoming was approaching, and two friends of Sture and Haynes were planning to attend. Teeny Lincoln, an instrument-man at NACA and a sometime resident of the apartment, and a friend of his known affectionately as Queeg were planning to make the homecoming weekend a true celebration, regardless of the Eighteenth Amendment.[13] With several local young men, Teeny and Queeg

Teeny Lincoln, Sam Eaken, George Bulifant and Carter
Glass, NACA, 1928. Sigfred collection.

---

[13] The Eighteenth Amendment to the Constitution, approved by Congress in December of 1917 and ratified in January of 1919, prevented the manufacture, sale and transportation of intoxicating liquors in the United States. The amendment was repealed by ratification of the Twenty-first Amendment in 1933.

developed a plan to transport and sell liquor at the game in Roanoke. The least courageous of their group acquired an old Hudson to transport the alcohol, and beefed it up with heavy springs to support the weight of their intended payload. The less intelligent developed a plan to collect their bounty. Though Teeny did not actually participate in the appropriation of the liquor, he heard rumors of the plan and agreed to let the boys store some of the alcohol in Sture's apartment until the weekend of the game.

The boys, as Sture found out with a tub of unopened bottles sitting before him, had stolen the liquor from several river pilots' houses that fronted the James River. The pilots in Hampton were a select and close-knit group of men. Raised to read the river, bay and sea, they navigated ships in and out of the channel that led to the shipping port at Norfolk and the shipyards at Newport News and Portsmouth. Each pilot, like his father before him and his son after, was allowed one appointment to the rank of pilot. The appointment normally went to the oldest son, and the group maintained its unique status in the community as impenetrable and omnipotent. They were also among the most influential and highest paid workers in the area. At a time when $5000.00 a year was considered a good income, the river pilots made as much as $15,000.00. They were the lifeline to the region's lifeblood and were allowed certain liberties, even during Prohibition, that other, less important men were forbidden. The community revered and protected the men. Among their fringe benefits was access to the best wines, lagers, and liquors in the world, and many of the pilots, discretely but proudly, possessed some of the best-stocked cellars on the middle-eastern coast. Rum from Jamaica, vodka from Russia, and scotch from Scotland were common in the cool basements beneath their large, ornate homes.

The local boys were proud of themselves when they snared enough of the liquor to pay their way to the game. While they acknowledged some danger in their theft, they suspected that even if they were caught they would not get into serious trouble, because local authorities would likely consider their breaking into the pilots' homes and stealing their best spirits merely a prank of young manhood. When Sture heard how the liquor had been obtained, he was furious. A little liquor was one thing, he told Teeny, but theft was another. He demanded that the liquor be removed from his apartment and threatened to dump it in the street. Teeny and Queeg quickly interceded, and a few of their young friends lucky enough not to have been caught retrieved the liquor after dark.

Unfortunately, some of the young men who had stolen the spirits were caught, and the authorities considered their prank anything but youthful folly. The boys had not counted on the sitting judge being close friends with several of the pilots whose cellars they had robbed. They had also not counted on the influence that the pilots wielded over the judge and that resulted in their receiving sentences of twenty years each for breaking and entering, and larceny.

In late 1928, NACA received a request from Henry Ford to fabricate a newly designed wing section. He wanted the section two feet by ten feet, approximately one-quarter the size of the Ford Tri-Motor wing, with corrugations ¼" apart instead of 1" as on the original tri-motor wing. Ford suspected that the increased number of corrugations in the wing would correspond to an increase in its strength. The job of developing the wings was assigned to Sture. With the skill he had gained over the past two years, he attacked the job with vigor. Working well past normal working hours, he first had the Pattern Shop make a wooden section of a wing, exactly three corrugations wide. The shop fabricated the sections from walnut, an extremely hard, if expensive, wood. Next, the machine shop added to Sture's select tools by fabricating a special roller, also three corrugations wide, to impress three corrugations at a time into the wing section, then to be moved forward a corrugation and to roll out three more corrugations in the section, until the whole ten-foot wing span was completed. In its world-renowned wind tunnel, NACA tested the new wing for lift and drag against a section of wing the same size without corrugations. Though the exact results of the tests have been lost with time, the Ford Tri-Motor never again appeared without corrugations.

In all aspects of his life, professional and personal, Sture pursued aviation with a single-minded purpose. No occasion was more worth his time than that which involved flight. On December 3, 1928, as the 25th anniversary of the first successful manned flight approached, he and two of his coworkers, George Bulifant and Raymond Braigh, decided to attend the dedication of a memorial to the Wright Brothers in Kittyhawk, North Carolina. NACA planned to provide a parachute

Propeller Research Tunnel, 1928. Inside this building, the cowling and the Ford Tri-motor corrugated wing were tested. Sigfred collection.

to cover the large block of granite from Mt. Airy that would sit at the point of takeoff of the first flight, near the largest dune in Kill Devil Hills. The parachute would also conceal the carrier pigeons that were to be released when the rock was uncovered. Amelia Earhart and Orville Wright were expected to attend the ceremony, and the Navy Band was scheduled to provide suitably jubilant music. The event promised to be a grand occasion, and for weeks Sture and his friends eagerly anticipated the celebration.

When the big day finally arrived, the three friends climbed into Sture's Model-T and drove to the ferry landing at the Outer Banks. After their trip of several hours, they discovered that the large ferry was out of service. The smaller ferry could carry only three cars at a time, and if the three waited in line to board it, they would miss the ceremony. With no other choice, they hitched a ride with a local Coast Guard crew to the north end of the island. From there, they walked several miles to the ceremony and arrived just in time to witness the dedication. After numerous long speeches, a team of several men attempted to hoist the parachute from the rock to release the pigeons, but it caught on a corner of the granite block. Their faces flushed with exertion and embarrassment, they continued to tug at the parachute for several minutes, but the parachute refused to budge. None of the men checked to see if the parachute had caught on the block, and they continued to tug without success. Finally, with many of the luminaries of aviation watching, Sture tipped his hat and smiled. He leaned forward and with no effort at all pulled the parachute away from the corner of the jagged rock, revealing the memorial and releasing the pigeons. As the chute billowed in the wind and the pigeons flew gracefully toward the clouds, the Navy Band broke into music more boisterous than melodic, and the celebration began.

After the ceremony, as the crowd thinned and the noise of the wind overcame the noise from the assembled voices, Orville Wright purposefully folded the parachute. Recognizing Sture from the hangar at NACA, he handed him the parachute. "This belongs to NACA," he said. "Take it back with you." He smiled at Sture, but his face looked drawn and tired. As Sture thanked him for the parachute, Wright stared past the dunes and toward the ocean. Remembering, perhaps, the days of his glory when his brother had stood at his side,[14] the man seemed diminished by age, and his smile looked to Sture like grief.

A strong wind at their backs and the memory of the celebration fresh on their minds, Sture and his friends crossed the channel back to the mainland and headed toward Langley Field. Through the silence of their drive to the north, the memory of the sad but proud face of Orville Wright played in the recesses of Sture's mind.

Sture and George Bulifant on their way to Kittyhawk for the 25th anniversary of the Wright Brothers' first flight. 1928. Sigfred collection.

Again, along the nearly deserted road leading away from the Outer Banks, the goal of becoming a pilot hounded him as surely as did the solitary face of his hero. Sture yearned for his share of glory, for his chance to fly, but as always before, his dream was dashed by the realization and reality that his eighth grade education limited his options. He had faced it in the Navy and heard it in the halls at NACA: "*Only* an eighth grade education." It was his albatross.

---

[14] Wilbur Wright passed away on May 30, 1912.

Though his position at NACA assured him of future security and a lifetime of interesting work, he finally understood that his goal of becoming a pilot had slowly, without his realizing it, evolved into an obsession. It gnawed at his consciousness. It weighed him down and obscured his thinking. He was, he knew, blinded with the desire to become a pilot. After the granite obelisk had long disappeared from his view, he saw clearly that this goal, this dream, this unyielding desire was as permanent as the stone from which the memorial had been quarried, and he knew that whatever he had to do to make it so, his adventures in aviation had only just begun. Compelled to prove that he could accomplish his goal in spite of his limited education – perhaps even to spite all who claimed he could not – he once again pushed himself to the brink of another approach.

Sture beside the original granite monument to the Wright Brothers in Kittyhawk. Approximately 1985. Sigfred collection.

In the summer of 1929, Sture boarded a steamer at Old Point Comfort in Hampton, bound for Washington DC. The purpose of his trip was simple: to see Minnesota's Senator Shipstead in an effort to obtain a commission in the Navy and receive flight training. Senator Shipstead owned a summer home on Lake Irene, only eight miles south of Parkers Prairie, and Sture felt confident that the Senator could help him. But the Senator was ill when Sture arrived in Washington, and he had to speak to the senator's secretary. Though they enjoyed their conversation and reminiscences of Minnesota, Sture left without his commission and any hope of getting one.

"If you had only graduated from high school." The secretary shrugged and raised his open, empty hands.

The opportunity to speak personally with the senator never again presented itself, and Sture was forced to admit that not even a senator could change the fact that his education was, at best, limited.

Disappointed and disillusioned, he requested time off work, away from the stifling humidity of the middle Virginia summer and the daily reminder of what he had not yet become. In the new Dodge for which he had traded his Model-T, he drove to Minnesota for a much-needed vacation and the chance to sort through the few options he had. He lost himself in thought throughout the several days he drove west, viewing his dilemma from different perspectives, trying to determine a new plan that would move him closer to the cockpit. Returning to school seemed out of the question. He was almost thirty years old, far too old to return to a high school classroom. He could try to get into college, but that would mean quitting his job, and without an income he could not afford to go to college. His attempt to rejoin the Navy had proven fruitless, and NACA remained a secure but dead end path to what he had already accomplished.

Walking the NACA flight line, 1928. Sigfred collection.

As the landscape around him slowly changed from flat coastal plains, to rolling foothills, to mountains, to foothills and back to plains, his thoughts returned to where they had begun. He had come to the end of a road, and he felt lost. Any chance he had of becoming a pilot seemed to hinge upon his giving up what little security he had gained since leaving the Navy. And maintaining any security, launching into the adulthood that his brothers and sisters had long since begun, meant giving up on the one thing that had sustained him for more than twenty years – the dream of becoming a pilot, as irrational and irresponsible as it might seem to anyone else. After his long drive and all of his thinking, he simply didn't know what to do next.

As he had not done in what seemed many years, he thought of his father. Unable to speak English, John August had boarded a steamship in 1888 to come to a new country. With little more than a dream and a willingness to work, he had saved enough money to bring Sophia to the United States, to raise eight children and to build his own home. He had not been lucky enough to get to the eighth grade, yet he had overcome illness and all the other barriers life had placed in his way. He had accomplished his dream, a dream just as lofty and difficult as Sture's now seemed. And he had faced even greater risks.

The word bounced in Sture's head.

Risk. That was it. He had to be willing to take a risk, to give up his security and to lose everything, if necessary, in pursuit of his goal. It was, after all, as simple as that. Pounding the steering wheel with the heel of his palm, Sture turned his Dodge up the path that led to his parents' house, the house he had as a young man helped raise from nothing but earth and water and stone.

Current Wright Brothers Memorial, Kill Devil Hills, North Carolina.
Dedicated December 1, 1953. National Park Service photo.

NYRBA

1929 - 1930

A Consolidated Commodore glistened on the tarmac at Langley Field when Sture returned from vacation. Perched on the detachable wheels used to raise and lower it on a small ramp into and out of the water, the seaplane, with wings already attached, supported two 550 horsepower Hornet engines hanging above and outboard the cockpit between the hull and pontoons. The plane's hull extended sixty-two feet deep, and a coating of cream-colored paint over its aluminum skin accentuated red letters that announced "NYRBA Line," the shortened name of Ralph O'Neill's New York, Rio, and Buenos Aires Line

Sture marveled at the graceful plane sitting silently in the morning sun, a spray of dew sparkling on the wings. Shipped from the Consolidated Aircraft factory in Buffalo, New York on a flatcar, the seaplane seemed to bask in the Virginia sun, to rest briefly before flying from Langley to Back Bay in the southeastern corner of the state, site of NYRBA's Norfolk site. There, the plane would rest one more time before hopping down the southeast coast to Wilmington, North Carolina; Charleston, South Carolina; Jacksonville, Florida, and finally Miami, where it would await assignment to duty in South America.

Consolidated Commodore on the beach at Belem, 1930.
Sigfred collection.

Though sleek, the plane, Sture knew, was also among the most powerful in the air, capable of carrying thirty passengers and supporting over nine tons in flight. As powerful as it and her sister ships were, however, they could not overcome all of the forces of nature. Even as the late autumn sun warmed the clear waters of the James and York rivers around the Virginia Peninsula, ice forming on Lake Erie prevented the planes from leaving Buffalo in flight. In a manner unfitting their beauty and grace, the planes were loaded like refugees onto railcars and shuttled without wings from the factory to NYRBA's staging grounds in Virginia.

Like most of the men working in the hangar, Sture had heard rumors of NYRBA's goal to establish regular passenger and mail service between New York and Buenos Aires. It was the talk of the industry. He had even discussed the company's plans with the NYRBA agent in charge of assembling the planes at Langley, Louis B. Putney. He had known Putney during his Navy days in Pensacola and had joined the Odd Fellows with him, so he frequently took the opportunity to stop and share a few words with him when their paths crossed. A firm supporter of the company's plans, Putney had provided Sture with regular updates on its operations.

Front of NYRBA route card, 1930.
Sigfred collection.

Unlike the other men in the hangar, Sture did not scoff at Putney's explanations of establishing passenger service before establishing airmail service, on which all of the other major airlines depended. Nor did he scoff at the idea of securing foreign airmail contracts before domestic contracts. His youth had taught him that there was always more than one path out of the woods, and any path that led out was the right one. If NYRBA was getting passengers and contracts, he reasoned, they couldn't be doing all wrong. He merely shook his head and remained silent when his coworkers laughed. The whole NYRBA plan, they claimed, the very idea that a passenger service between New York and the southern coast of South America was possible, was just the pipe dream of another egocentric pilot. But Sture understood the importance of dreams, even pipe dreams, and when Putney spoke of NYRBA's plans, Sture listened.

Ralph O'Neill, America's fourth World War I ace, had conceived the idea of NYRBA's transcontinental service between New York and Buenos Aires while working in South America. Other airlines had pursued service between the United States and South America, but they limited themselves largely to land planes, to airmail cargoes, and to the less challenging, less prosperous routes along the west coast of the continent. O'Neill's dream was larger. He wanted to connect all of the major cities on the east coast of both continents with airmail and passenger service. Instead of land planes, he planned to use seaplanes, and to establish a string of coastal bases equipped with weather stations and radio towers to make the airline safer and more efficient.

By mid-1929, despite an obvious preference by New York's investors and Washington D.C.'s politicians for Juan Trippe's Pan American Airways, he had largely accomplished his goal. Argentina had granted him a lucrative airmail contract so long as he initiated service within a year of the contract award. With the assistance of Jim Rand, president of Remington Rand, and Admiral Moffett, Chief of the Navy Bureau of Aeronautics, he had

NYRBA route card, 1930. Sigfred collection.

raised approximately six million dollars to capitalize his venture. With these funds, he ordered six Commodore flying boats from co-owner Reuben Fleet's Consolidated Aircraft, and six amphibious S-38's from Igor Sikorsky's Aero Engineering Co.

On June 11, 1929, O'Neill personally initiated NYRBA's service with a flight from Norfolk, Virginia, to Rio de Janeiro. His S-38, the *Washington,* carried seven passengers and demonstrated that NYRBA was more than just a pilot's dream. Within six weeks, the airline initiated service between Montevideo, Uruguay and Buenos Aires. Only weeks after that, it commenced regular overland service between Buenos Aires and Santiago, Chile.

But, as Putney explained when Sture dropped by after returning from vacation, all was not well with the company. Several weeks before, on October 2, 1929, when Mrs. Herbert Hoover was scheduled to christen NYRBA's first Commodore in Anacostia, Juan Trippe had mounted the christening stand and announced that Pan Am would soon establish its own route to Buenos Aires, an extension of its existing Central American route. Additionally, Trippe seemed to have Irving Glover, the Assistant Postmaster General in his back pocket, and had been able to block all attempts by NYRBA to secure airmail routes to South America. Furious, O'Neill had declared virtual war against Pan Am.

The crash of the stock market in October of 1929 placed severe limitations on venture capital, thwarting O'Neill's efforts to maintain a steady inflow of cash. Despite O'Neill's successes, NYRBA was losing money at a phenomenal rate, and few in the aviation community truly believed in the commercial viability of air transport. If that were not enough, the Postmaster continued to display an obvious preference for Juan Trippe, Pan American Airways, and its plans to exploit the west coast of South America. Though NYRBA's future did not look exactly bleak, neither did it look especially promising.

Still, by the end of 1929, the New York, Rio and Buenos Aires Line had already accomplished more than most other airlines combined. The company had received shipment of four Sikorsky S-38s, a Consolidated Commodore and three Ford Tri-Motors. All of the planes were in regular service in South America, and five more Commodores and two more S-38s were on order. The company possessed Argentine and Chilean airmail contracts, with the promise of additional contracts from Uruguay and Brazil. The Buenos Aires-Montevideo passenger route had been successfully operating for over four months, and the company's airmail route over the Andes between Buenos Aires and Santiago had been in service for three months. Though still operating at a deficit, the company saw revenues increase daily and still held hope that it would earn a profit within two years. Unlike most other businesses in late 1929, NYRBA was hiring.

Disillusioned with the dismal prospects at NACA that grew more apparent each day, Sture stopped by the NYRBA office one afternoon in late November to speak to Louis Putney. The two men shared small talk into the early evening, swapping reminiscences of their Navy days and advances in aviation since the World War. Finally, with little left to talk about, Sture got to the point.

"Louis, I understand that NYRBA is hiring pilots. You know as well as I do that most folks think this talk about a passenger and airmail service between New York and Buenos Aires is a lot of hot air, but I think it can be done, with the right people, of course. I just believe the time has come. You know I have a commercial transport license, have had since '26. I've flown my share of miles, too. That and my experience as a crew chief on the flying boats - well, I just think you won't find anyone better than me to help you get this company off the ground. Excuse the pun."

Putney leaned back in his chair. Sture glanced out the window. For almost a minute, the office was silent except for his breathing and the creaking of Putney's chair behind the large walnut desk. When the silence had grown intolerable, Sture turned back toward Putney and spoke so loudly it surprised even him.

"You know as much about my days in the Navy as anyone. You know I've done a damned respectable job here at NACA, too. If I had more education, I'd be in charge of most of these people or I'd have a commission, but I don't. No use fretting about it. I can't do anything about that now. But I can do something about my situation. I want you to recommend me for a copilot position with NYRBA. You know you won't find anyone any better."

Putney leaned forward and crossed his arms atop his desk. He looked Sture in the eyes and was again silent for several minutes. Then, never taking his gaze from Sture's face, he jerked open the right-hand drawer of his desk and pulled out a stack of NYRBA letterhead. Brandishing his pen with a flourish, he began to laugh and write at the same time. Barely able to speak over his laughter, he wrote as he spoke to Sture.

"Nothing would give me more pleasure than to recommend you. I was wondering when you would tire of the hangar and return to the plane. Finally, you've come to your senses. I'll tell you, we are going places, no matter what Pan Am or anyone else says, and you can join us."

Putney looked down at his page and wrote furiously for almost a half-hour. Then he blotted and folded several pieces of stationery that comprised his letter and placed them in a company envelope.

"I will mail this first thing tomorrow morning, Sig. You have my highest recommendation, and I only hope it will help. Please let me know if there's anything else I can do for you. We Navy men must stick together."

Several weeks later, Sture learned that Putney's letter had not only been long, it had also been effusive in its praise for the man Putney claimed was the best mechanic he had ever met and a fine pilot to boot. Two NYRBA executives who had visited NACA to observe operations earlier in the year received Putney's letter. They remembered the young Swede in the metal shop, and though they chuckled at the exuberance of Putney's letter, they agreed that Sture was a first-class mechanic. Cabling their regrets that there were no copilot positions available, they added that they had a desperate need for a metal smith. If Sture were interested, he would be placed in charge of all metal working operations at NYRBA's Miami location at a salary of $2400 per year.

Sture reported to NYRBA's Miami office in early January of 1930.

Work in Miami was harried. Preparations were underway for meeting the requirement of the Argentine airmail contract that NYRBA begin weekly flights between North and South America. In addition, legal arrangements had been completed for establishing a Marine base at Dinner Key, and condemnation of the existing facilities at the Key was in progress. As one of the two most important NYRBA sites in the United States, Miami witnessed the arrival and departure of all NYRBA planes bound for their South American routes and the arrival from the south of many damaged planes for repair. The site was also used for test flying planes before they embarked upon some of the most dangerous flying in the world, along the eastern coast of South America.

Upon his arrival in Miami, Sture became shockingly aware of the enmity between NYRBA and Pan Am. Trippe's company was known among all levels at NYRBA as the "Coyote." Rather than damaging morale, however, the enmity made NYRBA's workers especially dedicated to succeeding. Far more negative were the effects of rumors of a power struggle among NYRBA's executives. Sture obstinately ignored the rumors and stayed busy - so busy that he had no time to notice his increasing esteem and importance within the company. In May, however, his status became clear, even to him. After only four months with the company, he was directed to prepare for overseas duty and assigned as the base manager at Buenos Aires. He also received a salary increase to $3000 per year. Though the raise pleased him, he was most proud that he was being placed in charge of the company's largest and most important South American base. He wasted no time preparing for his departure and had to force himself to remain calm when he was informed that the Commodore that was taking him to Buenos Aires would be grounded in Trinidad for two weeks because of engine trouble.

NYRBA hangar at Belem, 1930.
Sigfred collection.

Engine trouble became the least of Sture's concerns when he finally arrived in Belem, Brazil in early June. Luke Harris, NYRBA's manager for the southeastern Trinidad to Buenos Aires region, met him at the air base. Explaining that he had heard of Sture's expertise as a mechanic, he informed him that he regretted delaying his arrival in Buenos Aires, but he had an S-38 that desperately needed the attention of a good mechanic. He placed Sture in charge of repairing the damaged seaplane, the *Pernambuco*, and informed him that he had until

September to finish completely overhauling the plane, repairing her control cables and recovering her wings with new fabric.

Though it was not one of the planes he had worked on in the Navy, Sture was familiar with the S-38 from his time at NACA. Originally produced in early 1928, the Sikorsky S-38 was a ten-seat amphibian, capable of takeoffs and landings on both water and land. The plane was powered by two 400 HP Pratt & Whitney Wasp engines and cruised at 100 mph with a maximum speed of 130 mph. With a long nose and blunt tail, the plane had a seventy-two foot upper wingspan and a thirty-six foot lower sesquiplane. The engines were suspended from the upper wing, outboard the hull. The hull was manufactured of aluminum up to the cabin windows, with rubberized fabric completing the top of the hull. The sesquiplanes, or lower wings, like the upper wings, were covered with doped fabric. Like most seaplanes, the wing controls were cable-operated.

When Sture saw the damaged S-38, his heart sank. Looking at the stricken ship, he understood why the previous mechanic had given up on the repairs and requested transportation for him and his family back to the United States. It appeared that the plane had not only been wrecked, but that the previous mechanic had scavenged parts from her. Even worse, he or someone else, in frustration or desperation, had simply cut with wire cutters, rather than repaired, the plane's control cables. Noticing Sture's expression, Harris shook his head and explained to Sture that the first mechanic had somehow believed that money was unlimited and that it would be easier for the company to buy a new plane than for him to repair this one.

NYRBA hangar under construction at Belem, 1930.
Sigfred collection.

"But," he added, "the depression is having its effect - even down here. Between that and the pressure that Postmaster General Brown is putting on us and everyone else to force a merger with Pan Am, it's getting harder than ever to capitalize. It looks like we're just going to have to get by with what we have for as long as we can. When we turn a profit, we can think of new planes."

Harris looked at the damaged plane and again shook his head. "A damned shame," he said. Then he wiped the perspiration from the back of his neck with a damp handkerchief and lowered his eyes. "I hope you can do something for her." He nodded toward the plane and walked away.

Sture gazed at the plane a final time before turning and following Harris toward the relative coolness of his office. "I'll need to hire some people and to move the plane closer to the machine shop. You'll also have to find me a tailor."

"A tailor? I'm sure there are some fine ones in town, but the clothes you have will be suitable for the work you have to do here. We're relatively informal in the jungle. You'll find much better tailors when you get to Buenos Aires."

Sture laughed. "The tailor isn't for me. He's to help me replace the fabric on the wings."

He looked back toward the *Pernambuco.* The plane seemed to wilt in the heat. "September's pretty early, but I suppose, with your support, I can have her flying."

Harris tucked his handkerchief into the front pocket of his white linen trousers and nodded. "I'd heard that if anyone would give it a try, you would. I'll do whatever I can to help." He wiped his hand on the front of his trousers and held it out. Sture shook it vigorously.

"May I suggest, Sig - may I call you Sig - that you rest before beginning work? We have a room for you at the Grande Hotel, and, frankly, the plane has waited quite a while to be repaired. I don't believe one more night will destroy it."

Sture nodded. "That's fine, but tomorrow I must begin work."

"Agreed."

Harris busied himself with a stack of various papers strewn across his desk as Sture turned and walked into the afternoon heat and humidity.

"Surely this can't be winter," he muttered as the door closed behind him. "The whole damned world's turned upside down."

The *Pernambuco* after repairs, Belem, 1930. Sigfred collection.

This Man We Keep

1930

The following morning, Sture rented a large shed beside the Port of Para building near the docks in Belem. The workshop and surrounding yard were completely fenced, and a gate in front of the shop led onto the street. To his surprise, a long line of men stood outside the gate only hours after he had rented the workshop. The line formed every morning thereafter. The men had heard that he might be offering work and gathered from miles around to offer their meager but inexpensive services. Because none of them had any experience in mechanics or aeronautics, Sture found himself eliminating most of the candidates on the spot. Of those who remained, he was compelled to

The Belem overhaul crew of the *Pernambuco*, 1930. Sture stands at the far right of the back row. Sigfred collection.

keep any who showed an aptitude for mechanics, including repairing the wing fabric or cleaning the corrosion off the wing frames.

The fact that he did not speak Portuguese made his task of selecting the most capable workers more difficult. Fortunately, with the job of repairing the S-38, he had inherited, in addition to a new Model-A touring car, an English-speaking chauffeur named Andrade who had lived with his parents in Brooklyn until he was thirteen years old. He had moved back to Brazil with his family several years before and spoke both English and Portuguese fluently. Together, the two accomplished the hiring with relative ease.

124

Only a few days into the repairs, however, when the crew finished removing the old linen from the wings of the S-38 and began to clear and paint the metal spars in preparation for applying new linen, it became clear that teaching the men to repair the Sikorsky without speaking their language would be almost impossible. Though Andrade had proven a great help to him, Sture knew he must learn Portuguese.

He purchased a small ledger that he carried in his rear pocket wherever he went. When he wanted to tell one of the men what to do or to explain a particular concept of flight, he asked Andrade how to say the phrase in Portuguese. He then repeated the phrase to Andrade until he could say it perfectly. Finally, he entered the phrase into his ledger and continued to study the entries until they came to him by second nature. In only a few days, he had completely filled the ledger and was regularly speaking Portuguese with the men. Within two months, he told his coworkers, he was dreaming in Portuguese.

The first phrase in his ledger concerned him greatly while the men prepared to install new linen on the wings. Not only could dirt and grease from their hands mar the appearance of the wings, more importantly, it could inhibit the ability of the fabric to adhere to the frame. For this reason, he cautioned each of the men to "work with clean hands."

"Trabaje con mano limpia," he scrawled in his ledger.

"Trabaje con mano limpia," he repeated to each man until the wings were safely doped.

Trabaje con mano limpia, he believed, were the four most important words in repairing and maintaining a plane.

Sture continued his work on the plane throughout the winter of 1930, his body slowly adjusting to the southern hemisphere's schedule in which summer and winter occurred opposite the seasons in the northern hemisphere. He also became more aware of the hatchet job the previous mechanic had performed on the control cables. Control of the various surfaces on the wing was among the most important features of flight, and Sture could not trust the work to men who had never seen, let alone installed or maintained, the control cables. Though his training of the men had proven effective for most repairs, this was one operation that he believed required *his* attention and unique skill. Unlike many of the other NYRBA managers in South America, he knew he must remove the white linen suit that had

125

NYRBA hangar and offices, Belem, Para, Brazil, 1930.
Sigfred collection.

become the trademark of the Anglos in Brazil. The suit he had purchased for $10.00 from the tailor who sewed the linen for the wings and that he had worn at all times since his arrival in South America hung in his closet as he dirtied his hands with his workers, always reminding them to wash up.

"Trabaje con mano limpia," he repeated day after stifling day. "Trabaje con mano limpia."

Beside his men, in coveralls much of the time, he passed the

Pernambuco repair crew, Belem, 1930. Sture stands second from left of the back row. Sigfred collection.

126

winter repairing the control cables and supervising the overhaul of the S-38. Rumors of continuing power struggles at the NYRBA home office in New York continued to surface at the Belem station, but Sture did his best to ignore them. Believing that his job had more to do with keeping pilots and passengers alive than with keeping abreast of corporate politics, he also tried to ignore the persistent reports that the Postmaster General was holding hostage several major South American mail contracts until NYRBA merged with Pan Am. He focused his attention on the S-38 and managed to convince himself that there was nothing to worry about in the fact that he went five weeks without a paycheck.

While he busied himself with repairs to the stricken S-38, NYRBA completed regular Commodore flights between Miami and Buenos Aires for over five months - without an airmail contract from the U.S. Though the company did its best to maintain the Commodores ready for safe flight, they could not predict mechanical and personal failures that could result in the downing of one of the flying boats. The company, therefore, maintained a contingent of S-38s to replace the Commodores when necessary. The S-38s, however, did not have sufficient range to fly the distance from Cayenne, French Guyana to Belem, Brazil without stopping for fuel. To ensure that even the S-38s could make the flight, NYRBA and Standard Oil Company placed a refueling barge on Montenegro Lake halfway between Cayenne and Belem. The barge was stocked with two five-gallon cans of gasoline in a wooden case. Both the cans and the wooden boxes in which they were shipped became almost-legal tender among the natives of the rainforest. The cans were used like buckets to haul water, and the boxes furnished many of the natives' homes where they were used as both tables and stools.

Pan Am's existing South American airmail contracts ended at Paramaribo, Dutch Guyana. But to demonstrate that they could fly the entire distance to Rio, and later to Buenos Aires, they began flying regular, though empty, flights from Paramaribo to Brazil's most famous city, Rio de Janeiro. The Pan Am planes, like many of NYRBA's, were S-38s, and the pilots landed at Montenegro Lake to refuel from the NYRBA-Standard Oil supply barge.

As the antagonism between NYRBA's and Pan Am's boards increased over the winter, several executives from NYRBA headquarters in Rio flew to Belem, determined to stop Pan Am from using the fueling facilities on Montenegro Lake. In the late winter of 1930, they held a conference at the Grande Hotel to discuss the problem and invited Sture, the senior NYRBA representative in Belem, to attend. Despite the attempts of some of the senior officials to keep the meeting calm, it soon degraded into a raucous free-for-all, with each man trying to outdo the other in his outlandish plans for denying Pan Am access to the refueling barge. After several hours of heated discussion, the group decided upon a plan to protect their claim in South America. A NYRBA man would be stationed on the barge with provisions and a deer rifle to protect the NYRBA fuel. The first Pan Am plane to land was to be blessed with a shot across the bow, a reminder that Pan Am had better leave the disputed NYRBA facilities. Tired, but satisfied, the men seemed joyful when they approved the plan.

Sture, however, was silent until the members had completed their discussion. Then, without raising his voice, he spoke slowly to the group.

"Gentlemen, I agree that it is incumbent upon us to protect the assets of our employer. I also agree that it is necessary to remain loyal to the company that has thus far protected our livelihoods, and to a great extent our lives. But I cannot agree that this loyalty should include planning and executing unnecessary acts of violence against men who are no more involved in the squabble than we are.

"To the best of my recollection, the Pan Am pilots flying the evening run to Rio include Red Williamson, Bill Cluthe, Jack Tilton, Germany Schultz, and Rod Sullivan. I know each of these men. I served with many of them in the Navy, and consider more than one a friend. If any of you believes that endangering the lives of these men will endear NYRBA to the Postmaster General and win us an airmail contract, you are very much mistaken.

"There is nothing to gain and very much to lose in the plan you have just agreed to - not the least of which are the lives of men I count as my friends. I strenuously object to this plan and encourage you to develop another."

The group overruled Sture's suggestion. As the Base Maintenance Manager, he was ordered to prepare an S-38 for the flight to the barge and invited to accompany the group of executives to Montenegro Lake where implementation of their plan would take place. Politely, he declined. A young flight mechanic named Skinny Glaze, displeased with the plan but unwilling to make waves among the men who controlled his career, flew the executives to the barge and was charged with protecting NYRBA's property on the lake. After ensuring that the barge was suitably provisioned, the group returned to Rio, and Skinny Glaze began his vigil.

The first Pan Am pilot to take a shot across the bow of his plane was Germany Schultz, a friend of Sture's in the Navy. Quickly applying power after realizing what had happened, Schultz took off from the surface of the lake and headed toward Belem. Only a few minutes later, he ran dangerously low on fuel and was forced to land in the thick Brazilian rainforest. He was fortunate enough to have a radio onboard and quickly notified Pan Am of the incident. The company rescued him several hours after he landed the plane, angry, dismayed and almost eaten alive by mosquitoes. Pan Am wasted no time notifying the Postmaster General of NYRBA's aggressive actions.

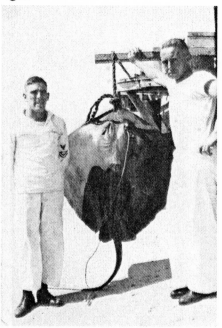

Navy photo of Matt Kandle and Germany Schultz taken at Pensacola, 1921. Schultz would be the Pan Am pilot to take the shot across the bow that ultimately led to NYRBA's takeover by Pan Am. Sigfred collection.

News that NYRBA had resorted to violence did the company little good in Washington. Within days, NYRBA was patently denied any hope of an airmail contract from the US government, and the Board of Directors was unofficially notified that the Postmaster General considered it in the best interest of the country that NYRBA merge with Pan Am. On August 19, 1930, NYRBA founders Jim Rand and Ralph O'Neill grudgingly signed a preliminary agreement of merger with Juan Trippe, and Pan Am officially absorbed the larger and more successful company. Pan Am was awarded pending airmail contracts and within a month became the supreme aviation presence in South America.

Sture with the *Pernambuco* after repairs, on the dock at Fortaleza, 1930. Sigfred collection.

On August 29, 1930, Sture was still unaware that Pan Am owned what had formerly been NYRBA. Back in his white linen suit, freshly cleaned and pressed the evening before, he surveyed his work: a completely overhauled Sikorsky S-38, looking as good as new and ready for flight. He shook hands with his men - not an American among them - and congratulated them on work that rivaled that of the finest craftsmen in the United States. While others may have been caught up in the intrigue of international business, he thought, he had done what he had been hired to do.

NYRBA pilot Johnny Harlin and Sture test flew the repaired Sikorsky and reported back that it flew as well as if it were new. The following day, he and Sture flew the Sikorsky on the regular run to Fortaleza. While topping off their fuel tanks in Fortaleza, they learned that revolution had erupted in Brazil. They returned to Belem the following day to wait out what they hoped would be a short war. As Sture sat at his desk completing paperwork on the repaired Sikorsky, he noticed a Commodore flying low over the river. It shone silver and blue in the afternoon light. "Pan Am colors," he thought, returning to his paperwork. Then realizing that Pan Am owned no Commodores, he looked up again and watched the plane, unmistakably a

Commodore, bank to the left and slowly dip to the surface of the river, a spray of brilliant white foam issuing from beneath her hull. The plane slowed and taxied to the NYRBA barge where she stopped and floated buoyantly on the water. From an open hatch in the side of the hull, several men and women stepped into a low boat that shortly made its way for the hangar on shore.

Sture set his pen on the desk and watched as the boat pulled to the dock beside the hangar. He watched as the men and women stepped from the boat and peered around the seaplane base. For several minutes, until the group had climbed into waiting taxis and left the base and Robin McGlohn entered the office and began to speak, Sture stared out the window, a realization growing in the back of his mind. Though nothing could have prepared him for the awareness, he knew that his understanding was a part of history, a human moment in a myriad of moments that forever changes and defines the course that time will take from that instant forward.

It's final, he thought. I am now part of Pan Am.

He reached for his pen and finished the report on the repaired Sikorsky. Then he leaned back in his chair and listened to McGlohn's explanation of how all of them had become a part of the largest commercial airline in the United States and what was certainly destined to become one of the most famous. As McGlohn spoke, all Sture could think was that he was lucky to be employed and lucky to still be in aviation.

McGlohn, the former NYRBA pilot and manager of the company's Trinidad-Belem Division, explained with a resonant lack of pride that he had been designated the new Operations Manager for Pan Am, and that he had just had the pleasure of flying a delegation of Pan Am officials from Paramaribo, Dutch Guyana. His voice broke when he spoke the word pleasure. The group included Andre Priester, the company's Operations Engineer and General Manager, and Hugo Leuteritz, the head of communications. The entourage also included several of the Pan Am officials' wives with their extensive wardrobes in tow.

"This was not the most pleasant flight I've ever made. William Grooch joined up with Priester in Trinidad; apparently he already has a job with Pan Am. I flew the whole bunch to Paramaribo. The plane, as you might expect, was overloaded, and I ran out of fuel just as I landed in Paramaribo. One of the engines actually quit right before we touched down. They don't know how lucky they are, how lucky we are, to be here. Anyway, Grooch flew the rest of the way from Paramaribo."

Through the window, Sture saw Germany Schultz, the Pan Am pilot who had recently been shot at on Montenegro Lake, on the barge taking command of the Commodore and preparing it for its flight to Rio. McGlohn continued his explanation. As a former Division Manager for NYRBA and Operations Manager for Pan Am, he would act as the liaison officer between the NYRBA employees and Pan Am officials in Belem. Priester would set up an office at the Grande Hotel in Belem and interview each employee. Some, McGlohn added, would surely lose their jobs.

Though he did not tell Sture at the time, McGlohn knew all too well that many of the men would lose their jobs, for he had barely escaped with his own.[15] When he informed Priester that the plane had run out of fuel, as he believed was his professional responsibility, Priester immediately relieved him of command of the Commodore and had Grooch take over. Refusing to listen to McGlohn's explanation of the excess weight resulting from the women's luggage, Priester berated him in front of his crew and passengers, threatened to fire him, and assured him he would never again fly for Pan Am.[16]

---

[15] Sture would have gained this information second-hand from McGlohn during one of the many flights they made together after this. Other accounts of the same events differ from this, primarily in the claim that Grooch flew the plane that ran out of fuel when it landed in Paramaribo. The best reconstruction of events seems to be that after Ralph O'Neill fired Grooch from NYRBA, Grooch followed O'Neill's advice to see George Rihl at Pan Am. Rihl promised Grooch a job, but when Priester found out, Rihl rescinded the job offer. Without employment, Grooch was returning to South America via Trinidad, when he ran into Priester, on his way to South America to survey Pan Am's new assets. Because McGlohn was the NYRBA Operations Manager for the Trinidad to Belem route, it is not only likely, but also probable that McGlohn flew Priester's group to Paramaribo where the plane ran out of fuel. This actually seems the case, since Grooch was shortly appointed to McGlohn's former position for Pan Am. McGlohn was relegated to copilot status for several months. He returned to pilot status for the Cuban subsidiary of Pan Am, and ultimately flew both the Clippers in the Pacific and cargo planes for the Air Transport Command during World War II.

[16] Though he did not continue to fly for Pan Am, he was later allowed to fly for the Pan Am subsidiary, Cuba Airlines, in Havana. His encounter with Priester, only hinted and whispered about in the company of Pan Am brass, became the first in a

The following morning, September 1, 1930, McGlohn met Sture in the lobby of the Grande Hotel and escorted him to Priester's office. The stern Dutchman sat behind a large mahogany desk that gleamed in the tropical light filtering through an open window. To his right, an assistant scrawled notes in a large ledger and checked names off a list of NYRBA employees in Belem. In front of him stood an empty chair that looked as though it had not been sat in all morning. Priester looked Sture up and down when he entered the room. As McGlohn introduced the two men, Priester referred repeatedly to a list on his desk and never offered Sture the empty chair. So Sture remained standing throughout the short meeting. When McGlohn finished speaking, Priester tapped his finger on the roster before him and looked again at Sture.

"Do you want to stay with Pan Am, or do you want transportation to go home?" He labored over the words.

"I would like to stay on with Pan Am."

Priester looked at McGlohn. "This is the man who repaired the S-38?"

McGlohn nodded and answered, "That's right."

Priester again looked at Sture. "Is it true that you speak Portuguese?"

"Yes, sir, it is."

Priester turned to the aide at his right. The assistant looked up from his page as the Dutchman stroked his jaw. "This man repaired the seaplane we spoke about yesterday and may interpret for us while we are here. Write his name down. Sigfred. S-I-G-F-R-E-D. Sigfred. This man we keep."

---

long string of stories Sture would hear and witness regarding Priester's temper, passion and apparent lack of reason. Worshipped by many outside Pan Am as a key to the company's success, Priester was disliked, if not despised, by many in the company's rank and file, and his no-nonsense, no-excuses approach to management proved a bane to company morale during the boom years of rapid change that would follow.

133

The Grande Hotel, Belem. 1930. Sigfred collection.

Propless Planes

1930-1932

Sporadic gunfire echoed in the night, shaking the limbs of mimosas in the river valley and silencing the shrieks of tapirs in the brush. The rebel forces of Getúlio Dornelles Vargas picked their way through the darkness around the city of Belem. The valley was alive with the scurrying of those who sought shelter and the strutting of those who sought trouble. The morning, however, was still. Steel doors rolled down over all entrances blocked the sun from the cool, dark lobby of the Grande Hotel and muffled occasional shouts from

Pan Am pilots gathered at the Grande Hotel in Belem, 1930.
Sigfred collection.

the street. In the light of day, the residents of the hotel tried to forget what had been all too clear the previous night: a war was snaking its way through Belem.

A loyalist Brazilian general, his entourage gathered round him like beggars, sat in the lobby of the hotel. While revolution passed across the countryside, the supporters of President Luiz Pereira de Souza reveled in a luxury reserved for only the military and the upper classes. In whispers, they plotted strategies for dealing with the insurgents around Belem. As the general spoke, employees of the hotel moved quietly among the guests and dispensed refreshments and snacks, as though nothing were wrong outside. Trying to ignore the bluster of war, Sture sat in a large cane rocker opposite the general and his aides. Rocking slowly, he explained his recommendations for securing the local base to a group of Pan Am employees. The group, sent from Miami to perform a physical inventory of the NYRBA equipment, included airport manager Fritz Blotner and two Pan Am engineers, "Mac" McGregor and Johnny Nash.

McGregor, preoccupied with the threat of imminent violence, stared toward a shattered window and paid little attention to the other men. "I hear the SOB's have taken over all of Brazil. Soon they'll take Belem," he said. "Are you sure Priester and his crew got away in time?"

Sture leaned back in his chair. "They've been gone for several days. Hopefully they stayed ahead of the fighting, but you never know." He glanced toward the door beyond which lay the hot, vacant streets.

McGregor wiped his forehead with a damp handkerchief and stared again toward the window. "I don't like this. Seltzer has been hanging around like a vulture with those damned forms of his," he said, referring to the American consulate. "He wants to know who he

Work tents Sture constructed for repairing engines, Belem, 1930. Sigfred collection.

should notify in the event something should happen. That's what he says, 'in the event something should happen.'"

Ignoring McGregor's complaints, Sture turned toward Blotner and again began his explanation of what Pan Am needed to secure their operations in Belem. As well as they could, the staff of the Grande Hotel maintained the appearance of normality and made the guests comfortable. A well-stocked larder promised food for several days. A well-stocked bar promised the same for spirits. Drinks flowed as freely as predictions on the progress of the revolution, and as afternoon approached, the hotel seemed the scene of a celebration. Only the barricaded windows and doors hinted at the violence in which the celebration occurred. Briefly forgetting the revolution outside the hotel walls, the kitchen staff began to mimeograph menus for the evening meal. Laughter sprang from a corner of the lobby. The voices of men in heated discussion rose over the afternoon calm.

Then a bullet hit the metal door at the lobby entrance. The door shook violently against its frame.

The men fell silent.

In the kitchen, workers exchanged frightened glances. The chef scratched through one of the entrees on the menu and directed his workers to make new copies. "We don't know how long the fighting will last," he said to the frustrated worker who manned the handle of the mimeograph machine. "We must save what food we can."

The afternoon progressed in a play of restless relaxation and frightened tension. When all of the guests had calmed sufficiently to continue normal conversation, another shot sounded from across the lane. Again the guests fell silent, the workers' hands froze in midair, and the chef removed another entree from the menu.

Pan Am maintenance facility at Belem, 1931. Sigfred collection.

From across the room, Sture caught snippets of conversation from the general and his adjutants. Occasionally the words "escape" or "withdrawal" drifted over the whispers of the military men whose faces became more grave and worried with each hour. Once, when he glanced toward the group of loyalists, he saw a thin, young man, somewhat sickly looking, bend toward the general and point toward Blotner who wore the uniform and emblem of a Pan Am pilot.

137

Sture signaled for Blotner to meet him outside the lobby, and the airport manager followed him into the hall near the front desk.

Sture leaned toward him and spoke quietly.

"I think the loyalists are getting frightened or restless."

"You're right."

Sture leaned closer. "It seems to me that they'll want to try and get out of here quickly if the fighting gets any worse. Let's walk down to the hangar and get rid of the propellers from the S-38s. We don't want them misappropriated by the loyalists *or* the rebels."

Blotner thought for a moment.

"We don't want to take sides in this fight, but you're right. We can't afford to lose either one of those planes to either side in this fracas. The fighting is bound to end, hopefully sooner rather than later. We'll need those planes for the mail that's piling up. Let's go. It'll be safer if there are two of us."

"You really ought not come dressed like that."

"What do you mean?" Blotner looked confused.

"We should look as casual as possible before we leave. If they see you looking like you just stepped from the air corps, both of us are in trouble."

Blotner nodded and hurried to his room to change. Taking care to avoid the glances of the general and his men, Sture returned to the lobby. Blotner joined him after changing his clothes.

After almost an hour without a gunshot, Blotner nodded toward Sture. "Let's go." The two sneaked through the gate of the hotel courtyard and hurried toward the docks. Both repeatedly glanced over their shoulders to ensure they were not being followed.

Once safely inside the Pan Am hangar, Sture explained his concerns more thoroughly. "I didn't like the way those men were looking at us. They want to save their necks, the government be damned. I thought it was just a matter of time before they demanded that you fly them out with one of these planes."

"Well, I am a pilot," Blotner answered. "I could have flown them out if it came to that."

"So could I, for that matter," Sture said, "but not in one of these planes. They're not flyable right now - problems with the engines. Try explaining to a desperate man that an airplane won't fly. With the propellers on, we'd have a hard time convincing anyone that they won't get into the air. But with the propellers off, any damn fool could see they're not flyable."

Blotner looked at Sture and laughed. "Good thinking, Sig. That's all we'd need is some frightened soldier trying to force us out of

Commodore on survey flight, 1930. Sigfred collection.

Belem in a plane that won't fly."

Sture ran to the stockroom and retrieved two wrenches. He and Blotner set to work on the S-38s. They removed a single propeller from each of the planes, immediately and clearly immobilizing them. First, they hid the propellers outside the hangar, and returned to remove the second propeller from each plane, which they hid in a different location from the first. More relaxed than before, they began the short walk back to the Grande Hotel.

Dusk descended on the river-city as the two men made their way, conspicuously pale, up streets that hours before had been deserted. As on the previous day, most of the city's residents had remained inside their homes, behind the drawn shades of their small but protective houses, while the sounds of angry shouts and errant bullets echoed across the valley. Only when darkness promised the same shelter from the eyes of an unrecognized enemy did they venture from behind the walls. As night fell upon Belem, whole families crept into the street to share rumors of the rebel advancement and to trade stories of the gunshots that had pounded the city throughout the night and much of the day. Women with children bouncing on their hips speculated on who would win the revolution. Men, the grime of labor pressed into the folds of their weathered faces, laughed at politicians who resorted to petty violence for the sake of power. Most of the faces seemed strangely detached from the fighting, as though it were a mere distraction when compared with the demands of feeding a family and caring for the young.

Commodore at the dock in Belem, 1930.
Sigfred collection.

As Sture and Blotner foraged their way through the streets, they passed several makeshift barricades made of cobblestones stacked several feet high before ditches where the stones had previously lain. Ruddy-faced young men, several who had worked for and recognized Sture, manned the barricades. They waved and called to him through the haze of late afternoon. He greeted each of them, smiling, and shook their hands. While speaking with them in Portuguese that only occasionally revealed he was not a native, he noticed that each of the young men gripped tightly in his fist one of the cold black carbines that had echoed through the night. In the barrel of more than one of the guns, he noticed unmistakable brown rust that completely sealed the bores.

When the two men finally ducked back into the courtyard of the Grande Hotel, they could not help remarking on the fearless faces of the Belem natives and the excited faces of the young soldiers at the barricades. Unlike the general and his friends in the hotel, these common people were not frightened by the war - bothered perhaps, in some cases even hopeful, but not frightened. Though it was a revolution, fear was only for the career soldiers, those with the least to lose.

The citizens could save fear for another day, so they huddled a respectable distance from the loyalists. The farmhands-turned-soldiers guarded the streets with rifles that would not fire. And a full moon climbed high over the dark and silent streets. The citizens retired behind walls that would protect them for another day from the shots of angry and misguided soldiers. The soldiers braced their backs against cold, hard stones. And the jungle came alive in the moonlight. The young men, still clutching their rusted carbines, closed their eyes and dreamed of wars where glory - and never blood - ran through the streets of Belem. The night was silent, and like the soldiers at their barricades, the guests of the Grande Hotel slept without stirring.

Within three weeks, the war was over. President de Souza resigned, and Getúlio Dornelles Vargas assumed power as the provisional president. Pan Am returned to its pattern of regular flights, and Sture threw open the doors to the Pan Am hangar and inhaled the scent of a

Commodore in the air over Belem, 1930. Sigfred collection.

breeze off the Amazon River. There, in the blazing light of a springtime afternoon, he personally replaced the propellers on the downed S-38s. Then he readied his men to repair yet another plane on yet another day.

With the revolution over and spring looming in the air, scores of Pan Am employees flooded into South America. They took up residence in the cities and villages that marked the former NYRBA routes from Georgetown, British Guyana, to Buenos Aires, Argentina. Though many of the new employees were pilots, most seemed to be managers, directors and superintendents of some type or other, and Sture quickly found himself back with his tools. He did not mind what others considered a demotion, for he had always enjoyed his work on the seaplanes. Unlike men - especially the Pan Am men, somewhat spoiled by their preferential treatment in Washington, D.C. - the planes responded predictably and appreciatively to the concerned hands of a skilled mechanic. The reciprocating engines did not complain about the heat or argue that overhead must be reduced. The sight of one of his planes soaring through the Brazilian sky pleased Sture more than any number of profit and loss statements.

All in all, he considered himself lucky to be working when much of the world was strangled by the Depression - despite the fact that many of the Pan Am employees from the states made things difficult for him, the only former NYRBA employee left in Belem. Still, he could not let go of his desire to become a pilot. Thinking there was little the company could do but say no, he requested reassignment as a copilot on the route from Belem to Rio de Janeiro. Though he expected to have to repeatedly fight for the appointment, he was surprised when his request was granted. Apparently, despite the growing Pan Am presence in South America, the company was in desperate need of skilled pilots and copilots – regardless of the status of their formal training. Despite the long hours and hard work, he was overjoyed to finally be a member of the flight crew on his beloved seaplanes.

The route with which Sture was to grow most familiar consisted of eighteen stops for passengers and mail between Belem and Rio. Two overnight stops along the way provided the opportunity for him to service the engines himself and to top off the gas tanks with fuel poured from five-gallon cans. As often as not, he would return to Belem, only to be put to work servicing one of the planes that was due to fly north to Miami at daybreak. The three-day route often stretched to four days, and Sture seldom had a day off. But he enjoyed his work so completely that neither the tropical heat nor the lack of sleep diminished his enthusiasm for aviation or for Pan Am.

Sture arriving at Pan Am facilities in Rio, 1931. Sigfred collection.

In the months he had spent with NYRBA before it merged with Pan Am and before the Brazilian revolution, Sture had established a reputation as one of the finest aviation mechanics in South America. This reputation spread quickly among the small and sometimes incestuous aviation community. His work on the S-38 upon his arrival in Belem had done much to establish that reputation, and it seemed only natural when another S-38 overhaul was required that he be removed from flight duty and assigned to repair it. Though the assignment kept him from copiloting, he realized the importance of his work and the opportunity it could provide. He refused to complain. None of the men pouring into South America from the United States could splice and install control cables, and Sture was sure that the assignment would demonstrate his importance to the company.

He was right. As soon as he completed the overhaul of the S-38, he was promoted to Chief Mechanic and placed in charge of all maintenance operations at the Rio base. His assignment, however, left no one who could repair control cables in Belem, and his promotion was delayed until he could make arrangements for a replacement. He assured the superintendent of the Belem base that he could train a Brazilian to perform the delicate work on the control cables in a matter of weeks. After his assurances, Sture was grudgingly allowed to transfer to Rio with specific instructions to expedite the hiring and training of the new mechanic. Even without his instructions, Sture realized that all of his hopes for advancement and his only opportunity for returning to flight duty rested in obtaining a qualified replacement for the cable work. He hired two Brazilians on his first day in Rio. Seldom sleeping, he spent the better part of the next three weeks training the two men in all aspects of control cable installation, maintenance and repair. As soon as he was sure that the men could handle the work by themselves, he transferred one to Belem and assigned the other to work for him in Rio.

Despite his success in maintaining and repairing the fleet of S-38s and Commodores, the New York office made it clear that they were dissatisfied with Sture's assignment as Chief Mechanic in Rio. The former Chief Mechanic, Mr. J. Garcia, was one of the first men Pan Am had hired, back in 1927, and his being replaced by Sture did not set well with the executives. For his part, Garcia was bitter about the assignment. He longed to remain in Rio, despite the fact that he was neither so good a mechanic nor so effective in dealing with the Brazilians as Sture. The climate in Rio seemed heavenly when compared to the hot jungle that surrounded Belem. Rio's city life was far more entertaining than the day-to-day grind of Belem, and Garcia did not want to give any of it up. Sture attempted to keep his dealings with the former Chief Mechanic cordial, but their relationship quickly degraded. The situation reminded him of the discomfort he felt during his final months at NACA.

Still, just as he had refused to let NYRBA's politics affect his work, he also refused to allow personal differences to keep him from accomplishing his assigned tasks. When he had arrived in Rio, the base employed sixty-seven men. Within days, he had been ordered to cut the ranks to forty-two. The depression maintained a constant pressure on the Pan Am executives. They transferred that pressure equally to all of their divisions. Orders to cut employment in Rio continued throughout Sture's first few months. Ultimately, he was allowed only $425 per month for payroll and was forced to cut employment to fifteen men. Though the task proved difficult, he was able to maintain first-class maintenance and readiness on the fleet of seaplanes within the financial constraints the company placed upon him.

The S-38 Sture repaired in Rio. 1931. Sigfred collection.

His first task was to cut the number of men working at the base. This he accomplished easily enough by asking some of the single men to resign. Although they were often senior to many of the other workers, Sture pointed out that most of the junior workers were relatives of the senior men and had small children to feed. None of the men relished the idea of unemployment, but they recognized the importance of keeping the family men working and cooperated in reducing the roll.

Sture's second task was to reduce costs by cutting the work week. Normally, the men, who were paid for six days, worked only five. Sture convinced them to work round the clock on the three plane arrival days and to take the remaining four days off. The company, he explained would still pay them for six days, but would save money through reduced facilities maintenance and operations costs. This reduced by half the amount of time the men lost commuting to the boat landing and translated directly into increased productivity. Additionally, the reduced workweek

allowed the struggling workers to spend less of their meager salaries on streetcar fares.

Sture with Pan Am workers in Rio. 1931. Sture stands at the far left. Next to him is the former Rio Maintenance Manager J. Garcia. Sigfred collection.

The change in working hours, though good for the men and the company, also presented logistical problems. He solved the problem of ensuring that the men were sufficiently rested to safely perform their work simply by cycling the men through breaks during which they could nap in the darkened recesses of one of the hangars. The most significant problem, however, was feeding the men during the long working hours. He solved this problem by installing a large sheet of aluminum over two blowtorches to serve as a grill in one corner of the workshop. He had groceries delivered from a market in Punta Caju, a short distance by water from the base. The scent of food cooking in the corner distracted some of the men, but it also seemed to make them more productive. Sture paid for the groceries himself, but saved the cost of meals he had previously taken at a German restaurant in Rio. He quickly found himself developing close friendships with his men. He believed that, all in all, the arrangement was a winning one.

Sture spent the next several months overseeing the maintenance and repair of Pan Am's fleet of seaplanes and enjoying life beside the Atlantic. His days settled into a predictable but enjoyable routine of maintenance on the fleet of S-38s and Commodores and occasional trips to nearby Pan Am facilities to inspect or assist in difficult repairs. Though his duties as Chief Mechanic kept him from serving as a pilot, they did not keep him from flying. He served regularly as a crewmember on flights throughout eastern Brazil, and was often away from the Rio base for days and weeks at a time. Between January of

1931 and March of 1932, he logged almost 243 hours of flight time, most on regularly scheduled operations or test flights. However, a few of the flights offered him the opportunity to explore the less inhabited

Sture with his Rio maintenance crew, 1931. Sture, the only American in a crew of Brazilian and German technicians, kneels before the men, gesturing to the dog. Sigfred collection.

regions of the country's interior.

He found these trips especially enjoyable and volunteered for them whenever the opportunity arose, pointing out that the flight crews would be so far from regular supply depots that they might need his skill in case of engine problems. In December of 1930 and again in February of 1931, he accompanied survey and motion picture crews to the Ford rubber plantation on the Rio Branco near Boa Vista in the foothills of the Pakaraima Mountains. On his way to the mountains, he watched in amazement the gentle evolution of the landscape as his plane worked its way inland. Leaving Rio, the flights hugged the Atlantic coast to Carabello, Natal, Fortaleza and Belem. Vast tracts of mangroves and cacao dotted the land along the coast. In Belem, the flights turned to the west and tracked the Amazon River where rainforests of bignonias, myrtles and mimosas formed a canopy over the river basin.

Further inland, at Santarem on the confluence of the Amazon and

Sture on tiger hunt at the Ford rubber plantation. He returned with only his camera, having lost the horse and found no tigers. 1931. Sigfred collection.

Sture and his friend Davey, bottom, at Corcovado under construction, 1930.

Sture holding a snake in the Amazon rainforest, 1932. Sigfred

Rock formation in the flatlands upriver from Rio. 1931. Sigfred collection.

Tapajós Rivers, the flights landed to refuel. Here he witnessed the dense undergrowth that carpeted the terrain and made land navigation almost as difficult as flight. From Santarem, the planes flew northwest over the Rio Negro and turned north at the Rio Branco. In the foothills of the northern mountains, the vegetation thinned, and deciduous trees and conifers replaced the exotic plants of the Amazon basin.

Outside the highly developed coastlands of the country, life slowed to a snail's pace. Sture in his uniform or white linen suit was as much an oddity to the barely-clad natives as they were to him, and the land was as wild as the urban storytellers – forever returned from the Amazon's jungles - claimed. It was not uncommon to hear the howls of jaguar and puma as he walked among the rubber trees, or to glimpse a tiger stalking its prey. His excursions into the heartland of Brazil were like excursions into his own heart. Though he had long before given up his childish fantasies of becoming an explorer or pioneer, the wilderness remained one of his greatest loves.

Believe It or Not

1932 - 1933

In March of 1932, barely aware that almost two years had passed since his arrival in South America, Sture returned to the United States with a pocket full of money to spend in two months of well-deserved vacation. Within hours of debarking from the Commodore that had transported him from Belem to Miami, he purchased a small, two-cylinder Aeronca, and informed the Civil Aeronautics Administration inspector from whom he expected to get his license that he planned to fly the plane to Minnesota to visit his family.

The inspector pulled his cap toward the back of his head and stared over his glasses at Sture. "That's an awfully long ways to be flying this plane. How many hours of cross-country flying do you have?"

Sture looked at the inspector and lowered his head. "Well, not that many in a small plane, but I've got hundreds of hours over the jungle in South America as a seaplane copilot."

"This isn't South America," the inspector said, "and that ain't a seaplane." He nodded toward the Aeronca. "Solo flight is a hell of a lot different than copiloting. I think it's just a little too dangerous for you to be flying this plane all the way to Minnesota. This thing only weighs 468 pounds. There's birds between here and there that outweigh it."

Sture did not smile.

"Your family ever been to Florida?"

"No sir," Sture answered.

"Why don't you just send the money you've saved to your folks and invite them to Miami for your vacation."

Sture frowned. "I had my hopes set on flying to Minnesota. I haven't seen my family in over three years, and I wired them I'd be flying in."

The inspector leaned against the Aeronca. He pulled his cap back over his forehead and squinted into the sun.

"You know, you could accomplish a lot of things in Miami in two whole months. You could have your family come visit. You could get some time under your belt in this plane. You could even get a Limited Commercial License when your folks go back home. But I understand you want to fly. And to fly, you have to get a license. From me. And well, I don't think it's safe to give you a license today. You could come back tomorrow, and I might give you one then. And maybe I won't. I might give you one the next day, too. But then again..." His voice trailed off into silence.

"Your folks ever been to Florida?"

"No sir," Sture answered quietly, "they haven't. But I think they might want to see it."

The Sigfred family in Miami, 1932. Left to right: Tony, Ebba, Helen, John August, Alpha, Sophia and Sture. Sigfred collection.

"I think they might too."

Sture left the inspector standing in the sun. He wired money and an invitation to his parents. He then drove into Miami to rent an apartment that he quickly and half-heartedly stocked with food and linen. When he was finished tidying up, he received a telegram from his parents telling him that they would drive from Parkers Prairie to Miami. A week later, they arrived with his brother Tony and his sisters Alpha, Ebba and Helen. For the next several weeks the family enjoyed a time they had never before experienced. Though pleased to show his family a good time, Sture was most pleased that he had passed what was perhaps the inspector's most difficult test.

Sture satisfied the inspector's requirements and passed his flight test only two days after his family returned to Parkers Prairie.

150

"You know, this is a much better license than I could have given you a couple of months ago," the inspector said, handing Sture his Limited Commercial License. "You need ten solo hours for a private license. You need fifty hours for this. By the way, how did your family like Miami?"

Sture now owned his own plane and possessed a license to go with it, but he had little time to enjoy them. His vacation drew quickly to a close. Disappointed, he placed his Aeronca in storage in Miami Springs and returned to South America. By the time his family reached Parkers Prairie, he was back in Brazil and assigned to duties as a traveling airport manager. For the next year, he relieved airport managers and other men in key positions along the coast, enjoying especially his assignment as superintendent of the largest shop in South America at Belem. But standardizing procedures at facilities up and down the eastern seaboard quickly grew tiresome, and he counted the days until he was once again in the cockpit.

Pan Am facilities in Fortaleza before and after remodel. 1930 and 1932. Sigfred collection.

The year was relatively uneventful. He concentrated on the practical matters of standardizing maintenance and business practices at each of the airports he managed. He spent the greatest portion of his year as manager of Pan Am's facilities at Bahia, the colonial capital of Brazil. A large city, Bahia was built partially on a cliff atop a peninsula between the Atlantic Ocean and All Saints Bay, and partially at sea level on the eastern shore of the bay. A seawall with a large opening in the center protected the bay. Pan Am's facilities were located at the northern end of the bay so that the pilots could take full advantage of the protected waters for their takeoffs.

His routine in Bahia was much as it was in all of the other South American cities. He attended to administrative matters when work was slow. And on plane arrival days, he spent his time at the airport overseeing maintenance. When he finally left the airport, normally well after dark, he joined a recently arrived crew for drinks and conversation at a local hotel. One October evening, only a month after his arrival in Bahia, Sture stopped as usual at the hotel. When he sat at the table with his friends from Pan Am, a waiter tapped him on the shoulder and informed him that he had an urgent call from the airport. Sture excused himself from the table and picked up a phone near the bar.

Bahia, 1932. Sigfred collection.

Before he had finished stating his name, an excited voice on the other end of the line interrupted. In a rush of words, a young mechanic explained that he had been using gasoline to clean the engine of the newly arrived plane when he touched a hot line to the starter. The young man broke into a flurry of apologies.

Sture told the mechanic to be quiet. "Did you start a fire?" he asked.

"Yes," came the soft reply.

"I'll be right there."

Sture hung up the phone, and without stopping to explain to the Pan Am crew, rushed out of the hotel and grabbed a taxi.

"It's a fire," he said to the driver, "so hurry." The driver accelerated through the narrow streets of Bahia. "I want the taxi by the hour," he added. "I may have to keep it all night."

With that, the driver immediately slowed. "I've heard that before," he said in Portuguese. "You get lots of miles for the hour, and I get nothing."

"It's a fire on one of our planes," Sture shouted. "I'm not trying to rob you of a few Brazilian reys."

"I've heard that too," the driver responded and slowed the taxi even more.

Sture tried to argue, but the driver refused to cooperate. Sture knew that he would have scant chance of catching another taxi this late in the evening and did not relish the idea of walking to the airport through the city's poor neighborhoods, so he stayed in the taxi, cursing under his breath.

By the time he arrived at the airport, the fire department and police were already there. Stopping only long enough to ensure that the foamite truck was operating properly, Sture rushed to the police and complained of the driver's behavior. The police immediately confiscated the driver's license and contacted the cab company for a man to replace him.

The driver, noting the foamite truck and activity near the hangar, skulked away, turning momentarily to Sture and apologizing. "I hear so many lies from Americans that I don't recognize the truth." He shrugged his shoulders and walked into the darkness. Sture felt a surge of sympathy for the driver and for several seconds considered calling him back. But other concerns demanded his attention.

First, he inspected the inside of the plane. Though the fire had started in an engine above the fuselage, it quickly traveled down a strut

Bahia, 1932. Sigfred collection.

and into the passenger compartment. The fireproof upholstery did not burn, but the smoldering fabric had left a strong odor in the plane. Even with the hatch open and all smoke cleared, Sture felt the stinging in his chest of the pungent fumes that clung to the inside of the cabin.

He summoned his chief mechanic and asked what he thought they should do. "Well," the mechanic drawled, "I heard one of the older boys say that he once worked in a drug store, and the ladies of the night would come in to purchase what they called 'toilet water.' You know," he winked, "those ladies always smell quite nice. Of course, all of the drug stores are closed, but if we find where these ladies live, we could purchase some toilet water from them."

Sture nodded without speaking.

"Of course, they will charge an inflated price. How high can I go?"

Sture looked at the man's face as he handed him a fist full of bills. The mechanic flushed beneath his swarthy complexion.

"You hurry back," Sture warned him. "I don't want any excuses about being detained."

154

Sture, 1932. Sigfred collection.

The mechanic returned in less than an hour with a large bottle of perfume in his hands. "I found a place right away," he said. "I did not have to search far, at all. We were very lucky tonight."

Sture nodded, and the men began spraying and dabbing toilet water throughout the cabin. He hoped that by morning it would smell more like a plane than a brothel.

Traveling across South America quickly took its toll on Sture, and by June of 1933, he was again ready for a vacation. This time, despite protests from anyone to the contrary, he planned to fly to Minnesota in his Aeronca. From Rio, he cabled Fred Richards in Miami and asked him to get the Aeronca out of storage and to have the windshield replaced. Because the plane had to be relicensed each year, he also asked Fred to take care of that. Fred wired back that he would take care of everything and that he looked forward to seeing his old friend when he arrived in Miami.

For the next several days, Sture could think of nothing but the adventure that lay before him. Though the Aeronca C-3 was not an attractive plane, it offered all he needed for his journey. The flying bathtub, as the C-3 and her older sister the C-2 were commonly called, had a thirty-six foot wingspan and a twenty foot, tubular steel fuselage tightly wrapped in muslin, doped and polished to a hard finish. The angle at the spine was so sharp that she was often referred to as "the razorback" as well as the flying bathtub. Her Aeronca 113 engine provided thirty-six to forty horsepower to the 468-pound plane with a compression ratio of 5.1 to 1. The engine bore was 4 ¼ inches, and the stroke 4 inches. Though the crankshaft had proven historically susceptible to failure, the engine was still highly reliable and cost only a few cents per mile to operate - an economy Sture looked forward to for his 1800-mile flight to Parkers Prairie. With an average cruising speed of sixty-four miles per hour, exceptionally long wings and a thirty-five mile per hour stall speed, the C-3 would quickly and safely carry him to his destination. The open cockpit could be a bit uncomfortable in extremes of weather, but Sture expected mild temperatures throughout his early summer flight.

Pan Am facilities at Dinner Key – from the land. 1933.
Sigfred collection.

On the evening of June 9, 1933, near Dinner Key, Sture and Fred Richards stood outside a hardware store that had catered almost exclusively to NYRBA employees back in 1930. Sture had often purchased supplies at the store, taking advantage of the wholesale prices the proprietor offered to NYRBA employees. Still, he had long since forgotten the friends he had made among the store's owners and employees. But as he and Fred stood outside discussing his plans for the trip to Minnesota, the owner of the store stepped onto the sidewalk for some fresh air. He looked at Sture and smiled broadly.

"Mr. Sigfred," he called. "How have you been for the past three years?" The man grabbed Sture's hand and pumped furiously.

Sture recognized the man as soon as he spoke. He returned the handshake and introduced the owner to Fred. He answered that he had been well since they had last seen each other and told him of his duties with Pan Am. Almost as an afterthought, he added that he was planning to leave the following morning on a flight to Minnesota.

156

"Then you'll probably need a machete to hack your way through those amber waves of grain." The owner winked. "Wholesale, of course."

"You may be right," Sture said and walked into the hardware store to search through the machetes. Fred and the owner followed him, and the owner repeatedly asked Sture if the stories he had heard of the diamond tooth were true. Sture avoided the question and looked though the largest selection of machetes he had ever seen in the United States. He quickly chose a simple machete with a blade approximately eighteen inches long, and asked the owner to sharpen and wrap it for the trip.

Sikorsky S-40, amphibian, loading on land, Miami, 1931.
Sigfred collection.

After they left the shop, Fred stopped on the sidewalk. "What's this about a diamond tooth the old man was going on about?"

"It's nothing," Sture answered. "I just have a tooth inlaid with a diamond. It's good for identification purposes."

Fred seemed incredulous, so Sture stuck his finger into his mouth and hooked his cheek away from his teeth. Laid into the cap on one of his eyeteeth was a small diamond.

"I've got to hear the story behind this," said Fred. So Sture told him the story as they walked in the cool evening.

"Somewhere I heard or read the slogan, 'Be true to your teeth, or they will be false to you.' So I've tried like the devil to take care of my teeth. When I was washing dishes in a restaurant in Minneapolis, one of the first things I did was look up a dentist to take care of a small cavity that had started. My brother Berger did too. When I got to Brazil, finding a good dentist was number one on my list. The hotel manager in Belem recommended one who spoke English, and I made an appointment.

"He didn't find much wrong. But the filling in my left eyetooth, the one I had taken care of in Minneapolis, was loose, and he thought it should be capped. He told me that teeth are normally capped with silver or gold, but said that nothing is better or more expensive than diamonds. I thought he was joking. He looked at my teeth again and said the tooth with the loose filling was the perfect place for a cap with a diamond.

"Well, he didn't have a diamond, and I forgot about the incident until that night. A few of us were sitting at the sidewalk café at the Grande Hotel when the dentist showed up and called me aside. He showed me an oval shaped diamond that would fit perfectly on the cap. I agreed on the price, and the next day he put it in.

"It didn't cause much trouble until Mr. Ripley of the '*Believe It or Not*' books was on one of my flights from Rio to Belem. He found out I was the only airman registered with the Department of Commerce who had a diamond in his tooth for identification. Ripley printed it in a cartoon in one of his books. It upset the company for a while. They put out a memo on not wearing decorations or adornments in public, and it's pretty much died down now. I just don't want to stir it up again."

He shrugged and looked at Fred, bent double with laughter. "Come on now. I don't want to make a scene."

Sikorsky S-40, amphibian, loading on water, Miami, 1932.
Sigfred collection.

Flying Home
1933

The next morning at 8:00, Sture flew out of Miami, equipped with a full eight-gallon tank of gas, an extra two-gallon can for those places that might not have gas, a compass, and a pair of pliers. Tucked between the two seats in the cockpit was the gleaming new machete, and carefully wrapped and stowed in the luggage compartment to avoid questions, a shrunken human head he had purchased in Brazil.

License for the Aeronca, 1933. Sigfred collection.

Though he hoped to fly all the way to Jacksonville before refueling, he was forced to land for fuel in Vero Beach. He was fortunate to have a quick turnaround, and within a quarter hour was back in the air. He was enjoying the calm, bright day when he noticed a Stearman rapidly approaching off his port wing. Knowing the Aeronca could travel only 65 MPH, the pilot of the Stearman pointed the nose of his plane into the sky. Quickly dropping airspeed, he settled into a leisurely flight parallel to the Aeronca. Sture noticed the Department of Commerce Aeronautics Branch logo on the Stearman, and quickly returned a wave to the pilot. The Stearman paralleled

Sture's small plane for several minutes, then abruptly banked to port, added power, and disappeared into the distance.

When he landed in Jacksonville, Sture recognized the Stearman on the tarmac. Entering the coffee shop, he saw the Department of Commerce logo on the badge of an inspector sitting at the counter. Sture sat beside him.

The inspector turned to the window and nodded toward Sture's plane. "That isn't the Aeronca I licensed for a man named Richards in Miami last week, is it?"

Sture's temporary copy of his 1933 transport license. Sigfred collection.

"Yes sir," Sture responded, "it is. Fred is a friend of mine. He had it licensed while I was still in Rio."

"Well, I hope you're not going too far in it. Like I told Richards, there's a lot of time on her engine."

"No, sir," Sture answered. "I'm just going up into Georgia a little way." He reached for his cup of coffee and sipped, burning his lip on the steaming liquid.

"Well, you be careful until you get that engine overhauled, you hear?"

Sture nodded and thanked the inspector. The inspector placed a penny, the standard tip of the day, on the counter and walked out of the coffee shop. Sture rubbed his tongue over the tender spot on his lip. He waited for the inspector to board his plane and taxi toward the runway for takeoff. Then he too placed a penny on the counter and nodded at the cook. "Time to head for Georgia. A little way." He walked into the afternoon sun, blinking in the glare, and inhaled deeply before climbing into the cockpit.

The afternoon flight went smoothly, and Sture quickly found himself landing in Savannah to refuel. After only a few minutes on the ground, he took off for Charleston. In Charleston, he topped off his fuel tank and wired ahead to the CAA Weather Station for a weather report. Within minutes, the report came back to the Western Union office that all was clear. Sture again climbed into the cockpit and flew toward Florence, South Carolina, approximately 100 miles north. The afternoon light reflected off railroad tracks that ran straight north between the two cities. Sture maintained his altitude low enough to keep the tracks in sight.

After only a few minutes in the air, Sture noticed storm clouds ahead of him. Hoping the storm would blow out to sea, he lowered his altitude and forged ahead. The storm refused to budge. Only minutes after he spotted the clouds, the sky opened in a flood of dark, heavy rain. Raindrops blasted the windshield. Wind buffeted the small plane. Sture was forced to lower his altitude to about 50 feet in order to keep sight of the shining railroad tracks. The wind threatened to drive the small plane into the ground, and Sture gripped the control stick until his knuckles turned white with pain. Perspiration drenched his clothes. Still the storm pressed around him. For over an hour there was no respite.

161

Then, as quickly as it had started, the rain stopped, and Florence glistened on the horizon. Sture was pleased with the Aeronca's performance even though the storm had taxed his energy. As the company had advertised, the plane was inherently stable, and if worse came to worse, he could simply let go of the stick, and she would seek a stable track and position. She had endured the beating of the storm and had responded quickly and capably to his manipulations. He exhaled with relief and patted the instrument panel. Then he added power, gained altitude and turned into the wind for his approach to Florence, fewer than twenty miles away. Below him, the ground glistened like quicksilver.

At the airfield, Sture taxied to a stop in front of the only building and killed the Aeronca's engine. Wiping his hands on his trousers, a young man stepped from the building. Before Sture could introduce himself, the young man raised one grease-streaked hand and began to speak.

Sture with his Aseronca C-3 in Parkers Prairie, 1933. Sigfred collection.

"I am so sorry, sir. You must be Mr. Sigfred. I'm the radio operator. I wired you just a couple of hours ago that the weather was clear between Charleston and here. I swear to you it was. The storm just blew in. I don't even know where it came from. Just blew in, I tell you. I can't tell you how sorry I am and how relieved I am you made it here safe."

Sture looked at the young man, again wiping his hands nervously on his trousers.

"Last I knew, God was the only one controlled the weather. It wasn't your fault. Besides, this was the first time I had a chance to fly my plane in anything but ideal conditions. I'm pretty happy with it. It may have been only an hour in heavy rain, but it sure did a lot to reassure me about her ability to weather a storm."

On the perimeter of the airfield sat four small houses used by visiting pilots for overnight stays. Sture pulled the Aeronca in front of one of the houses, braced its wheels, and set forth on foot for the Western Union office downtown. He had walked only a couple of hundred yards when a car pulled off the road, and the driver, a man in his late twenties, asked if Sture needed a lift.

Sture nodded at a young woman with a small child in the back seat. "I'd like to go to the Western Union office, if it wouldn't be too much trouble."

"No trouble at all." The man leaned over and opened the passenger door, and Sture climbed into the car.

The couple, the husband explained, had been out for an evening drive when they noticed Sture's plane heading toward the airfield. Hoping their son might get to see the plane land, they had headed toward the airfield but missed Sture's landing. They drove Sture to the Western Union office and waited as he went inside and wired a message to his parents in Parkers Prairie. Then they drove him back to the airfield, stopping at the building beside the runway.

The radio operator again stepped from inside and told Sture that he would get a weather report and tie it to the control stick of the Aeronca so that he could have it in the morning. Then he grinned and added, "This one, I'll get right."

Sture led the couple and their son to his plane and proudly displayed it.

"Is this a government plane?" the wife asked.

"No," Sture answered. "It's mine. I bought it last year, but this is the first chance I've had to fly it cross country."

"Where are you going," the boy asked.

The woman placed her hands on the boy's shoulders and told him not to pry.

"It's all right," Sture said. He stooped so that his face was level with the boy's and explained that he was flying to Minnesota to visit his family. "The telegram I just sent was to them, to let them know I'm safe and still on my way. I'll send them a message every night so they won't worry about me."

"How far have you come?" the father asked.

"Well, I just flew up from Miami today, but I really started out last week flying on a company plane from Rio de Janeiro in South America."

The boy's eyes grew wide. "My brother told me about South America. That's on the other side of the world, isn't it?"

"That's right," Sture answered. "Where is your brother now?"

"He's in school, but he likes airplanes. He'll be really sorry he didn't get to meet you."

"Well, I'll tell you what." Sture pulled two five-milrei notes from his pocket and handed them to the boy. "Why don't you keep one of these for yourself and give one to your brother. Tell him it's a gift from a real pilot." The notes had been printed by the American Banknote Company and were engraved with large 5000s on their face. The numbers denoted their value in reis, the national currency of Brazil.

The mother quickly shook her head. "Thank you. Really, it's very kind of you, but we couldn't let the children accept such a large sum of money."

Sture laughed. "Well, maybe I should caution you to be careful where and how you spend it. In the United States, this is worth only twenty-four cents."

The woman smiled. Her husband laughed along with Sture. The young boy stashed both notes into the front pocket of his knickers and, standing on tiptoe, kissed Sture on the cheek.

That night, Sture drank a pint of milk and ate a jelly doughnut for supper. But for the croaking of bullfrogs in a nearby marsh, the night was still. He composed a letter of thanks to the couple. Then he sealed the letter and placed it beside his cap. Switching off the electric lamp beside his bed, he noticed through the silence the hum of mosquitoes outside his screen. He closed his eyes and listened to them, imagining that the sound came from the thrashing of thousands of microscopic wings. Soon he drifted to sleep, the mosquitoes serenading him with their song of flight.

The next morning, he found the weather report tied to the control stick of his plane as the radio operator had promised. Quickly skimming over the lines of text, Sture shook his head. He didn't need the report to tell him what he already knew. He stared up into the dull gray sky where whorls of fog ebbed and flowed across the horizon. Glancing to the east, he noticed a circle of lighter gray trying to break through the clouds hovering around the tiny city of Florence. Every now and then, a puddle of blue glistened beyond the pewter of the sky, but was quickly lost in the sea of fog.

"Heavy fog until late in the morning," the report said.

"He got that one right," Sture murmured.

He filled the gas tank and took off from the Florence airfield. Quickly, he gained altitude and broke through the clouds into the blinding whiteness atop the fog. Below him, clouds of fog stretched like miles of snow, brilliant and white-hot, completely obscuring the ground, and he made a point of not venturing too far from his current location. His plane was not equipped for instrument flying; it included only an altimeter, an oil temperature gage, an oil pressure gage, a tachometer, and a compass. He was navigating simply "by the seat of his pants," practicing the ancient craft of dead reckoning. Only by sighting stars at night or by maintaining visual contact with an earth-bound landmark during the day could he navigate the plane. He felt that appropriate. It kept him in touch with the earth. Dead reckoning or not, he could not escape the feeling that this was the most alive he had ever been, the most alive he could ever be. A man, alone, with nothing but the earth and the sky, the sun and the clouds to guide him. The scene below him struck Sture as one from his youth, the rolling plain of Parkers Prairie blanketed in a thick layer of snow. He was awed and humbled by the beauty that nothing man-made could approach. He flew for almost a half hour before sighting a tree through a hole in the cloud cover. He began his descent back to the Florence airfield.

Once again on land, the gnawing in his stomach reminded him of his meager dinner the evening before. So he walked to a general store just two blocks from the airfield and purchased another pint of milk and a jelly-filled doughnut. Around 9:00, the fog cleared, and Sture departed for Raleigh, North Carolina. For almost two hours, he followed the rail tracks that led north from Florence. Then he began to look for a place to land so he could put the two spare gallons of gas he carried onboard into the tank. The ground below was lined with trees except for a wide swath cut by the railroad. Only after searching for several minutes did he find a narrow field that appeared to be long enough for him to land.

The field was laid out in what looked from the sky to be undulating rolls of soil that Sture found strangely attractive. He was so engrossed in staring at the ground and the rolling earth, trying to keep the Aeronca level, that when he finally looked up he saw that he was heading directly for a house. Before he could react, his landing gear touched terra firma. Quickly, he applied hard left rudder and pushed the throttle as far forward as it would go, applying maximum power to the loping plane. He spun like a top across the field until he finally came to rest in the middle of the green, manicured lawn.

Two men ran from the house waving their arms and shouting about his safety and sanity. He jumped from the cockpit and explained that he had been forced to land so that he could pour the spare two gallons of gas into the tank. He needed the extra gas, he explained, to make it to Raleigh where there were suitable refueling facilities. The two men looked at the lawn and saw that there was little damage except where the landing gear had originally touched down. Then they looked at Sture and made sure he was not hurt. Finally, apparently relieved, they began to laugh and, each speaking over the other, to describe to Sture what the landing had looked like from their vantage point.

Between their heavy southern accents and the volume of both men talking at once, Sture barely understood a word, but he smiled and nodded his head until they were finished. Then he poured the two gallons of gas from the spare can into the gas tank and asked the two men to help him pull the plane far back into the brush so that the tail was actually sitting in the woods. He explained to the two men that he needed all the distance he could get for a clean takeoff.

Then, climbing into the cockpit, he directed the men to hold onto the tail of the plane until he signaled for them to let go. He ran the power up to full throttle and waved at the two men. They dropped the tail as he had instructed. The Aeronca lurched forward and began to gather speed. Sture counted off the yards as the plane's tachometer inched up and the distance from the tree line fell rapidly away. Finally, with only inches to spare, Sture felt the last bump of the earth as the Aeronca took to the sky. The plane shuddered a final time as the landing gear brushed against a hedge at the tree line, but the plane was safely in the air, and the bush suffered more damage than the plane.

Only after clearing the tree line, as he gained altitude, did Sture realize he had not asked where he was. Without knowing his location, he would have to sense his way toward a landmark, guided only by the sun's position. He noticed a rusty rail track running beside the house he had just left. Because it ran northwest, which he believed was the general direction to Raleigh, he followed the track. About twenty miles down the line, he came to a junction with another railroad whose shining track ran in a more northerly direction. He adjusted his course to follow the new track, and within two hours touched down in Raleigh. Wasting no time in the capital of North Carolina, he topped off his gas tank, filled the spare two-gallon can, and took off again for Langley Field in Virginia.

After two hours and ten minutes in the air, he noticed the gas gage dipping lower, and decided it was time, once again, to land and pour the spare two gallons that he kept in the baggage compartment into the plane's gas tank. He soon spotted a field and decided to circle it to ensure it was long enough for him to land and subsequently take off. He banked sharply to the left, and the engine began to sputter. Fearing that he was about to lose the engine, he pulled the throttle back and pointed the nose of the plane into a long, steep dive. His airspeed carried him low over a field of timothy hay, rapidly robbing him of much needed length for takeoff. Only about three feet from landing, the plane stalled and dropped the remaining few feet to the ground. To keep the plane in the field, Sture applied a hard right rudder and the plane landed on its right wheel first. From inside the cockpit, Sture heard the metal of the landing gear give way when the wheel hit the earth.

When the plane came to rest, he climbed from the cockpit to survey the damage. As he had suspected, the landing gear had sheared. He looked around him, at fields as far as he could see, wondering how far he would have to walk to find help. As he stood in the hay, trying to formulate his plan, he heard an engine growing louder. When he turned to locate the source of the sound, a truck driver sped into the field, throwing a cloud of gravel and dust and hay behind him. He jumped from the cab of his truck and ran toward Sture.

"I saw you land, and I thought you might need some help," he said, panting, as he stopped beside Sture.

"You're right about that," Sture answered. "I hope you can stay a while. I'm in trouble."

The strut above the right wheel on the landing gear had completely buckled, so the truck driver lifted the left wing, and Sture removed the nuts that held the landing gear to the fuselage. When the truck driver lifted the right wing, the struts and landing gear fell to the ground. Sture asked the driver to take him to a welding shop, and the two men climbed into the dusty truck for the short drive into Franklin, Virginia. The driver took Sture to the local garage, which had once been a blacksmith shop, and Sture presented the landing gear to the mechanic.

"That's awfully thin metal. I don't know if I can handle it," the mechanic said, looking at the damaged strut.

"Sure you can," Sture said. "It's not that hard if you use the right size welding tip. The one you have on right now is too large."

"Are you a welder?" The mechanic tilted his head forward as though he were peering over glasses.

"Yes," Sture responded. "I can handle it, if you have the right supplies."

"Go ahead then," the mechanic said. "There are other tips in that case. Use whatever you want."

Sture selected a tip from the case and welded the two pieces of broken strut back together. The three men then looked at the repaired strut and decided that it needed reinforcement. The mechanic offered two blades from the front-end spring of a Model-T. Sture placed one blade on the top of the strut and bolted it to the second blade on the opposite side - in effect covering and strengthening the weld. Then the three men stood back from their work and admired the new, better looking, and stronger strut. The mechanic turned to Sture and asked for $3.00 to cover the cost of parts and materials. Sture gave him a $5.00 bill and thanked him for his help.

The truck driver then drove Sture to the local Western Union office where he sent a wire to his friend "Mac" Maconahey at NACA explaining that he had been delayed but would be in Hampton in a couple of hours. The two men walked to a soda fountain near the Western Union office where Sture treated the driver to a Coke. Though Sture was thirsty and wanted another, he suspected that his takeoff from the hayfield might be so precarious that even another Coke would make a difference. He declined the driver's suggestion of a second round.

Sture and the truck driver returned to the field and attached the repaired landing gear. Sture poured the remaining two gallons into the gas tank, stowed his pliers in the cockpit and pulled out the machete he had bought in Miami just two days before. He had grown accustomed to using a machete in South America where the tool was used for everything from harvesting sugar cane to cutting brush and clearing paths in the thick jungles of the Amazon River basin. He and the truck driver moved the plane to the extreme south end of the field, and Sture quickly cut a wide swath in the timothy hay for a takeoff.

He tried once to take off, but the cleared path was too short. So he cut down more of the hay to lengthen the strip. Then he stepped off the distance from the spot where the plane stopped to the brush at the end of the field. Counting out the same number of steps at the opposite end of the field, he told the truck driver to stand where he stopped. "You," he explained, "are going to be my beacon." Sture believed that he would know if he was going to succeed in his takeoff by the time his plane drew even with the truck driver. If he was not going to succeed and he killed his engine when he reached that point, he would have sufficient room to stop the plane before running into the brush.

Before getting back into the plane, Sture paid the truck driver for his help with a $10 and a $5 bill. To lighten himself, he emptied his pockets of all change and gave that to the man as well. Because he was planning to build an auxiliary gas tank when he arrived at NACA, he gave the shining two-gallon gas can to the man as a souvenir. And finally, to ensure he had the minimum weight on the takeoff he could possibly achieve, he excused himself and visited a nearby tree where he relieved himself of a few final, but precious, ounces.

In the cockpit, he reached to the left of the windshield and heaved on the propeller. It sprang instantly to life, increasing its speed as he settled into his seat. He tested the throttle and quickly accelerated down the field. Though the ground passed rapidly below the plane, Sture feared that it would not pass quickly enough for him to takeoff. But when he drew even with the man standing in the field, he felt the plane lighten. With only one or two more jolts, the Aeronca lifted slowly into the air. Sture quickly applied more power and gradually gained altitude. Then, as he had done when he arrived, he circled the field. Waving to the truck driver, still standing in the center of the path he had cut, Sture dipped his wings and established a northeast heading.

With his repaired landing gear glinting in the sun, two gallons and a quart of gas sloshing in his eight-gallon tank and a flight of about one hour and fifteen minutes looming before him, he made his way toward the Chesapeake Bay and Hampton where his friends and a large part of his past waited at NACA and Langley Field.

Sture flew much of the next hour over the Elizabeth and James rivers. The deep blue waters glistened in the afternoon sun. When he started his descent for Langley Field, he found himself regretting that he had to leave the sky once again for the earth. His disappointment soon melted, though, as he taxied to the new NACA hangar and his old friend Sam Eaken ran out to greet him. The two men stood on the tarmac catching up on each other's lives as though weeks and not years had passed. They arranged to get together before Sture left Virginia. Sam informed him that Maconahey, another good friend he had worked with at NACA, was waiting for Sture at Little Langley, an auxiliary airfield several miles from the Army airfield.

Little Langley, southeast of the area that personnel at NACA called Big Langley, lay in the direction of Buckroe Beach. It doubled as an airstrip for private planes and a cow pasture. Sture flew the short jaunt to Little Langley, and only after the cows had scattered did he decide to land in the field. Maconahey, having noticed the Aeronca searching for a place to land, ran across the field to meet his old friend.

Maconahey pulled his cap to the back of his head and shook his head. "So you *are* Fred. I thought it might have been you"

Sture jumped from the cockpit and grasped his friend's hand. "What do you mean?"

"This morning I got a telegram from a man named Fred. Said he had been delayed down in Franklin, but he would arrive in Hampton shortly. I wondered who the hell Fred was."

"I sent that message, but I sure didn't sign it as Fred. I'll have to speak to the clerk at Western Union about that. They apparently made a mistake."

"At any rate, you're here. I believe this deserves a celebration. You'll have to fill me in on South America and the great Pan Am we hear so much of."

Sture remained in Hampton for the next three days, looking up old friends and catching up to date on the research NACA had performed in his absence. He stayed in his old apartment on Armistead Avenue, still furnished with his belongings and still one of the few apartments in the city. Between his visits with friends, he also fabricated a spare gas tank for the Aeronca. Made from extra, galvanized tin laying around the shop at Langley, the tank held approximately seven gallons of fuel and almost doubled both his capacity and mileage. He had already grown dissatisfied with having to land so frequently to refuel, and he expected the spare tank to shorten the remainder of his trip. He placed the spare tank on the cushion of his seat and, when he was in the cockpit, passed the safety belt over himself and the tank to hold it in place. Sam Eaken gave him a wobble pump that he installed between the spare tank and the installed tank at the forward end of the cockpit above the instrument panel. All he had to do to transfer fuel in flight was simply operate the pump handle.

On his first evening in Hampton, Sture stopped at the Western Union office as he had told Maconahey he would. The clerk looked through his messages from earlier in the day and, after finding a record of Sture's telegram, explained that the clerk in Franklin had simply misread "Sigfred" as "signed Fred" when he sent the message. He apologized for the mistake, and Sture explained the importance of his messages being sent and received correctly. He was wiring his family every evening to report his location and his safe progress. Any mistake in the message might unnecessarily worry them. The clerk assured him that the mistake would not happen again, but to make sure, Sture began signing all of his messages "Sture" instead of "Sigfred." His regular nightly wires, phoned from Wadena, the closest Western Union office to his home in Parkers Prairie, were delivered without incident for the rest of his trip.

On the morning of June 15, 1933, Sture bid goodbye to his friends in Hampton and took off from Langley Field. With the sun over the Chesapeake Bay at his back, he guided the plane to a north-northeast heading and quickly discovered that he was having trouble pressing his foot on the right rudder. The front left corner of the new gas tank took up so much room on the cushion beside him that it prevented him from stretching his leg. Though he considered the oversized tank only a minor inconvenience, he knew it could prove to be a safety problem in worse flying conditions. So, after approximately three hours in the air, he made an unscheduled stop in Gettysburg, Pennsylvania to modify the tank. Safely on the ground, he drained and vented the tank and then sawed off one corner of the galvanized tin. After ensuring that it didn't interfere with his ability to reach the rudder or control stick, he soldered the modified corner back in place.

Sture topped off the two tanks, and with clouds gathering in the west, took flight for Warren, Pennsylvania. As he gained altitude, the clouds began to gather more quickly and heavily, and within minutes of taking off, he was forced into a narrow corridor of flight. His altitude was limited by mountains thrusting their way into the sky and a low ceiling frequently pressing down upon the tops of the mountains. As he flew further west, he found himself precariously navigating the crests of mountains to his right and left. He fought to avoid cloud cover above him and the threatening granite floor below him. Within a half-hour, he had completely lost his bearings. For the remainder of his two-hour flight, he fought the clouds and his plane.

After struggling more than an hour, he also noticed that the spark plug on top of his left cylinder seemed to be vibrating in place. He thought at first that the vibration might actually be flexing of the windshield Fred had replaced in Miami, and that the vibrating spark plug was just an illusion. But after placing his palm against the windshield and ensuring it was not moving, it appeared more likely that the spark plug itself was moving. To make sure, he stuck his head out the left side of the cockpit and peered through stinging eyes at the plug. Sure enough, it was loose. The Aeronca engine was equipped with only one spark plug per cylinder, and if he lost the plug, he lost at least half his power. He was afraid the plane would not survive the weather on only one cylinder. His first thought was to land and tighten the spark plug, but a few groves of trees sprinkled between sheer cliffs of granite prevented this.

With nothing to do but handle the problem in the air, he grasped the control stick with his right hand and lifted his left foot over the ledge of the cockpit. He planted his foot as firmly as he could on the landing wheel of the Aeronca and pushed his knee against the support frame that rose from the wheel. Bracing his shoulder against the cockpit frame and bending slightly forward, he reached around the

Plexiglas windshield and attempted to tighten the spark plug with his left hand. He was unable to gain a firm hold on the vibrating plug, however, and could touch it for only a fraction of a second before it burned his fingers. Frustrated, angry and starting to worry for his safety, he refused to acknowledge the burning in his hand. He reached again toward the taunting plug and grasped the top with his thumb and first two fingers. Immediately, he felt the snap of current on his skin and the tingling of his nerves as he jerked his hand away from the energized plug.

Shaking his left hand in an effort to regain sensation, he looked toward the ground and saw that his perch was more unsteady than he had realized. In order to reach the spark plug, he was forced to lean so far out of the cockpit that he was several times in danger of tumbling from the plane. The summer wind tore at his skin and clothes. It pulled against him and threatened to pry loose his grip on the control stick and send him tumbling to the hard, dark earth below. As he stared at the ground hurtling in a blur below his fuselage, reality seized him. He realized how crazily he was behaving. Stupid, he thought, just stupid. A fall from the plane, more likely with each inch he stretched from the cockpit, would provide a more abrupt and final end to his trip than even a forced landing should the spark plug fail.

He pulled back into the cockpit and strapped himself into his seat. Then he pressed his head against the seat back and closed his eyes. "Just fly the plane," he repeated to himself. "Just fly the plane."

When he opened his eyes, wisps of gray that he was sure must be smoke curled on the horizon. Where there was smoke, he knew, there was a city. So, almost two hours after leaving Gettysburg, he pointed the plane toward the smoke and prayed that the loose spark plug would continue to fire until he landed. As he flew toward the smoke, the sky began to clear, and the midday sun glinted on a river below. He continued to fly toward the haze of gray that hovered over the earth, the river growing larger and larger below him. On the opposite shore appeared a thin line of gray. As the Aeronca pulled closer to the city, Sture noted that the line of gray became a landing strip, and a control tower rose from the earth like a lighthouse from deadly shoals.

With sweat dripping from his face and a throbbing in his head, he descended toward the landing strip. Only when his landing gear touched the pavement and he heard air escaping from his lips did he realize he had been holding his breath. He pulled the Aeronca to a stop beside a large hangar at the end of the runway and rested his head in his hands. Finally, when his breathing and heart rate returned to normal, he looked around. Though the airport seemed well equipped, there appeared to be no flying activity. Sture secured the plane and walked into the hangar.

From across the bay of the hangar, a man called to Sture.

"You look lost. Can I help you with anything?"

Sture peered in the direction of the voice. "Yes you can," he answered. "Can you tell me what state I'm in?"

The man walked to Sture and stared questioningly into his eyes. "If you have to ask what state this is, then your flight must have been as bad as you look. I'm the airport manager here. And by here I mean Williamsport, Pennsylvania." The man held his hand out to Sture.

"It wasn't the best of flights, no sir," Sture answered. "When I saw that haze, I thought I was heading into Pittsburgh."

"Try 200 miles northeast of Pittsburgh."

"Exactly where I wanted to be." Sture smiled and shrugged.

"You look exhausted," the manager said. "Why don't you take a cot in the corner back there and get a little sleep." He nodded toward the back of the hangar. "We'll talk about where you are and where you're going when you're rested."

Two hours later, over coffee and conversation, the airport manager told the refreshed and wide-awake pilot that he had fallen fast asleep before he ever lay down on the cot.

Without thinking, Sture responded. "Well, sir, there are worse places I could have fallen, I suppose." He looked toward his Aeronca still sitting at the end of the runway.

The manager too looked toward the Aeronca and nodded. "I suppose there are."

When he was sure that Sture was sufficiently rested, the manager gave Sture directions to Warren.

"Fly straight north 120 miles, about two hours, and you'll come to a road that runs east and west. Take that road west, and you won't be able to miss it."

Sture followed the directions as well as he could in the rough woods of Pennsylvania, but after almost two hours in the air, he saw the road disappear into mountains and woods. Rather than risk getting lost again, he landed at a small airport in the valley on the outskirts of Kane. At the airport, he asked for directions to Warren and was told to head straight west. He would come to a wide brick road heading off to the right, but he should ignore the road to the right and continue going straight over the road leading west. Sture repeated the directions to make sure he understood them and headed back to his plane.

Within minutes of taking off, he found a brick road leading to the right, slightly northwest, but did not see the road that was supposed to lead straight ahead. So he followed the brick road. Several miles down the road, he came to a factory that appeared to make the bricks that lined the road. Again, the road ended in the side of a mountain. The dark pinewoods stretched as far as he could see beyond the factory. More than slightly frustrated, he returned to Kane for better directions.

The airport manager at Kane leaned against the side of the Aeronca and peered at the ground.

"Well," he said, "I guess you missed the road because of all them trees. It's happened more than once. Go back like I told you. Keep flying straight ahead and

Sture landing the Aeronca in a field during his 1933 trip to Parkers Prairie. Sigfred collection.

you'll see glimpses of a small brick road through the trees. Follow that road and it will run into a two-lane blacktop highway. Follow the highway to the right. That'll take you north, and you'll see the Allegheny River and a bridge. Fly over the bridge and turn left. A few more miles down the road will be Warren."

This time, Sture jotted notes on a small slip of paper and tucked the paper into his pocket. Once again, he climbed into the cockpit and guided the Aeronca into the air. He kept a closer watch on the road, the woods, and all that the woods revealed.

Nine years before, there had been no airport in Warren. Pilots had landed their planes on a racetrack, and Sture expected to have to do that now. So barely clearing the tops of the trees, he looked for the bridge and what would appear to be a small earthen oval in a clearing beside the town. Before he got to the bridge, he noticed a purple reflection in the rotating propeller. Without pondering its source, he realized that it was the reflection of the exhaust from his two-cylinder engine, a phenomenon made possible only in the gloaming, the setting of the sun. For an extra margin of safety, he increased his altitude slightly and began to look more feverishly for a place to land.

To his surprise, just ahead was what he thought must be the most beautiful airport he had ever seen. At the end of the gleaming runway, stood a large, new hangar. He had no idea where he was, but he landed the plane and taxied to the hangar. He cut the engine and stepped from the plane as a young attendant walked out of the hangar.

"Where am I," Sture asked the attendant.

"Warren, Pennsylvania, sir," he answered.

Sture looked back to the east, at the granite-faced mountains looming behind them. He laughed and looked back at the attendant. "Really, where am I?"

The attendant again answered that he was in Warren, and only after describing the town and its surroundings did he satisfy Sture that he had indeed landed in Warren.

"Well, I'll be a son of a gun. I wasn't expecting an airport."

"Most people don't," the attendant responded. "But here she is."

After the usual greetings, the attendant asked where Sture was from. He repeated what had become his common response, and told the man that he planned on staying in Warren for a few days. For a few minutes, he recounted the times he had barnstormed in Chandlers Valley and asked the attendant if he could drive him to Chandlers Valley, fourteen miles west of the city. The young man enthusiastically agreed and didn't stop talking for the fourteen-mile trip. By the time they made it to Chandlers Valley, Sture felt as though he had never left.

In Chandlers Valley, Sture visited his friend Brownie. He told him he was checking into the Carver Hotel in Warren, and Brownie offered to pick him up the next morning. The two men spent the following morning together, and after catching up on the nine years that had passed in his absence, Sture flew to Jamestown, twenty-five miles north of Warren, to visit his old barnstorming partner, Slip

King. Slip, though no longer a barnstormer, had a flying school in James-

The Aeronca flying over Parkers Prairie, 1933. Sigfred collection.

town and, despite the depression, was reaping the benefits of a renewed interest in aviation.

On June 18, Sture left Warren and headed for Akron, Ohio. After a brief stop to top off his fuel tank and visit the facilities in Akron, he pushed through to Cincinnati. He spent the night in Cincinnati, and early on the morning of June 19, as the sun first peeked over the mountains to the east, he left for Chicago. After four hours and five minutes in the air, he had to land at Culver, Indiana because he was so thirsty.

Though he searched for an airport, he could find none within a twenty-mile radius of the small Indiana town. He did, however, notice a circle of rocks that had been painted white in the center of a large cow pasture. Clearly, someone intended this to be a sort of a landing spot as well as a pasture. He taxied the plane up to the road that ran into town and killed the engine as a cab pulled to a stop beside him. The driver got out of the car and held his hand out to Sture.

"Name's Ginsberg," the man told him. And without pausing, he added, "Every time I see a plane land here, I come out because they, the pilots, they always need gas."

"I appreciate your coming," Sture said "but I don't need any gas. I landed to get a drink. I am really thirsty."

Just then, a young boy ran out of a nearby house and toward the two men. Sture noticed some cattle wandering toward the plane. He told the boy that he was going into town and that he wanted the boy to keep the cows away from the plane. He pulled fifty cents from his pocket and pressed it into the boy's hand.

"We'll be gone only a short time, and when I come back, I'll give you another fifty cents," he told the boy.

Then he and Ginsberg left for town. After Sture drank two Cokes, they headed back to the plane. When they arrived at the field, the boy was nowhere in sight. To Sture's horror, a large cow had worked her head under the flying wires and was standing with her head in the cockpit, licking the dash. Sture was angry that the boy had taken the fifty cents and left, but Ginsberg said that it was probably the first fifty cents the boy had ever seen.

"Couldn't wait to spend it. So he left. Simple as that. What you should have done was take a one-dollar bill out of your billfold, torn it in half, and told him you'd give him one half now, and the other half when you got back. Live and learn, right?"

As Ginsberg spoke, Sture began to imagine the cow bolting away from the plane. Because she was bigger than the plane and undoubtedly weighed more, he was sure she would wreck it. So he began to pet her. As she nuzzled his hand, he maneuvered her away from the plane and lowered her head below the crossed wires. Peacefully, she ambled away. Sture scattered the rest of the cattle and took off for Chicago.

An hour and forty-three minutes later, he landed at Midway Airport in Chicago. Upon disembarking, he learned that air traffic into the airport was controlled from a tower. The controller in the tower had a light gun that he aimed at the cockpit of incoming planes. If the light shone green, it was okay to land. If the light shone red, it was not. When Sture heard this, he was surprised. He had not seen a light when he landed. He had, in fact, not even noticed the tower.

After checking in at the airport, Sture called his former Navy buddy, Matt Kandle. Matt was surprised and pleased to hear from his friend, and invited him to his home. "You'll have to take the streetcar, though," he said. "I still don't have a car." Sture took one of the streetcars that left the airport every few minutes, but still had to walk over a mile to get to the small house. The two friends talked for several hours, and at about 7:30, a friend of Matt's arrived to drive the two to Matt's parents' home in Edison Park, about 40 miles northwest.

Matt's parents were as happy to see Sture as Matt had been. They enjoyed the reunion and talked until after 1:00 in the morning. Much of their conversation involved the unusual gift Sture had brought for Matt's parents: the shrunken head. Relishing the attention, Sture relayed the story of how he had traded his portable typewriter for the head. He explained that the chemist in Brazil with whom he had made the trade traveled on a riverboat up and down the Amazon, buying timber root used to manufacture an insecticide called Rotenone.

"Shrunken heads are prizes in Brazil," he added. "The natives collect the heads of their enemies and shrink them by applying hot sand until they're the size of baseballs. These are the trophies of the jungle, the spoils of war."

It had been eight years since Sture and Mr. Kandle had spoken. The last time they had seen each other, Mr. Kandle had sternly advised him to decide what he wanted to do with his life and to do it. "Driving a yellow cab or a mail truck should be only a start," he had said. "You can do better. You need to do better. Much better."

As Sture sat talking, he yearned to prove to Dad Kandle that he had taken seriously his advice from eight years before, that he had done better. And he beamed with pride when Mr. Kandle noticed that he had grown during the passing years. Mr. Kandle, for his part, had been so excited when Sture arrived in his own plane that he looked up how many other people in the U.S. also owned planes. When Sture arrived, Mr. Kandle told him that he was in the ranks of very few who had reached that point. Sture understood that the proclamation somehow meant more than his being among those who owned their own planes. In Mr. Kandle's eyes, he had finally achieved some status.

Mr. Kandle's excitement over the plane, the shrunken head, the diamond tooth, and the stories of adventure in and over the jungles of South America made Sture giddy with pride. For a moment, he basked in the feeling that he had finally reached his goal in life, that he had finally pleased this man who, for a moment eight years before, had judged him harshly. There, in the sitting room of the home of his best friend's parents, with the sound of the summer night tinkling through the darkness, he felt as though he had finally grown up.

At 8:00 in the morning on June 21, 1933, Sture left Chicago for LaCrosse, on the Minnesota-Wisconsin border. A light rain fell as he picked up a Northwestern Railroad track and headed in the general direction of Minneapolis, following a train heading in the same direction. As the morning passed, the rain began to fall more heavily, and visibility diminished to only a couple of miles. At Baraboo, Wisconsin, the track he was following disappeared into a long tunnel. Sture made a quick 360-degree, climbing turn to avoid the mouth of the tunnel. A road, barely visible beyond the hills, provided Sture with a new path to follow. So he quickly accelerated over the hill to outrun the rain. Just outside LaCrosse, he burst from the clouds into a brilliant sunshine that illuminated his descent into the city. After almost five hours in the air, he touched down at the airport on the outskirts of the city. After topping off his gas tanks, he wired a message to his sister in Minneapolis advising her of his estimated time of arrival. He had forgotten about the change in time zones, however, so no one was home when his message arrived.

After wiring the message, he left the LaCrosse airport and again flew toward Minneapolis. Within two hours, he landed at the airfield in Minneapolis and went to the operations office to announce his arrival. To his surprise, a letter from his father waited at the office. The letter included a warm welcome from his father and a diagram of a landing strip on the shores of Lake Adley that John August had built. Just as he finished reading the letter, his sister Ebba and her husband arrived at the airport. They took Sture back to their home and treated him to lunch. After lunch, they briefed him on the landing strip that his father had built. Paul, Ebba's husband, thought the strip was too close to the trees for the Aeronca's thirty-six foot wingspan and cautioned Sture to fly clear of the tree line. Sture thanked him for the information and promised to remember it as he landed.

Sture did remember his brother-in-law's advice. Rather than risking damage to his plane from clipping the trees, he opted to land closer to the water. Though the landing area was clear of brush, it was also situated in soft earth. The landing gear Sture had welded first in Franklin, Virginia, and later at Langley broke once again, and as the plane rapidly decelerated in the mud, it flipped up onto its nose, but not so far that the propeller hit the ground.

A farmer watching Sture's landing nudged Mr. Sigfrid. "I've seen many airplanes land in Alexandria, but none of them stopped as fast as your boy did."

Sture's father beamed. "My boy is good."

Sture jumped from the cockpit and tiptoed through the mud to the crowd of relatives and neighbors that had gathered to greet him. For several minutes they milled about and pressed their way toward the young man who had made his way from South America to Parkers Prairie. He was, for the afternoon, their favorite son. Only when the crowd began to thin were Sture and his brother Ed able to remove the broken landing gear from the plane. They took it into town and had it repaired at Fortwengler's Welding Shop. By early the next morning, the plane and Sture were ready for flight.

Sture quickly discovered that by taking off in the opposite direction from his arrival, he had the whole north end of the lake, almost a mile, without obstruction, at his disposal. The shore of the lake, however, was strewn with rocks that made his takeoffs and landings far more treacherous than Sture wished for his tiny plane. He promised a ride to each of the scores of children who had arrived to watch his exploits if they helped clear his airstrip. For almost an hour, stones of all sizes and colors sailed through the air and pocked the surface of an otherwise still lake.

Landing beside Lake Adley in Parkers Prairie, 1933. Sigfred collection.

One of the most excited of the children was Sture's nephew Paul Ryden. Gathering stones by the handful, he tried single-handedly to clear a path for the plane. For hours, he sat enraptured, listening to the stories of his uncle's exploits and imagining what it would be like to fly his own plane. When his turn in the Aeronca came, he watched his uncle's every move, memorized each step in the process of taking off and landing a plane, pressed his feet to the floor as though he controlled the rudder. Finally, when Sture circled over the lake in preparation for landing, Paul looked at his uncle shyly. "When I grow up, I'm going to be a pilot just like you."[17] Then he turned his head away and watched the earth rise to meet the plane.

Sture on vacation in Parkers Prairie, 1933. Sigfred collection.

For the next several days, Sture flew his relatives and neighbors over the lake and Parkers Prairie. On each trip, he made note of the terrain and planned the flight that would be the hallmark of his visit. Though each ride was special for the person he flew, Sture reserved his excitement for the one flight he had waited thirty-three years to make.

The previous year, his father John August had retired from the Parkers Prairie Post Office and the route he had served for twenty-seven years. Sture believed it would be meaningful for his father to fly the thirty-two mile route he had known so well and bid hello to the ninety-four customers he had previously served so faithfully. He told John August to notify all ninety-four of his patrons that he was going to come around sharply after dinner at the week's end in a flying machine. Just as he had stopped at three or four locations for prayers or coffee each day he had delivered mail along the route, he would fly over and circle three or four areas above the route so his friends could

---

[17] Paul Ryden went on to a long and fruitful career with Pan Am. He was the flight engineer for the 50th anniversary flight of the *China Clipper II* on which Sture and Mildred flew as Pan Am's guests and one of thousands of employees who saw much of their security wrested from them when Pan Am finally went out of business.

get a good look at the plane. John August bought ninety-four penny postcards, one for each farm, and informed his former clients of the four locations he would circle and the scheduled time of his arrival above each.

Sture and his father spent just over an hour in the plane, surveying the woods and plains around the city and acknowledging the waves of friends and well-wishers along John August's old route. They barely spoke to each other during the flight. Sture kept his attention on the roads and rails below him, realizing that navigating the area where he had spent over half his life was far different in the air than it had been on the ground. John August simply stared out of the cockpit in amazement as the landscape curled and folded below him in vibrant shades of blue and rust and green. Occasionally Sture sensed his father's gaze directed toward him and hoped that he was proud.

Sture left Parkers Prairie on the fourth of July and landed in Minneapolis after only two hours and forty-three minutes in the air. For the next two days, he enjoyed the holiday festivities and visited old friends before heading for Chicago on the sixth. He arrived in Rockford, Illinois four hours and nineteen minutes after leaving Minneapolis and departed the same afternoon for Chicago. One hour and twenty-one minutes later, he landed outside Chicago at Curtis Reynolds Field, where he laid over for almost a week, practicing for the test for his commercial transport license.

On the eleventh of July, he flew the Aeronca to Municipal Field in Chicago. On the twelfth, he rented a Travelair with a Gypsy, inverted engine and had a pilot check him out in the new and unfamiliar plane. He made four practice flights in the Travelair before he felt comfortable to take his transport license test. On July 14, 1933, he took the test, and passed it the first time.

That afternoon, he turned the Travelair back in and returned to Curtis Reynolds Field in his faithful and trustworthy Aeronca. For about thirty minutes, he soloed a Stinson over the airfield and, later, gave rides to several of his friends in Chicago. On July 15, he flew Matt's sister Gladys over the Italian fleet of ten seaplanes that had landed on Lake Michigan for the Century of Progress World's Fair. On July 17, he flew the Aeronca to Cincinnati, and on the eighteenth made his last flight in the Aeronca as he turned it in at the Aeronca factory in Cincinnati, Ohio for a $500 deposit toward the purchase of another plane.

Ebba and Alpha in the cockpit of the Aeronca, Parkers Prairie, 1933.
Sigfred collection.

From Cincinnati, he took an overnight train to Atlanta since the airlines still lacked the ability to fly safely at night. From the train station in Atlanta, he called Pitcairn Airlines and asked about a flight to Miami. The ticket agent told him that the scheduled flight had just taxied out but that he would call it back to the ramp. Sture quickly flagged a taxi and told the driver that there was a plane waiting for him at the airport. The driver raced through the city at breakneck speed and deposited Sture at the foot of the ramp to the idling plane.

When he boarded the plane, it became immediately clear why the airline had held the ship. Sture was the only passenger onboard. He lowered himself into one of the chairs bolted to the floor and glanced at the wall before him. A sign announced: "An experienced air traveler fastens his seat belt." Without thinking, his hand went to his waist to ensure that the metal clasp of his belt was fastened.

With Sture safely buckled into his seat, the pilot pushed forward on his throttle, and the noise of the plane's two engines grew louder. Sture shut his eyes and recounted the fifty days he had been away from Miami. In that time, he had carried sixty passengers in his Aeronca. He had flown over sixty-seven hours and had earned his transport license. But of the entire trip, the hour of which he was most proud was his father's last flight over his old mail route. The vacation had been a success.

Route of Sture's 1933 outbound and return trips in the Aeronca, from Miami to Parkers Prairie and back.

Sture reported to the Pan American office in Miami as soon as he arrived and requested a flight back to Brazil. He was informed by the agent that there was no space available on a flight to South America and was instructed to go to the hangar to go to work. Before leaving the office, he requested to be placed on an expense account during his time in Miami. When he arrived at the hangar, the supervisor instructed him to install an extra seat in the front of one of the Commodores. As soon as the seat was installed, the supervisor in the hangar explained that it was Sture's seat for the flight to South America. He was taken off expenses and assigned to leave on the next southbound flight for Rio in the seat he had installed in the plane.

He shook his head as the Commodore gained altitude over the Atlantic Ocean. This, it seemed, had forever been and was destined to remain his history in aviation. Repairing, building or installing his own transportation - he was, more than most, responsible for what was quite literally the movement of his career. With a red sun glistening on waves breaking on the Florida coast, Sture smiled, knowing that his vacation was, at last, truly done.

Repairs

1933 - 1937

During Sture's absence, Pan Am had been granted a 1000-mile extension on its airmail contract to Manaus on the Amazon River. Because all of the Commodores were filled to capacity on regularly scheduled flights between Belem and Buenos Aires, the company needed an S-38 to cover the extension. The company reassigned a

Harbor in Manaus, 1933. Sigfred collection.

plane to the region from Pan Am's Eastern Division, though the region was still without a spare.

Since his return to Brazil, Sture had been working diligently to be removed from the ground jobs he had been assigned and to go on regular flight duty. His requests had been so emphatic and frequent that, after two months, they were granted - on the condition that he rebuild a discarded S-38 that lay in a pile of dismantled parts in a shed behind the company's maintenance hangar in Buenos Aires. Sture had to laugh aloud when informed of the company's decision.

"I did it for NYRBA," he told his supervisor, "and I've already done it once for Pan Am. If it means I'll get to fly, then I'll do it again, and again, and again. But I must be the only pilot in the world to have the distinction of resurrecting from the junk pile every plane he gets to fly."

The next day, he began his first steamer ride, traveling from Rio to Buenos Aires on a three-day respite from the endless line of planes requiring maintenance in South America. Upon his arrival in Buenos Aires, he discovered that, as each time before, he indeed had his work cut out for him. The mechanics had dragged the S-38 into the hangar, and had started cleaning all of the parts. Though the job was essentially a repeat of what he had done for NYRBA three years earlier, this time he had good, experienced mechanics to work with.

Sikorsky S-38 Sture repaired in Buenos Aires. 1933. Sigfred collection.

All they required was direction and close supervision when reassembling the plane. Sture targeted sixty days to complete repairs to the plane.

In late November of 1933, he met his target and radioed Rio that the plane was ready. Captain R.J. Nixon flew a one hour and ten minute test flight of the plane on December 1 with Sture in the copilot's seat. On December 4, 1933, with the successful test flight behind them, Sture officially accompanied Nixon to Rio as the copilot of the newly refurbished S-38.

A week later, he began regular flights along the east coast of Brazil and 1000 miles up the Amazon. He flew both Commodores and Sikorskys, including the S-38 he had refurbished in Buenos Aires, and remained on flight duty in South America until September 1, 1937. Though no stranger to flying, he learned during those four busy years what it truly meant to fly by the seat of his pants.

1934 and much of 1935 passed without major mishap, and Sture learned the tricks of the trade of seaplane flight. He weighed each person and piece of luggage, each bag of mail before he allowed it onboard. He calculated how much fuel he needed to make it to the next stop, and when necessary politely removed cargo or passengers from his plane. He watched each move made by the various pilots with whom he flew, learning how best to fly a plane from those who were the best, and more importantly, learning how not to fly a plane from those who were not so good. Between January of 1934 and early October of 1935, he amassed 1583 hours and 18 minutes of copilot time and was as respected as a copilot as he had been as a mechanic. He could hold his own as both, a fact that saved him and his crew on more than one occasion.

On October 5, 1935, on a regular flight along the northeastern coast, the starboard engine in a Commodore carrying Captain Cyd Wildman and his copilot Sture came to a dead stop halfway between San Louis and Belem. Wildman managed to guide the plane over the edge of the jungle before he was forced to land on the Gurapa River.

Sikorsky S-42 at the dock in Belem. 1932. Sigfred collection.

As the two men regained their bearings after the rough landing, Sture turned to Wildman.

"You know you've placed us in the middle of cannibal territory."

Wildman laughed, but he also repeatedly checked over his shoulder as he taxied the plane on one engine upriver to the town of Vizeo. He anchored the plane, and Sture climbed out of the cockpit to inspect the damaged engine. Within minutes, he poked his head back into the cockpit and told Wildman to radio Belem and have a new engine flown into Vizeo. He wasted no time preparing for the engine's arrival. With the help of some natives, he cut down two large trees and built an "A" frame to support the hoist he would use while removing the old engine and installing the replacement. That afternoon, the plane from Belem arrived with a replacement engine, and Sture set to work. While the crew that delivered the engine looked on, he separated the new engine into sections and began its installation by securing the rear section to the motor mount. He installed each section, moving forward until the entire engine was in place. He then began to retime the engine.

While he focused all of his attention on retiming the new engine, the Pan Am agent at Vizeo ran up the riverbank, yelling and waving his arms. He shouted to the men that the stricken plane was anchored too close to the opposite shore and was actually within blowgun range of the cannibals. Though he was skeptical of the stories he had heard of flesh-eating Indians, Sture agreed to stop work long enough to

Sikorsky S-42 taking off from Belem. 1932. Sigfred collection.

move the plane closer to the adjacent shore and further from the range of what he suspected were mythical blow guns.

He worked throughout the following day and the morning of the day after to repair the engine. On December 5, he informed the crew of the other plane that he had no additional need for their services and they could return to Belem. With only a few glances toward the jungle lining the opposite shore, they pulled their anchor, started their engines and taxied into the current for takeoff. With the sound of their engines fading in the distance, Sture began to perform his last repair to the plane, installing the oil sump at the bottom of the newly installed engine. The sump was commonly referred to as the elephant sump because it looked like an inverted elephant. In a hurry to get the sump installed and get back into the air, Sture clumsily handled the sump, and it fell into the river in twenty feet of dark, muddy water. By that time, the other plane was on its step, about to be airborne. Afraid of becoming stranded, Sture scrambled onto the wing of his plane and ran toward the tip flapping his arms madly. Jimmy, the pilot of the second plane, pulled back on his throttle. He taxied back to Sture, stuck his head out the cockpit window and asked what was wrong. Sture yelled for the men to remove the elephant sump from the old engine and gestured that he had dropped the other sump into the river. Jimmy rolled his eyes but held the plane steady as Sture sent his rowboat out to the plane to retrieve the sump.

He was more careful with the second sump and directed one of the natives to hold the rowboat directly under where he was working until he finished the job. Then he opened the oil shut-off valve to the engine to add oil, checked the gas, and informed Captain Wildman that the plane was ready to go. Cyd congratulated Sture on his performance while installing and retiming the engine. He grabbed him by the elbow and leaned close, telling him he would remember his work as long as he lived.[18]

"Now let's get away from these cannibals." Within minutes, the plane was back in the air.

---

[18] Cyd did, in fact, remember Sture and his work for as long as he lived. He returned to the Navy when World War II broke out and rose to the rank of Captain while also earning a distinguished war record. The two corresponded until Cyd's death at ninety-one.

The following year, 1936, passed in an endless string of normal flights. Sture's log recounts a regular procession of flights up and

Sikorsky S-42 at Dinner Key. 1932. Sigfred collection.

down the eastern coast of Brazil: from Rio, north to Victoria and Carabello to Bahia to Aracaju to Maceio to Natal to Fortaleza and back along the same route to Rio; from Rio south to Santos to Paranagua to Florianopolis to Porto Alegre and back along the same route to Rio. During the year, he amassed 996 hours and 31 minutes of flight time with few mishaps. On one occasion in late July, his plane had to return to base because of ice buildup on the wings, and twice his plane had to turn around due to fog, but other than these, his log notes only an occasional school of whales playing or mating off the Brazilian coast as items of interest. It was, quite simply, an uneventful year that allowed him to study and develop his skills. 1937 was not so tame.

At 2:00 in the morning of February 8, 1937, Sture awoke from a fitful sleep. Feeling under the weather earlier in the evening, he had gone to bed early to fight off his cold. When he awoke with a fever and drenched in sweat, he realized that he was terribly sick. Though he tried to fall back to sleep, the fever and pounding in his head kept him up until the morning. When Joe Hart, captain of the Sikorsky S-43 Sture was supposed to copilot, saw him, he asked if Sture thought they should remain in Victoria long enough for him to seek medical attention. Because it was the last scheduled mail flight before the two men were to return to Rio, Sture informed Hart that he would tough it out. He strapped himself into his seat and braced for the rough ride over Victoria Harbor.

Sikorsky S-43 at Dinner Key. 1937. Sigfred collection.

When the Sikorsky finally reached its cruising altitude, both Sture and Joe smelled the smoke of burning insulation. With little conversation, they turned the plane around and landed in the harbor at Victoria. Each held his breath in tension as the plane rapidly descended toward the glass-like surface of the water. Sture had barely exhaled after Joe stopped the plane's forward momentum when the right engine burst into flames. Joe pulled the large red handle on the fire extinguisher for the right engine, and Sture grabbed two portable extinguishers. He rushed aft in the cabin toward the rear hatch and climbed onto the top of the hull. From there he scrambled on top of the wing and hurried to the air intake of the starboard engine. Barely able to stand, he discharged both extinguishers into the engine, but the flames continued to grow. Realizing that gas in the wing tanks was feeding the fire, he wasted no time. He quickly removed his uniform and laid it on the wing. He then placed the two extinguishers on top to keep it from blowing away.

He pounced to the wing top opposite the flames above one of the 200-gallon fuel tanks. The plane exploded as he dove into the bay. He swam under the surface of the water as far as he could, to what he believed would be the wing tip and the edge of the fire ring. His lungs burned from exertion and lack of air, and he surfaced for a gulp of air. The fire ring had grown, and when he opened his mouth, he inhaled gas fumes. In pain and very near unconsciousness, he fell back into the water and would likely have drowned had a native not pulled him into a dugout canoe and deposited him on the Pan Am barge where Joe Hart waited.

Joe quickly revived Sture who went with him in a small boat back toward the plane. With the right wing gone in the explosion, the left wingtip dropped into the water and formed a ramp on which the two men could walk toward the cockpit. When they reached the cockpit, they attempted to pull as many bags of mail from the plane as they could, but the flames were too hot. Frustrated and disappointed, they

Sikorsky S-43 in Belem; pilot, passengers and copilot Sture. 1937.
Sigfred collection.

retreated to the safety of their boat and watched as the plane lost her battle to remain afloat.

A German pilot with the Condor Line, one of Pan Am's competitors, also watched the plane and took a roll of pictures of the stricken craft as her crew struggled to save her and the mail. Among the pictures was a print of Sture in his undershorts, followed by Captain Hart, walking up the left wing that served as their ramp. Pan Am, in an attempt to avoid the negative publicity of the pictures of its burning plane, paid the pilot $150 for his roll of film. But somehow, Condor received a copy of the picture and, labeling it "Trying to Save the U.S. Mail," placed it in several local papers.

When the plane was raised and the partially burned mail removed from her hull, Sture discovered a letter from his mother. Though he lacked the words to fully explain why, the letter took on a special significance for him, and he placed it among his most prized possessions. He was distraught when several months later, after his transfer from Brazil, the trunk reached him in San Francisco without the letter.

Between February and July of 1937, Sture maintained his regular schedule of flights while developing the Portuguese ground school curriculum that Pan Am was conducting for new Brazilian Army and Navy pilots. He also pursued a transfer to California.

Crew of the *Brazilian Clipper*, Rio, approximately 1935.
Sigfred collection.

As the company repeatedly reminded its pilots and the world, in 1935 Pan Am had inaugurated the world's first regular airmail service across the Pacific Ocean. In October of 1936, it initiated regular passenger flights as well. Duty in the Pacific Division was one of the most glamorous assignments for a pilot at a time when all pilots seemed glamorous. It was also one of the most challenging and dangerous, and a necessary step on the path to becoming a Master Pilot with the company. Sture longed for assignment to the Pacific Fleet and lobbied for a transfer even more intensely than he had lobbied for flight duty in 1933.

He knew he had done everything he possibly could for the assignment. Though he lacked the formal education of other pilots, he had enrolled in 1935 in the International Correspondence School, officially sanctioned by Pan Am to train its pilots in everything from classical physics to geography and maritime law. The course was designed specifically for Pan Am personnel working toward promotions to Junior Pilot and ultimately Captain, and Sture devoted himself to his studies. Between November of 1935 and August of

The hoist Sture used in Rio to remove the engines from seaplanes. The tractor in the picture on the right is used to anchor the hoists during removal. 1932. Sigfred collection.

1936, he had completed most of the required course work. Already second nature to him were the elements of navigation, dead reckoning and nautical astronomy. Behind him were the courses in formulas, elementary geometry, trigonometry and logarithms. He had completed all of the classes in materials, heat transfer, statics and kinetics. Combined with his experience as a mechanic, the courses had made him an expert in combustion and fuels, gas engines, and aviation carburetors. He had even mastered electricity and magnetism, capacitance and inductance, principles of radio communications, radio receiving sets, and the generation of electromotive force. As he worked tirelessly for his transfer, little remained for him to do other than gain certification as a radio operator.

His possible transfer to California was contingent upon that certification. Because of job shortages in Brazil, foreign citizens were not allowed to become licensed in radio operations, so Sture faced a quandary. He could not transfer to California unless he had his license, and he could not get his license while in Brazil. With few other choices, he convinced his supervisor to let him take the qualification test on his transit from South America and hired a local radio operator to help him prepare for the test.

His instructor was a pleasant man, Sture thought when he first met him, but he quickly noticed that his tutor also had a tendency to take advantage of Sture's hospitality, even as he paid the man for his services. He frequently ate all of the food Sture had available and, on more than one occasion, demonstrated his propensity for draining every ounce of available liquid as well. Sture put up with his instructor's imposition, knowing that he was the key to Sture's transfer to California. Still, he could not deny himself the opportunity to play a joke on the man as his departure for California grew imminent.

Late on a June afternoon, the tutor rang Sture and informed him that he would drop by later in the day to finish their lessons. In his closet, Sture found a toy gun that resembled a Luger and sat beside the door waiting for the man to arrive. About forty-five minutes later, a knock sounded at the door. Sture stood beside the door and placed his left hand on the doorknob. Quickly turning the knob, he pulled the door open and thrust his right hand out the door, aiming the toy gun at the man's chest. The man, shocked and frightened, screamed loudly in a voice Sture did not recognize and dropped a carton of soap to the ground. Sture looked dumbfounded at the man, a soap salesman and not his instructor.

"I'm sorry," he stammered to the man, prone and panting on the ground. "I thought you were a friend of mine."

After helping the man up from the ground and collecting the samples of soap strewn across the yard, Sture bought what he believed must be a lifetime supply of bath soap, repeatedly apologizing but stifling his laughter.

On July 21, 1937, with his course work complete and only his checkout as a radio operator remaining, Sture made his last flight in South America, from Bahia to Rio. Though he somehow thought he should feel a sense of sadness or loss during his final flight, he could not muster the emotion. His pending transfer from South America and the prospects for his career made him too optimistic and excited to dwell on the loss.

In August, he packed his trunk and boarded a regularly scheduled flight for Miami. While in transit, at San Juan, Puerto Rico, he completed his exam and earned his radio operator's license. He was finally prepared to become one of Pan Am's elite—a junior pilot flying the famous clipper ships over the Pacific.

Rio from the air, approximately 1933. Sigfred collection.

Eugene M. McAvoy and Sture V. Sigfred Sr.

Part II: The Clipper Years

Pan Am ad for the B-314 run during the early 1940s. PAA

Eugene M. McAvoy and Sture V. Sigfred Sr.

Clippers

1937

Sture checked in at the Pan American Air Base on September 1, 1937. Actually an addition to the yacht basin that had existed on the north shore of Alameda for several years, the air base was homeport for the Pan Am fleet of Clippers that by the autumn of 1937 debarked regularly for the Orient and New Zealand. Pan Am flew two types of planes from its Alameda base on the San Francisco Bay: the Sikorsky S-42 made in Bridgeport, Connecticut, and the Martin M-130 manufactured in Baltimore, Maryland.

M-130 visits Dinner Key, approximately 1937. Sigfred collection.

Of these, Sture would become most familiar with the Martin M-130. With an all-metal construction, the high-wing flying boat had a 130 foot wingspan and was powered by four, 800 horsepower Pratt & Whitney, R-1830 geared, air cooled radial engines. She was ninety feet and ten inches long from nose to tail and twenty-four feet tall. Her top speed had been recorded as 180 mph, and she regularly reached a cruising speed of 157 mph. During daytime service, she could accommodate up to forty-six passengers in compartments that rivaled the best and most luxurious of passenger trains. For overnight travel, the passenger compartments could be converted into berths capable of comfortably sleeping eighteen to thirty passengers. As a passenger plane, the M-130 carried seven crewmembers. With the passenger equipment removed, the plane became a mail carrier with fewer crewmembers and an increased range from 3000 up to 4000 miles.

The most prominent feature of the M-130 was her size. At the time of her launch, she was the largest airplane in the world. Like this distinction - all aviation records in the 1930s were short-lived - the three M-130's purchased by Pan Am would serve relatively short but distinctive careers with the company. One of the many innovations her construction introduced was a unique hull and sea wing combination. The sea wings were primarily intended, like the sponsons they replaced, to produce lateral stability on the water. They also carried 950 gallons of fuel and held down the spray of water inevitably thrown up into the tail surfaces during operations on the water. The top surfaces and tips of the sea wing were shaped like airfoils and helped produce lift during taxiing runs, assisting the main wings in lifting the 51,000-pound plane into the air.

Hawaii Clipper in Hawaii, 1937. Sigfred collection.

Sture's flying experience in Latin America had been limited to the Consolidated Commodores and the Sikorskys. He understood those planes and the nuances of their behavior thoroughly; he had repaired, rebuilt and flown them between South and Central America for over five years. But the sight of the famous Clipper ships, especially the Martins - at rest on the bay or as they rose on their steps and climbed into the crisp blue skies surrounding San Francisco - filled him with the urge to climb into the left-hand seat in the cabin and to teach himself all at once everything there was to know about the powerful machines. He longed to know them as he had known the planes in South America, to become a part of the power that soared over the Pacific. So he set himself, almost without distraction, to the task of learning to fly the Pacific fleet's famous Clipper ships.

After six weeks of classroom training and becoming familiar with Clipper operations, Sture began air training on October 23, 1937 on

Crowds gathered for the *China Clipper's* inaugural flight across the Pacific, November 1935, San Francisco. PAA.

NC-14714, the *Hawaii Clipper*. For the next two weeks, he alternated between flights on one of the M-130's or one of the Commodores Pan Am maintained at Alameda specifically for training flights. While most of his training was conducted in and around San Francisco, he counted the days until he was able to join one of the crews for a flight to the Orient.

His wish came true surprisingly quickly. On November 1, 1937, he was assigned to his first Pacific crossing—a flight to Honolulu, Hawaii in the *Philippine Clipper*, NC 14715. Though he had checked out only on cockpit procedures during approximately ten to twelve hours in the Links Trainer, he had spent eight hours and twenty-six minutes flying in the Commodores and eight hours and fifty-two minutes on test flights of the Martin M-130 to familiarize himself with her arrangement and procedures. Still, his crewmates warned him, none of this could adequately prepare him for a scheduled flight of eighteen hours from Alameda to Hawaii. But Sture yearned for the chance to find out for himself. Most of his training had included cockpit time and flight engineer time. Cockpit time was spent in the pilot's seat, though the plane was normally on automatic pilot. He had also been frequently allowed to control the large ships and to make takeoffs and landings under the close supervision of the captain. He felt ready for the challenge of joining the crew for the flight. He knew that as a Junior Pilot on a Pacific crossing, he could also look forward to landing at either Midway or Wake under the supervision of the captain.

During the long crossings of the Pacific, the crew would cycle through various positions of responsibility. Usually, a position watch lasted an hour. This was followed by an hour of rest, which was in

China Clipper crew takes on first load of mail,
November 1935. San Francisco. Sigfred collection..

turn followed by another position watch. For Sture, this position

204

would normally be as the flight engineer. The flight engineer's station was located in the cabane, the area located between the wings and the hull. The cabane contained all of the instrumentation necessary to monitor the vital functions for which the flight engineer was responsible: fuel-flow, oil temperature and pressure, carburetor temperature and cylinder temperature. In the cabane, he would monitor and record these indications of engine performance, paying special attention to fuel flow to the engines and oil temperature and pressure.

Another of his duties would be to stop a windmilling engine in case of a problem. Because the props on the M-130 were not full feathering, if an engine stopped functioning for any reason, its propeller continued to windmill at the same speed as the three

China Clipper departs San Francisco, November 1935. PAA.

remaining engines. If allowed to continue, the windmilling would destroy the lift behind that engine and could worsen damage to the engine in many casualties. To prevent such occurrences, the backside of each prop was equipped with a brake drum. This drum in turn was equipped with brake shoes, just like an automobile wheel. A large hand pump bolted to the floor of the cabane furnished hydraulic pressure for engaging the brake. The flight engineer was responsible for operating the pump. It took significant amounts of muscle and perspiration to stop the rotation of a prop that often turned at speeds of approximately 2500 RPM.

Because Sture had not checked out on the radio in the M-130, he was not scheduled for the radio watch during his first crossing, though soon enough he would grow to hate it as much as most of the other pilots. The radio watch was one of the more demanding positions simply because it required the detailed memorization of complex rules that were often never used under normal flying conditions. The watch itself was simply boring, and the technology still proved frequently unreliable. So dreaded was the "Morse Code Watch," primarily for the boredom, that junior pilots often showered the Operations Manager's secretary with large boxes of candy to gain her assistance in remaining off the assignment. The watch rotation and assignments were normally made up in the Operations Manager's office, and it was rumored that a five-pound box of chocolates to his secretary could keep a crewmember off the radio watch for an entire trip. Though there never seemed any concrete proof of this, there was no denying that during the final few days before a departure, the secretary *did* receive an inexplicably large amount of candy.

Of all of the many tasks that each crewmember had to perform, the one most often joked about or completely omitted from conversation was tying the plane up to the buoy. Because of the difficulty involved in performing the tricky and often dangerous operation, this was one of the most abhorred tasks onboard the ship. The snubbing post was just exactly that, a short post around which the mooring line was cinched. It was stored inside and at the front of the hull during flight. After landing, the bowman placed it in a socket atop the hull, securing it inside the hull but allowing it to protrude six inches above. A twenty-foot float line attached to the buoy and held afloat on the water by several large corks evenly

B-314 tying up to buoy.
Sigfred collection.

206

spaced along its length were wrapped around the snubbing post to keep the plane from drifting in a swift current. The bowman was expected to snare the line with a boat hook and to wrap the line around the snubbing post to secure the plane to the buoy.

Under the best of conditions, the bowman found the operation difficult. Under the worst conditions, he found it life-threatening. During a landing at Aracaju in Brazil several years before, Sture had learned firsthand the risks involved in tying up to the buoy. Aracaju sat at the mouth of the Cotinguiba River. A brisk wind continually blew from the Atlantic Ocean, directly opposite the river's current. Inevitably the wind blew the line from the buoy, allowing the current to pay it out downstream toward the mouth of the river. The bowman was forced to balance atop the hull of the swiftly moving ship and try to snag the line with his hook. Because the current was so swift at Aracaju, there was little slack in the line stretched taut from the buoy, making it virtually impossible, however necessary, for the bowman to catch the line and wrap it around the snubbing post in the few available seconds before the plane shot past its mark. With luck, an unsuspecting bowman might miss the line entirely, but that merely forced him to attempt to grapple the line during another pass of the buoy. More frequently, he snagged the taut line and either lost his boat hook or was pulled overboard into the current.

Sture had experienced all three of these potential results on his first landing in Aracaju, and had grown to hate the job, no matter where the landing occurred. Most of the other pilots felt exactly the same way. Of all of the menial tasks associated with the seaplanes, being bowman was considered to be at the bottom of the totem pole, regardless of its importance to successfully docking the plane.

All of this Sture knew as he fastened his seatbelt and prepared for the routine takeoff on that Monday afternoon in November. While the crew considered the takeoff routine, the public did not, and Pan Am went to great lengths to provide the public with a show at each launch of the Clippers. It was not uncommon for radio stations to broadcast live during a takeoff, and newspaper reporters and photographers were regular fixtures at every launch. Glancing toward the shore, Sture watched throngs of people pushing against a rope barrier that had been set up to separate passengers from the curious public. Behind the crowds, scores of buses sat quiet in the parking lot, their passengers inching ever closer to the shore, jockeying for the best position from which to see the famous flying boat takeoff. Only after approval from Pan Am's public relations officials, two cameramen from the Pathe A News stood inside the rope barrier, their cameras focused on the *Philippine Clipper*, still quiet in the water. As they often did, the cameramen planned to film the takeoff of the Clipper for showing between features in hundreds of theaters across the country.

Though he had grown to take his position as a copilot almost for granted, the cameras and the crowds reminded Sture of how

Pan Am facilities in San Francisco

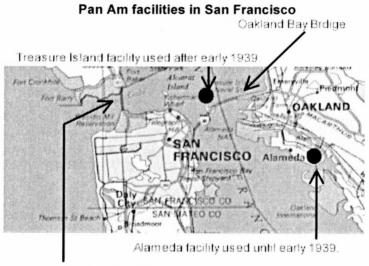

newsworthy this event actually was and in what esteem the country held the pilots. Less than halfway through the twentieth century and only thirty-four years after the first successful flight of a heavier-than-air craft, Pan Am and Sture Sigfred were making regular trips across the Pacific Ocean.

It was big news, and Sture was part of it.

The takeoff went as expected. First the captain and crew taxied across the bay to ensure the takeoff path was free of debris. Then he faced the plane into the wind and revved his engines to full power. When the plane approached sixty miles per hour, riding high on her step with just a slight spray trailing behind her, the plane pulled gingerly into the air. With passengers staring out their windows at the lush hills of San Francisco and the growing span of the Golden Gate

Bridge, still under construction, the captain banked the plane and made a slow turn back toward the air base for a pass over the cheering

Hawaii Clipper in San Francisco, 1939. Sigfred collection.

crowds. Then he pointed the plane to the southwest and sought his 9000 feet altitude, preparing for the long, loud flight to Hawaii.

When San Francisco had long since faded from sight, and the sun rested on the western horizon, splashing the sky with a thousand shades of red, the stewards covered the tables in the passenger cabin with cloths of linen and set them with fine china. The passengers sat down to a meal of prime rib or grilled tuna, potatoes, corn and rice. Over the dull roar of the engines and the hum of friendly conversation, they enjoyed a fresh salad, followed by dessert and, finally, a plate of fresh cheeses and coffee.

While the crew ate at their respective watch stations, the stewards served cocktails. For thirty-five cents, a passenger could enjoy a Gibson or Manhattan. For only twenty cents more, he could savor half a bottle of the best American Burgundies, Clarets, Chablis or Sauternes. The crew, of course, was forbidden from drinking within 24 hours of flying. They drank pot after pot of hot, black coffee as the endless darkness loomed ahead.

Only hours into his first crossing, Sture experienced the reality of international flight. Rather than the excitement the newspapers chose to emphasize, the night actually passed in a continuous drone of noise and exhaustion. The watch bill was posted on the wall next to the washroom, and as the long flight passed at 130 miles per hour, the

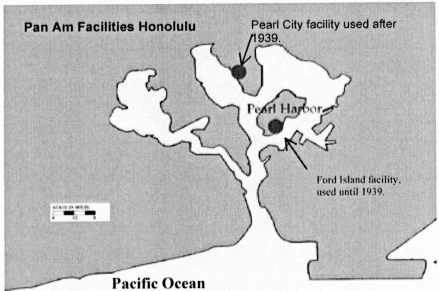

Pan Am Facilities Honolulu — Pearl City facility used after 1939.

Pearl Harbor

Ford Island facility, used until 1939.

Pacific Ocean

men cycled between their various assignments. With little conversation and much noise, tempers quickly shortened and nerves quickly frayed. To make matters worse, gasoline stored in the hull of the M-130 meant that smoking was forbidden for the duration of the flight. This only added to the discomfort that could grow in the crew's minds as night inched past the plane.

After five hours of flight, as the crew cycled through its fifth watch rotation, the passengers departed from the common lounge for their overnight accommodations. Atop freshly laundered linens, they lay down for the night. Soundproofing in the walls and ceiling offered the luxury of quiet, a luxury the crew could not share as they continued the long and often deathly boring process of guiding the plane across the Pacific.

As on most flights, there was on Sture's first flight a crew of nine: the captain and first officer, the first and second engineers, the first and second radio operators, two stewards and the navigator. Only four passengers received the combined attentions of the large crew. Though the planes normally carried more passengers, it was not uncommon for the crew to outnumber the passengers.

The 2400-mile, eighteen-hour flight between Alameda and Honolulu made gasoline the most precious commodity of the flight, even more precious than paying passengers. At rates of up to $2.00 per mile, the airmail contracts were also more profitable than the $278 fares passengers paid for transport to Honolulu or the $950 fares they paid for transport all the way to Hong Kong. On very long flights for which inclement weather had been forecast, the company actually removed seats and floorboards from the passenger compartment to accommodate a larger load of mail and shipped the seats by steamer to Hawaii. In Honolulu, shore workers reinstalled the seats for the shorter and less risky routes to the Pacific islands, where little mail, compared with that from San Francisco, awaited. The pilots often joked that if the company had to remove the crew in order to load more mail, they *might* cancel the flight. While the crew waited for the steamer to arrive with the seats and floorboards, they passed their time sunning on Waikiki Beach or dining at the Moana Hotel where the food was rumored to be the best in Hawaii.

The 2400-mile flight to Honolulu was the longest leg of the clipper's flight to the Orient and the longest over-water flight in the world. Of the eighteen hours of flight time, most passed in the dead of night. The nighttime flights were fraught with potential disaster, but they were necessary to ensure the crew could land the plane in Hawaii during daylight, and the experience and training of the Pan Am crews did much to mitigate the risk.

Early the following morning, already past the flight's scheduled eighteen hours, the sun peered over the eastern horizon and illuminated an ocean endless and blue. For several hours, the crew continued to the west with the sun at their backs. Then, without warning, the island of Maui seemed to spring from the sea, followed shortly by Oahu. As the islands passed below the hull of the plane and the stewards cleared dishes from breakfast, the passengers peered once again for a glimpse of the tropical paradise most had heard so much about but so few had seen. Despite their expectations, all seemed to inhale sharply as Diamond Head loomed into view. The extinct volcano thrust from the island like an angry hand reaching for the plane. Though Sture found the formation disappointing, the passengers seemed to thrill at the thought of a cauldron boiling beneath the surface of the earth so close to the plane. They seemed suspended for the moment in the most precarious position the earth could offer: the ancient heaving earth below them, constantly threatening eruption; the hungry sea stretching around them toward infinity, and the gentle sky, caressing for the moment this oddity of technology that bore them across the sea.

The flight ended well past noon as the plane touched down on the still, teal waters of Pearl Harbor and taxied to a long white dock at Ford Island. Diamond Head in the distance was a welcome sight to Sture and the other crewmembers, exhausted from the flight that had taken just over twenty-three hours, five hours longer than expected. The firm earth beneath his feet was reassuring, and only when he touched that ground did he relax. The launch and taxi rides from their berthing spot to the Moana Hotel in Honolulu, though short, took a surprisingly long time. In the quiet, several of the crewmembers slept, including the navigator who had been awake for the entire flight.

The navigator's long nights were the rule and not the exception during the transpacific crossings, since he was responsible for ensuring that the plane remained on course, day and night. During the day, locating the plane could be as simple as sighting a steamer on the ocean's surface. At night, however, it was quite a different story. Using an octant to measure the height of a star in degrees, the navigator obtained a line of position. He then measured another star ninety degrees from the first for another line of position. Finally, he plotted the two lines, and where they intersected was the plane's actual position.

Unlike the navigator, who had made the crossing before, Sture stayed awake during the ride to Honolulu, anxious to see how Waikiki Beach compared to Copa Cabana Beach in Rio. Several hours later, his toes digging into the beige crystals glistening in the sun, he tried to hide his disappointment. While the sand at Copa Cabana had been snow white, the sand at Waikiki was light brown, the color of regular silicon that could be found on almost any beach in the world. The water was not as clear as that at Copa Cabana, and the beach stretched only about a tenth the length. Still, the beach and pounding surf were a welcome respite from over twenty-three hours in the air. He leaned back and relished the sun on his tired and aching muscles, thinking that this was, in its way, a form of paradise - not Rio by any stretch of the imagination, but a form of paradise just the same.

He pulled his hat low over his eyes to block out the sun, and allowed himself to nap. The flight to Midway would come soon enough, and though much shorter than the flight he had just survived, he couldn't risk not being at his peak. No matter how short, any flight in 1937 was a dangerous undertaking, man against the heavens, and on this flight, man against the sea as well. He napped until evening lay like fog upon the beach, then walked back to the hotel where he enjoyed a large dinner and dancing in the open-air ballroom.

The crew laid over the rest of the day in Honolulu and departed the following morning, November 11, at 8:30 for the relatively short flight to Midway Island. Twelve hours for the 1380-mile flight was a short jaunt compared to the flight from San Francisco to Hawaii. En route, the plane flew over most of the small islands of the Hawaiian chain: Necker, French Frigate Shoals, Maro Reef, Pearl Reef and Hermes Reef, before the two coral islets of Sand and Eastern islands came into view after an exceptionally short flight of only nine hours and forty-six minutes.

A relay station for the transpacific cable, Midway had been inhabited only since 1903. Prior to Pan Am's arrival, it had been little more than a desolate strip of coral noted only for its location halfway around the world from the prime meridian at Greenwich, England. Captain N.C. Middlebrook had claimed the two islets for the United States on July 5, 1859, and named them for their location near the geographic center of the Pacific Ocean. The United States officially took possession of the islands of Midway in 1867 and commenced efforts to develop the coral atoll. Impeded by opposition from business interests in Honolulu who wished to reserve the bulk of Pacific trade for Hawaii, development efforts proved fruitless, and Midway remained uninhabited until the turn of the century when two crews laying the first transpacific cable met on her shores. President Roosevelt declared the islands a naval reservation the same year, and a small naval contingent had kept watch on the isolated atoll ever since.

When Pan Am had first undertaken establishing its Pacific bases, it became immediately clear that Honolulu, Guam and Manila would require far less attention than its other proposed stations. Facilities, labor and raw materials existed in sufficient quantities and at sufficiently low prices to allow adaptation of the islands' offerings to Pan Am's needs. Midway and Wake, however, were entirely different stories. Midway, the larger of the two island chains, featured a large deep lagoon on which the seaplanes could easily make their landings and takeoffs. A cable relay station had also been established on the island, but these meager facilities were all the island offered. Wake offered even less.

A possession of the United States since 1898, Wake had not yet proven a necessary key to the country's strategic and tactical defense, so little time and effort had been spent establishing facilities on the island. A Hydrographic Office chart tucked into the archives at the New York Public Library and a National Geographic article were all that Juan Trippe could find to help him determine the suitability of the island as a seaplane base. Like Midway, the island possessed a lagoon that seemed on the yellowed charts to be large enough

Juan Trippe. PAA.

and deep enough to accommodate the seaplanes, and the coral reef surrounding the island seemed to break sufficiently to allow landing cargo on the island.

Armed with more hope than confidence, Trippe assigned Captain L.L. Odell, Pan Am's Chief Airport Engineer, the task of designing and constructing the six bases needed to allow Pan Am to reach from San Francisco to Hong Kong. In a feat of engineering that rivaled the best the twentieth century would offer, Odell and his team of seven assistants made all arrangements necessary for constructing the bases. With fewer than four months of planning, on April 12, 1935, the 6700-ton *S.S. North Haven*, after taking on supplies in Alameda and Honolulu, arrived off the sandy beach of Sand Island of the Midway atoll. Normally with a light swell running, her cargo was offloaded on the open sea onto barges that were then towed five miles through a channel in the coral reef to the beach. The cargo was then loaded onto sleds and hauled 1200 feet toward the center of the island where the Pan Am facilities would be constructed. By the end of April, the crew and a construction complement of ninety-one assigned to the *S.S. North Haven* had succeeded in constructing on Midway a radio station with a fully functional direction finder, a temporary power plant, a windmill, and temporary refrigeration facilities. With an even more daunting task ahead of her at Wake, the ship sailed from Midway on May 1, leaving behind an anachronous tent city in the sand, eleven members of the station crew, twenty-three construction workers, and acres of land inhabited by curious but wary Laysan Albatross.

When the *Pan American Clipper* landed at Midway for a trial run on June 15, she and her crew witnessed startling progress toward establishing a city in the midst of the vast Pacific. Though the men still slept in their city of tents, they had completed construction of a mess hall and were well on their way to completing what would within a year be the famous Pan Am Hotel. Electric stills supplied fresh water for the island and were supplemented by a piping system that funneled rainwater from the roofs of the colony's few buildings to underground storage tanks. Long wooden docks were complete, and quarters for the station manager and ground and flight crews were well underway. By the time Sture reached the island for the first time, it was a virtual city in the middle of the Pacific.

The first thing he noticed during the *Philippine Clipper's* descent into the waters northwest of Sand and Eastern islands that formed the Midway atoll was a beach teeming with thousands of gooney birds. About the size of a tame goose, the birds made their home on Midway for most of the year. They had no fear of humans and entertained the passengers - a good thing since the island itself offered few amenities. In dozens of trips to the island, he would never lose his memory of that first sight of the gooney birds. It was always the first thing to greet him as the island drifted into view during his approach and the last thing he witnessed as the island disappeared in the distance after takeoff. For him, the island was the gooney birds and gooney birds, the island. It was one of the facts of the Pacific.

The crew laid over a day at Midway, and on the following morning, departed for Wake, a set of three islets, Wake, Peale, and Wilkes, almost 1200 miles west of Midway. As on the previous day, perfect weather and favorable winds allowed the crew to make the flight in a shorter than normal time: eight hours and sixteen minutes. Though the island was a virtual wasteland, the passengers seemed to enjoy what little tropical flora the island provided, and spent the few hours available to them basking in the sun and picking their way through the brush that lined acres of unblemished sand.

Just as on Midway, Pan Am had assembled a large prefabricated hotel on the island. Each room was equipped with a shower and a lavatory with hot and cold running water, despite a dearth of fresh water on the island. Chamorros from Guam comprised the majority of the hotel and support staff on the island. Small in stature, they proved efficient and willing employees, possessed of the intelligence necessary to survive in the island's harsh environment and the graciousness to make the short layover as luxurious and carefree for the guests as the small complex could offer.

All of the island's food was flown in, most of it from Guam. As a result, fresh meat, eggs and milk were standard fare at the island hotel. Though personnel on the island discussed for several years the possibility of keeping chickens on Wake and Midway, Guam kept the supply of eggs flowing to the breakfast tables, and the often-discussed coops never materialized. Since 1935, Pan Am had also been developing and expanding its use of hydroponics, the cultivation of plants by feeding them directly with weakened solutions of mineral salts in the absence of earth. The technique proved perfect for Wake, whose sandy soil produced only midget trees and scrub brush and lacked the nutrients to nurture a thriving plant life. In a hydroponicum of redwood tanks with a combined capacity of over 1260 square feet, the island's gardener produced over thirty pounds of tomatoes each week. Supplemented with fresh lettuce, cucumbers, peppers, onions and lima beans, the hotel's menu proved a drastic contrast to the stark landscape of the island.

Preparing the island for passengers, Sture knew, had been even more difficult on Wake than on Midway. The *North Haven* had arrived off the three islands that roughly formed a horseshoe around the atoll, on May 9, 1935. Though their original plans specified placing the station on Wilkes Island, directly accessible from the sea, the landing crew immediately noticed that the island bore signs of having been flooded. The island was also too far away for their tastes from deep water in the lagoon.

Rather than risk losing their facilities to tidal flooding or establishing an inconveniently distant and costly base, they turned toward Wake Island, between Wilkes and the lagoon, across a shallow channel. Wake, too, however, sat too far away from sufficiently deep water. The most acceptable alternative was to establish the base on Peale Island, directly opposite the lagoon from Wilkes.

The crew built a dock on Wilkes Island onto which they offloaded their supplies. From here, they transported the supplies to a storage yard halfway across the island. They also built a one-car railroad to transport the supplies downhill from the storage yard to the lagoon. At the lagoon, they loaded their materials onto a barge that had been

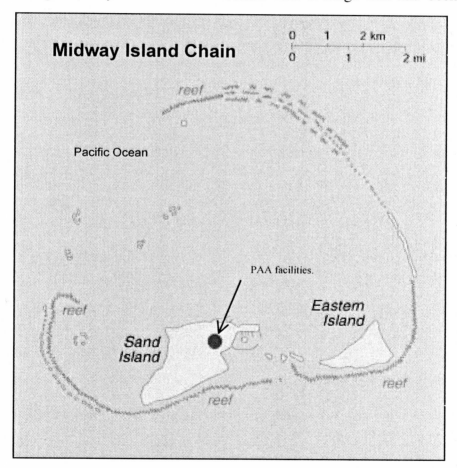

pushed and shoved at high tide across the channel between Wilkes and Wake. Once loaded onto the barge, the supplies were ferried across the lagoon to Peale Island where they were offloaded the final time. Because the supply ship was able to remain closer to Wake, unloading was accomplished more quickly than it had been on Midway. But the increased time needed to transport materials across Wilkes and Wake and then across the lagoon delayed completion of the power plant and refrigeration units necessary for bringing food ashore. Not until May 29 was the *S.S. North Haven* able to depart for Guam. Again she left behind a twelve-man station crew and forty-six construction workers to prepare the island for the Pan Am Clippers. Again a city of tents.

A complete survey of Wake performed shortly before the departure of the *North Haven* revealed a more treacherous terrain than anyone had expected. While the lagoon ran from six to twenty feet deep, several coral heads rose to within four feet of the surface. These had to be blasted with dynamite to accommodate the six-foot draft of the Martin M-130's. Additionally, a wedge had to be blasted from the coral reef that surrounded the islands to allow the seaplanes to access the lagoon and the facilities on Peale. The crew worked feverishly for the next two-and-a-half months, and on August 17, the *Pan American Clipper* safely landed across the wedge and taxied into the lagoon, despite a southwest wind that thwarted the efforts of the construction team. Oriented to make maximum use of the prevailing southeast winds, the wedge proved dangerously short for southwest winds, and was quickly enlarged to avoid disaster.

Though not a beautiful island, Sture felt a special appreciation for Wake - perhaps because it remained an island almost untouched by man, despite the hotel and hydroponic tanks; perhaps, simply because it was the most remote outpost he had visited, a place where he could ponder his deepest thoughts without the interruptions of the modern world. Here he was alone with only his thoughts and thousands of terns nesting on the island. Sitting on their nests, with only their black backs visible against the white sand, they seemed to form a line across the beach pointing away from the island, urging the crews of the clipper ships and all men to pass them by. The crews, however, saw no such sign and landed as instructed.

But each time Sture made the landing, staring at the line of black backs in the sand, he felt as though he were entering upon sacred ground. The feeling had nothing to do with religion or a deity. It was a feeling of awe, a sense of wonder at the majesty of the earth, a visceral reaction to the certain and spiritual knowledge of his place in the heavens. For him, the scrub palms and nesting birds, the greatest concentration of fowl he had seen in his life, were the most holy of icons, for they represented an earth that nurtured even in the most inhospitable of climates, and the ability of a life to temporarily break free from the bonds of dependence. On Wake, a dreary island in a dazzling sea, he could enter into himself and explore for a few brief hours the nature of his soul, before soaring to the heavens where all questions and problems fell effortlessly into the context of the cosmos.

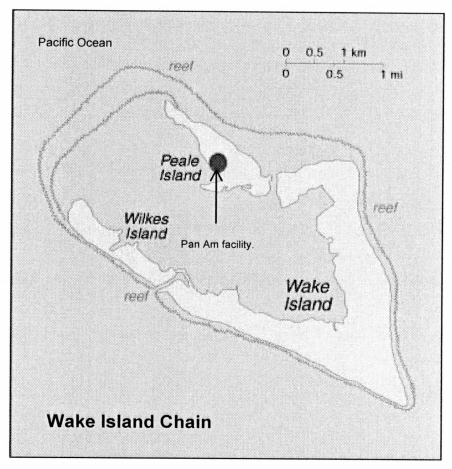

He had little time on his first visit, however, to relish the sacred. Early the next morning, the plane departed for its 1500-mile flight to Guam. Ceded by Spain to the United States after the Spanish-American War, Guam was a critical military post for the U.S. Navy.

The largest and southernmost island of the Mariana archipelago, Guam sat almost precisely halfway between Wake and the Philippines, and was surrounded by islands under Japanese mandate. The Pan Am base stood on the site of the former U.S. Marine Corps seaplane base of Patrol Squadron VP3M near the village of Sumay on Apra Harbor, six miles south of Agana, the capital of Guam. A small contingent of Marine and Navy personnel still remained on the island, providing a welcome encounter with Americans for the passengers and crews of the Clippers. Converted from buildings of the former seaplane base, the Pan Am facilities blended unobtrusively into the foliage of the island.

Hawaii Clipper at Wake, 1939. PAA.

The *Philippine Clipper* bearing Sture on his first transpacific flight, like all of the Clippers, landed on Apra Harbor outside a long, concrete breakwater after nine hours and fifty-eight minutes of flight. The plane taxied to the refueling barge alongside the breakwater where a company launch picked them up. The barge was moored in deep water where the threat of one of the Clippers running onto a coral shoal was slight. An encounter with the shoal could rip the hull from stem to stern, at best delaying and possibly killing all of the passengers and crew. The passengers and crew were carried by launch into Sumay Cove and deposited at a small dock at the foot of a path leading to the Pan Am hotel and administrative offices.

Sture had been looking forward to landing at Guam for several weeks. When his family discovered that he would be making the transpacific crossing, they informed him that a young man from Parkers Prairie, Admiral Lindahl was the commandant at Guam. A

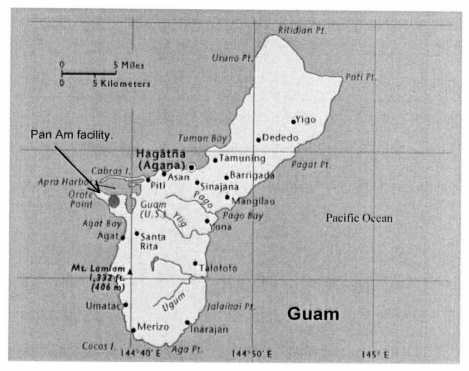

medical doctor as well as the commanding officer of the Navy forces in Guam, Admiral Lindahl had been confirmed in the same Swedish Lutheran Church as Sture, though many years before. When Sture arrived in Guam, however, he was disappointed to discover that the Admiral had departed the island only a few weeks before. With little else to do, he enjoyed an ample meal in the hotel restaurant and went to bed early.

The following morning, before first light, Sture boarded the *Philippine Clipper* while the passengers slept in their hotel beds. While the plane bobbed beside the breakwater, he read the latest weather information for the flight west and dragged his finger down the pre-flight checklist, preparing for the final leg of his western flight. He walked through the passenger compartments to ensure they had been properly cleaned and stocked. Then he stepped onto the refueling barge and walked up and down beside the plane, inspecting every visible inch of her aluminum hull and glass windows for damage. Finally, he verified that the fuel tanks had been topped off and that the ship glistened in the sun just peering over the horizon. When the passengers finally boarded, the sun cast the shadow of the plane toward Orote Point, and Sture took his position in the cabane where he awaited the takeoff. The captain powered up his engines and checked the few gauges in the cockpit for proper operation and indication. He then taxied the plane into Apra Harbor and, after ensuring that the harbor was clear of boats and the sky clear of planes, pushed the throttle completely forward. The plane cut across the water and rose quickly onto the step. Within seconds, she was in the air, heading west for the 1600-mile flight to Manila.

Arrival of the *China Clipper* in Manila, November 1935. The Manila Hotel is in the background. PAA.

Ten hours and seven minutes later, the captain began his descent toward the Pan Am base on Canacao Bay in Cavite. The cockpit buzzed as direction finders at Laoang and San Fernando guided the plane over Luzon Island and toward the southwest corner of Cavite Harbor. As the plane gradually lost altitude from 9000 feet to sea level, the captain banked the Clipper to the south and flew over whitecaps that raced across Manila Bay toward the western-facing city. The radio officer maintained constant communications with the radio station in Manila as Sture watched the gentle curve of Cavite Harbor become pocked with signs of life.

To the east of the Pan Am facilities, cranes at the piers of the Cavite Naval Base were bustling with activity, while to the north a large truck inched across the road toward the fuel depot. Eight miles northeast of the Naval Base, Manila, over which they had just flown, glistened in the afternoon sun. Sture sat enraptured at the beauty and amazed at the size of what he thought would be a small, impoverished and backward city. The captain guided the plane to a smooth landing on the protected waters of Cavite Harbor, then turned the plane to the west and taxied to the Pan Am base, another former Marine Corps flying-boat base, nestled in the arms of the U.S.'s western-most naval station. This was also the western-most point at which the Pan Am pilots could expect to receive major service and repairs.

Sture and the rest of the crew of the *Philippine Clipper* secured the ship in the harbor and disembarked with the passengers into launches that carried them to a long dock beside the Pan Am terminal. Once ashore, they climbed into several waiting taxis outside the terminal and drove around the southern and eastern shores of the Canacao Bay and along the eastern shore of Manila Bay to the Manila Hotel where they were scheduled to remain for a week.

Sture spent that evening exploring the five-story hotel that was the center of social life in the Philippines. In grand ballrooms and quiet walks on the beaches of Luzon, he basked in the sun at the gateway to the Orient. A week later, when it was time to return to the east, he felt a tug that he knew would bring him back.

On November 22, 1937, exactly two years after the first flight from San Francisco to Honolulu, the crew once again boarded the *Philippine Clipper* for the first leg of their journey back to Alameda. The flight from Manila to Guam occurred without incident, as did the legs from Guam to Wake, Wake to Midway, Midway to Honolulu and Honolulu to Alameda. On the morning of November 26, 1937, Sture peered from the cabane as the cables and joists of the Golden Gate Bridge grew larger. While the clipper circled over the bustling port of

San Francisco, steamers belched into and out of the harbor; two lines of traffic inched their ways across the Oakland Bay Bridge between Oakland and San Francisco, and a fleet of seaplanes and amphibians rested on the concrete pad adjoining the Pan Am terminal.

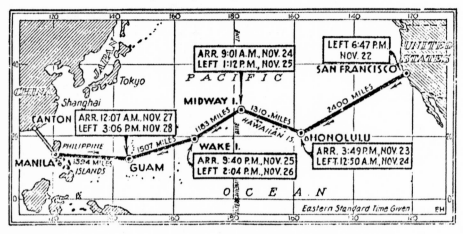

Original route of the *China Clipper*, typical of clipper flights in the 1930s. PAA.

China Clipper landing in Manila, November 1935. PAA.

Unlike his departure, there were no crowds to greet the crew as first the hull and then the seawings of their plane settled on the surface of the bay. It was just as well, for Sture and his fellow crewmembers were exhausted. They tied the ship up at the dock and embarked on various modes of transportation for their homes and the rest that each provided.

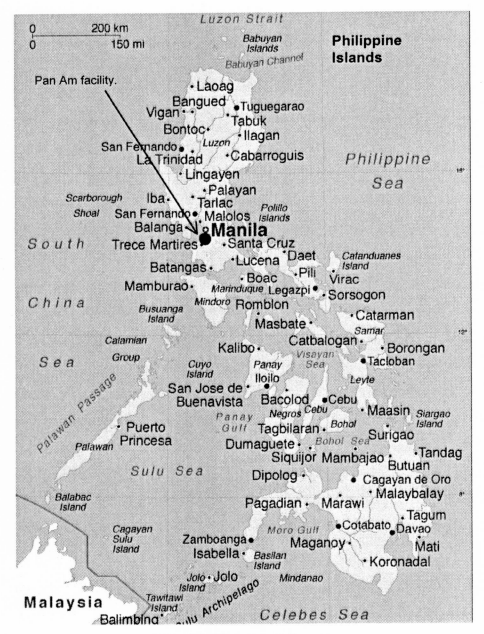

The Philippine Islands.

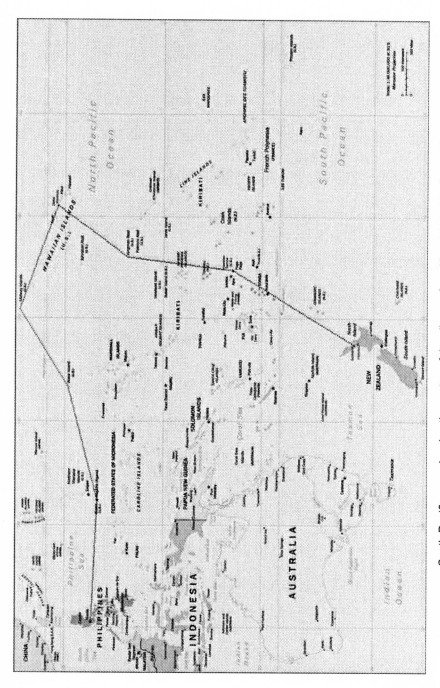

South Pacific map showing the routes of the clippers from Honolulu to Manila and the original southern route of Aukland, New Zealand

Routine Flights

1937 - 1940

By April of 1937, just months before Sture's arrival in San Francisco, Pan Am had successfully negotiated landing rights in Hong Kong, and her string of island bases extended completely across the Pacific. To ensure the M-130's could maintain their two-week round trip schedule between San Francisco and Manila, an S-42, the *Hong Kong Clipper*, became the workhorse for the company's flights

Martin M-130 over the Golden Gate Bridge, still under construction. 1938. PAA.

between Manila and Hong Kong, though M-130's were frequently forced to make the trip.

On March 11 of the same year, the company had also gained full commercial traffic rights in New Zealand, thus opening up the potential for a long planned southern Pacific route from Honolulu, 1100 miles to Kingman Reef, 1600 miles to Pago Pago, and finally 1800 miles to Auckland. In January of 1938, on Edwin Musick's third survey flight to Auckland, however, his plane, the S-42 *Samoan Clipper* exploded in the air between Pago Pago and Auckland, just a few miles out of Pago Pago. Within days, the Department of Commerce withdrew Pan Am's landing rights in Pago Pago, effectively, though only temporarily, shutting down the south Pacific route. Despite the publicity generated from the crash of Musick's plane, Pan Am's Pacific passenger traffic increased 39% in the opening months of 1938, and the small Pacific fleet was stretched to the limits.

The company, however, managed to hobble along fairly

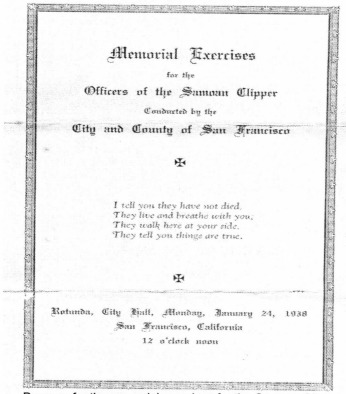

Program for the memorial exercises for the *Samoan Clipper*.
1938. Sigfred collection.

successfully until July, for on July 28, 1938, the *Hawaii Clipper* was lost at sea on a routine flight between Guam and Manila. The plane disappeared without a trace. Her last report, around noon, was that she was flying through rain at 10,000 feet and fighting strong headwinds.

The Panay radio tower acknowledged her message and asked to transmit the regular weather report. The last radio message from the Clipper was, "Standby for one minute before sending, as I am having trouble with rain static." She sent no more radio messages, and the details of her loss remain a mystery. All that is known is that she was lost over the Mindanao Deep, fewer than 565 miles outside of the Philippines, in the still, hot days of summer.

Pan Am publicity photo used to advertise the Clipper service. Sture stands at the far left. 1940. Sigfred collection.

Many speculated that the Japanese had hijacked the plane. The Japanese had made no secret that they resented Pan Am's presence in the Pacific. They had also indicated a desire for the design of the Pratt & Whitney engines to outfit their own warplanes. Additionally, a Chinese businessman was onboard carrying a suitcase with several million dollars for Chiang Kai-shek that surely would have been used to repel Japanese forces from China. The mysterious loss of the Clipper uncomfortably reminded Pan Am officials of the apprehension of two Japanese nationals who had tried to sabotage the direction finder of the *China Clipper* shortly before her maiden voyage in November of 1935. With evidence of strong Japanese motivation to hijack the ship and no evidence to refute the claim, the nation's newspapers ran the story that the *Hawaii Clipper* had been lost to the Japanese. The theory has never been proved.

Regardless of the cause, the loss of the *Hawaii Clipper* sent shockwaves throughout Pan Am, and the company slowed its expansion across the Pacific. The company refocused its attention on safety and tried to win back the passengers who had been frightened away by the loss of the *Samoan* and *Hawaii Clippers*.

Between September 31 and October 20, 1938, less than a year after his first flight to Honolulu, Sture made his first Pacific crossing as a flight navigator. On October 8, between Manila and Guam, the #4 engine of his beloved *Philippine Clipper* caught fire halfway between the two ports. In the cabane, the flight engineer, as he had been trained to do, braked the engine. The captain forced the plane into a rapid descent from 8000 feet to the churning waters of the Pacific where he hoped to land to extinguish the flames. At approximately 3000 feet, the fire appeared to go out, so the captain leveled the plane and continued on course at that altitude. A few miles to the east, the propeller on #4 engine suddenly started to windmill.

The flight engineer again tried to brake the engine, but to no avail. The brake drum grew red hot, and the fire seemed to burn in spurts, flames leaping toward the rear of the plane for several minutes only to disappear for several more, and to burn once again even more brilliantly than before. The crew kept an anxious vigil over the engine, the veins in their foreheads throbbing each time a flame leapt from the engine and lapped at the shining wing. But the fire never took hold. A few sparks that sputtered against a backdrop of blue and the weak, orange flames of a halfhearted fire soon gave way to an empty sky. On three engines, the clipper hobbled at 3000 feet into Guam. Nine days later, the engine had finally been replaced, and the crew hustled back to the states.

With problems such as these hounding the entire Pacific fleet, the company ended the year with the Pacific Division able to fly only 60% of its schedule and losing more than $95,000 each month. It petitioned the Postal Service for additional airmail contracts to make up for its losses, but what it desperately needed were replenishments for its remaining fleet of two M-130's, stretched dangerously beyond their limits.

Replenishments arrived none too soon, and no sooner had Sture become an expert on the M-130's than the new Boeing B-314 Clippers began to roll off the assembly line in Seattle, Washington. Partially because the Boeings were too large for the facilities at Alameda, and partially because the Navy wanted to construct a base at the site of Alameda's yacht basin, Pan Am moved its operations to Treasure Island on January 23 1939, in time to receive the B-314's and to coincide with the 1939 Golden Gate International Exposition. The man-made island had been constructed just north of Yerba Buena Island specifically for the exposition and to provide a site for a bay area airport. Its position offered takeoffs and landings throughout a 270-degree radius and near-perfect flying conditions throughout the year. Not even the famous San Francisco fog posed a problem at the site. The island was connected by causeway with the Oakland Bay Bridge, and planes were moored at Treasure Cove, a quarter-mile wide and two-thirds of a mile long, between Treasure and Yerba Buena islands, where the causeways afforded protection to the ships.

The Boeing B-314 seaplane was a four-engine, high wing, monoplane, with a two-deck hull of semi-monocoque construction and full cantilever wings, tail surfaces and stabilizers. Like the M-130 before her, the B-314 was the largest passenger-carrying airplane in

The B-314 *Yankee Clipper* takes off from San Francisco, 1939.
Sigfred collection.

232

the world. Among her many features were passageways through the wings to each of the four engine nacelles, allowing access to the power plants during flight. The main cargo, mail and baggage holds were located on the upper deck, aft of the control cabin in the center of the wing stub, and below the combination cargo hatch and navigator's observatory. The bow of the hull also provided cargo space, taking the B-314's total cargo capacity to over five tons.

The cargo capacity was the least of the B-314's features. The passenger deck was divided into nine sections with seating for up to seventy-four passengers. Berths were available for thirty-six passengers, thirty-eight if the central lounge was equipped with convertible seats instead of dining tables and chairs. The lounge was the social center of the ship with seating for twelve. In addition, six separate passenger compartments, a specially furnished deluxe compartment, and men's and women's dressing rooms were standard equipment on the plane. A spiral staircase connected the airplane's two decks. Interphone and signal light systems were installed to assist the crew in meeting all of the needs of their passengers.

The plane was a powerhouse as well as a showpiece. She could carry a 10,000-pound payload 2,400 miles at an altitude of 10,000 feet while traveling 150 miles per hour into a thirty mile-per-hour headwind. She was equipped with four 1,500 horsepower Wright GR-2600-A2, fourteen cylinder, radial engines with Hamilton-Standard propellers. The propellers were capable of being fully feathered, with their blades placed edgewise into the slipstream in the event of an engine shutdown to produce minimal drag and prevent engine damage. The plane carried 4,246 gallons of fuel and 300 gallons of oil, and her wings were supported by the internal structure of the hull, thereby eliminating the struts and braces that characterized the wings of most seaplanes. Still, she was not perfect. Fuselage-mounted sponsons, in strong crosswinds, allowed the wing tip to drag the water. Though wing-mounted sponsons would have prevented this, they would also have caused increased and unnecessary drag.

Despite her wing-dipping problem, most authorities, including the bulk of Pan Am's pilots, agreed that the B-314 was the fastest, sleekest and most technologically advanced passenger plane of her time. To prove so to themselves, the public continually flocked to the Treasure Island docks to watch the arrivals and departures of the famous and luxurious, state-of-the-art seaplanes.

Boeing B-314 at Treasure Island. 1940. Sigfred collection.

In April of 1939, Sture joined the crew of one of the new B-314's. With his old friend Robin McGlohn as his captain, he was assigned as first flight engineer for the christening flight of the *Honolulu Clipper*, NC-18601. Sture and the crew departed Treasure Island on April 13 for Honolulu where Pan Am planned for the ship to be christened by Helen Poindexter, daughter of Hawaii's governor. The flight between Treasure Island and Honolulu occurred without incident, and the crew was cautiously optimistic about the still unproven plane. For good reason, their optimism soon turned to doubt. The Clipper ship crewmen, a hybrid of sailors and aviators, shared with sailors a superstition for which their backgrounds could not account. So when Ms. Poindexter christened the hull of the gleaming Boeing with coconut milk, and announced, "I name you the *Honolulu Clipper*. May you always return to Hawaii," the crew took notice.

Only hours after the ceremony, the *Honolulu Clipper* departed Hawaii. Less than halfway to Midway, only three hours out of Honolulu, the ship developed engine trouble, and McGlohn turned her back to Hawaii. Already the blessing from the christening seemed a curse. As Sture would learn all too well, the B-314 would be plagued with problems throughout her life. The problems, though, had more to do with the fact that her design stretched the existing technological envelope than with forces beyond nature.

Boeing B-314 *California Clipper* over Treasure Island, 1940.
Sigfred collection.

In July of 1940, Pan Am was finally able to establish its southern route. With a route that stretched from Honolulu to Canton Island, to Noumea, New Caledonia and on to Auckland, on July 12th, the company inaugurated airmail service to New Zealand. By January of 1941, with tensions between the United States and Japan increasing, Sture was making regular flights to New Zealand, as well as to Manila and Hong Kong. In April of 1941, President Roosevelt authorized an extension of Pan Am's Pacific route to Singapore. Immediately the company began biweekly flights to the new facility. One week a B-314 would leave for Hong Kong, and the next for Singapore. By June, Sture was also among the crewmen making regular flights to Singapore.

Though he had long since realized or forgotten the dreams of his youth, Sture occasionally stopped to ponder how far he had come. At a time when most of his fellow pilots held degrees from prestigious universities or commissions in the military, he had accomplished through hard work and persistence what it seemed at one time his eighth grade education might prevent. Sometimes he even thought that his lack of education alone had been responsible for providing him with the motivation to continue his pursuit. Though he had met resistance toward his becoming a pilot at virtually every door he had knocked upon, he now stood on the threshold of accomplishing all of his professional goals. Yet even as he accomplished one goal, he quickly set his sights on another. Though he had accomplished by forty more than many of his contemporaries did in a lifetime, he never lost sight of his goal to become one of Pan Am's Master Pilots. He also turned his sights toward more domestic objectives as well.

Sture's friend and occasional copilot Captain Kit Smith, approximately 1940. Smith family collection.

Command Time

1940 - 1941

Approximately a year after he moved to California, Sture registered for a course in air navigation at the University of California at Berkeley. To his surprise, the wife of an old acquaintance was also taking the course. The two exchanged pleasantries, and Sture learned that Mildred and her husband had separated in the year since he had last seen them. Mildred was also, she explained, filing for a divorce. The two struck up a friendship over the next several months, and the friendship evolved gradually into love. They decided to get married when Mildred's divorce was final, after waiting one year as required by California law. So while the months dragged on until they could marry, the two divided their time between their jobs - Sture's at Pan Am and Mildred's at Western Union - and each other, and began making plans for what they hoped would be a long life together.

Sture and Mildred, San Francisco, 1940. Sigfred collection.

Not even Mildred, however, could distract Sture from his primary goal. By 1940, having met most of the requirements to become a captain, Sture faced the problem of acquiring solo command time outside the company. The Aeronautic Branch of the Department of Commerce in 1926 had established the requirements for licensing airmen at 10 hours for a private license, 50 hours for a limited commercial license, and 200 hours for a transport license. While he had earned the first two licenses many years before, and had obtained his Transport License #24813 on November 10, 1938, he desperately needed to gain additional solo hours to meet Pan Am's requirements for advancement to captain. Without a military commission and, as had always been the case, with only an eighth grade education, his promotion hinged upon accruing sufficient solo command time – and that time he would have to accrue on his own. But his plans for purchasing a plane to get the time coincided with a shortage of money. After several weeks of deliberation and weighing their various options, he and Mildred determined that getting command time was necessary for any of their plans to be realized, and both set to work on accomplishing the one thing on which their futures depended.

Mildred had long been impressed with Sture's dedication and drive, his stalwart resistance to even the staunchest opposition; it was one of the qualities that had first attracted her to him. And she was no stranger to opposition. As a young girl growing up on the outskirts of Baltimore, she had literally had to fight and cajole her parents into allowing her to attend high school; they simply could not understand why a woman would need or what she would do with an education. She won the battle with her parents, and was one of the first two girls from her parish to earn her diploma. The effort she expended working her way through school had made her surprisingly strong and independent for her time; she appreciated the same qualities in her future husband. But her strength and independence also had drawbacks. Some men were put off by her strength; others simply resented it. Their resentment, hidden or expressed, highlighted the other quality that attracted her to Sture. She was most impressed with the fact that he worked just as hard at making her feel good and treating her as she longed to be treated as he did to succeed professionally. She was devoted to him and did everything in her power to help him succeed in his many pursuits, sometimes even subordinating her own needs to his.

During one late night conversation, with Sture trying to discover a way to buy a plane to earn command time, she placed her hand on his arm and told him to stop his figuring and talking.

She removed her hand from his arm, picked up a pencil and jotted a column of figures on the pad in front of her. After several minutes, she looked up at Sture and smiled. "We can do this."

She suggested that they cut their expenses to the minimum necessary to survive - and she truly meant absolutely necessary to survive - that she chip in her savings toward the down payment, and that they purchase the new Stinson 105 Sture had been looking at. "Even though it will cost us $2995, it will still be less expensive than renting a plane like you've been doing."

Sture vehemently protested Mildred's spending her money on a down payment for the plane, but she persisted. When he continued to argue that they look for another way, she stopped him. "Well," she said, "no command time - no promotion. No promotion - no captain. No captain – no wedding."

Sture was speechless. This required at least another look at the column of figures. Finally, he grinned, "Play hardball will you? I can cut these figures by a quite a bit. I'll take delivery in Wayne, Michigan, save the shipping costs, and accumulate some command time flying the Stinson home. There is a catch to this though. I'll have to have a copilot, if only to watch and read the road maps and – that means you will have to go with me.[19]

Mildred knew he had trumped her hand, hardball as it was.

The next day Sture purchased two one-way tickets on Greyhound to Wayne, Michigan and a Stinson 105.

Sture took possession of the plane at the Stinson factory on February 14, 1940, and after having it inspected, went to the Aeronautics Branch of the Department of Commerce in Wayne. The building loomed over a vacant airfield, and when he opened the door,

---

[19] Aviation strip maps, far more detailed than road maps, with the locations of beacons clearly marked, were difficult to come by at the time. Additionally, they cost money – something neither Sture nor Mildred possessed in excess during the winter of 1940.

Sture was surprised to see six large, roll-top desks arranged in a semicircle near the center of a large room, vacant but for a sampling of office furniture. Beside each desk was a large file cabinet, and before each desk a large rolling chair in which sat one of the six clerks in the office posed in several different postures of relaxation. Their conversation and laughter vibrated throughout the room, but when Sture stepped from the cold morning air into the warm office, the men fell silent and turned their gaze as one to the stranger. Sture pulled his wallet from his pocket and walked to the first clerk.

"Excuse me, sir. I'd like to get my license updated."

Without looking into Sture's face, the clerk took the license from his hand and peered over his glasses at the faded print on the small card. He then looked up at Sture and back at the license.

"Well. Mr. Sigfred, I'm sorry to tell you this, but you don't have a license."

"What do you mean?" Sture asked.

"I mean that this license expired over two years ago. The Aeronautics Branch regulations state specifically that you must maintain at least ten solo hours a year and renew your license annually. From what I can see, you've done neither, so you don't have a license."

Sture looked toward the other clerks who by now had turned their heads toward their desks and lowered their faces over their ledgers. He looked down at the clerk.

"I hate to disagree with you, sir, but about two years ago, your office sent out a memo stating that pilots and copilots with a major airlines would be able to keep their licenses current by flying their regularly scheduled routes."

"I don't know what you're talking about."

"I know it's true. I have a copy of the letter in my files back home in California. Unfortunately, it's too early to call back there to get the information. If I wait until noon, it will be 9:00 there, but I'm sure you should have a copy of the memo."

The clerk turned to his coworkers and asked if they knew of the memo Sture had referred to. None of them could recall ever having seen or heard of it. The clerk turned back to Sture.

"I'm sure you're mistaken. We would remember a policy change as important as that, but I'll tell you what I'll do. We'll look through the files and see if we can find a copy of it."

He turned back to the other clerks and directed one to start going through the files by month starting five years before. He directed another to start going through the files starting the previous year, and another to start in the middle. While they worked through page after page of carbons and yellow and brittle pages, he leafed through the pages in his own file cabinet. As they looked, Sture paced back and forth from one pool of light cast through windows high in the wall to another. Finally, after almost twenty minutes of searching, one of the clerks slammed his file drawer shut and waved a yellow sheet in the air.

"Eureka! The man is right."

He carried the memo to Sture and the clerk. The clerk took the memo and peered at it over the top of his glasses.

"Well, I'll be."

He adjusted his glasses on his forehead and looked up at Sture. "Looks like I owe you an apology. May I see your license again?"

Sture handed the clerk his license.

The clerk pulled a form from his top desk drawer and rolled it into his Remington typewriter. With his two index fingers, he began to type. Several minutes later, he pulled the form from the typewriter, signed and handed it to Sture. Sture looked at the license. He saw that the clerk had given him a transport license that authorized him to fly single and multi-engine planes, land and sea craft, from 75 HP to 8000 HP. Few, if any, pilots could claim such a broad qualification, and with a sense of pride, Sture nodded to the clerk and made his way into the cold.

Upon obtaining his license, Sture and Mildred flew from Wayne to Chicago where they stayed overnight at Dad Kandle's home. Their arrival in Chicago coincided with St. Valentine's Day and the Kandle's wedding anniversary, so Sture and Mildred presented his close friends with a dozen long-stemmed roses to celebrate. The next morning, they departed for Minneapolis with planned stops for fuel at LaCrosse, Wisconsin and Winona, Minnesota. As they approached Lacrosse, covered in a blanket of snow, Sture reduced his altitude and flew approximately ten feet over the runway. As he was used to doing with the seaplanes, he took the last ten feet in one fell swoop, and when the plane touched the runway it shuddered as though it would fly apart. Clearly shaken, Mildred sat silently as Sture fueled the plane. When they were ready to take off, he asked which runway he should take. Mildred turned to him, her face impassive.

"If there's anything left of the one you landed on, use that."

Mildred smiled, and Sture snickered as he pulled to the runway. When he stopped for his instrument checks, however, he was overcome by laughter and had to sit several minutes before he could fly the plane. As he sat in the cockpit, trying to calm himself, a small white plane took off directly in front of the Stinson. Had he continued with his takeoff, Sture would have collided with the plane. He had never appreciated Mildred's humor more than at that moment.

In Minneapolis, Mildred and Sture spent the night with his sister. They had intended to fly 150 miles north to Parkers Prairie from Minneapolis, but poor weather forced them to remain in the city for four days, and with time bearing down on them, they canceled their jaunt to Parkers Prairie and headed back to California.

Mildred beside the Stinson, outside Minneapolis, 1940.
Sigfred collection.

They got as far as 130 miles southwest of Minneapolis when ice started forming on the wings and struts of the plane, and they were forced to land. Visibility was almost zero. They passed over a small field too late to land, then passed a red barn. Facing a possible crack up, they decided to go down near the farm so help would be available if they were hurt in the landing. As Sture was about to land, telegraph lines covered with ice loomed just ahead of the plane. He pushed the throttle fully forward and started a gradual left turn. When he came over the field again, he landed. When the plane finally stopped its forward progression, they noticed raised railroad tracks between them and the barn.

A farmer came running through the cattle pass in the fence that paralleled the railroad track. He had been hauling a wheelbarrow full of manure from a large pile on one side of the tracks, through the cattle pass to the opposite side of the barn. The plane, when it finally landed, had stopped rolling on the pile of manure.

"Are you cold?" the farmer asked, peering into the small plane.

"No," Sture answered. "I'm more scared than cold. That was a pretty close call with the wires."

Stinson covered in tarp outside Lakefield, Minnesota. 1940. Sigfred collection.

Upon seeing that Sture was not alone, the farmer invited Sture and Mildred into his house. His wife made coffee for the stranded couple and served them freshly baked bread. The farmer explained that the town of Lakefield was about 2 ½ miles from his farm and offered to drive them into town when they finished their coffee.

Sture and the farmer secured the plane in the corner of the field, and the farmer drove both of them into Lakefield where they checked into a small hotel.

On the way from the farm into town, Mildred noticed a Land O' Lakes creamery and remembered a story Sture had told her years before. When he was with NACA, a frequent visitor to his hangar had been Lieutenant Bissell, an attorney for General Billy Mitchell during his courts martial. Whenever the Lieutenant appeared in the hangar, all of the men stopped work and gathered around him because he always had some nugget of wisdom to pass on.

"One time," Sture had told Mildred, "he told us he had flown an Army De Havilland up to a football game in the northeast, and when it came time to leave, he discovered that his plane had completely iced up. The next day, he found it impossible to take off without removing the ice. The wings of his plane were made of fabric, so a blowtorch was out of the question. But Lieutenant Bissell solicited the help of some of the faculty members at the prestigious university where his plane sat stranded. They told him to cover the plane with a common tarpaulin, and even though the ground was covered with ice and snow, the heat from the ground would melt the ice from the wings."

Realizing that it was Boy Scout week and that if they had to freeze up, they couldn't have chosen a more convenient time or location, she reminded Sture of the story and suggested that Sture call the central operator and find out who the scoutmaster was.

The central operator informed Sture that the scoutmaster was also the postmaster and asked if he wanted to speak with him. She connected Sture with the postmaster.

"Comstock," the man answered gruffly.

"Mr. Comstock," Sture responded, "this is Sture Sigfred. I'm a Pan Am pilot heading back home to California."

"You're a bit off course, aren't you?"

Sture rolled his eyes and politely continued. "We've been sort of off our course ever since we left Minneapolis. Our plane iced up and forced us to land here. It's now sitting in a field just outside of town, covered in ice that must be removed before I can take off and return home. Do you think, Mr. Comstock, that you could get some Boy Scouts to help us build a tent in the morning? We have about an hour of 16-millimeter film of a flight I recently made crossing the Pacific. If you have a projector at the high school, I'd be more than happy to show the films."

"Why do you want to build a tent?"

Sture told the Lieutenant Bissell story.

Mr. Comstock told Sture that he would be glad to help. "We are isolated here in this town. Nothing ever happens. Then here you people drop in like men from Mars on a Saturday. I'm sure if I call my scouts, they'd cover the town with the news and it will turn out to be a gala night at the high school. And, of course, like I do in all situations of this sort, I'll enlist the assistance of our operator."

Sture and Mr. Comstock settled on a plan to show the film at 8:00 PM

When the time came, he and Mildred faced an auditorium crammed so full of people that there was no room left even to stand. When the film was finished, the two received a standing ovation as calls of Lindbergh and Amelia Earhart spread throughout the auditorium. Raising his arms high above his head, Sture quieted the audience and thanked them for their warm reception.

"I think the comparison with Amelia Earhart and Lindy are entirely incorrect. Our plane, even at this moment sits outside of town on a manure pile. I'm quite sure nothing like this has ever happened to our more famous counterparts."

Laughter spread throughout the room, as did promises for assistance on the following morning. So Sture and Mildred retrieved their film, bundled themselves against the cold night air, and returned to the hotel.

The next morning, they enjoyed a breakfast of ham and eggs before Mr. Comstock arrived at the hotel to pick Sture up. Leaving Mildred at the hotel, Sture rode with Comstock out to the field on the edge of town and saw that someone had already draped a tarpaulin over the plane. He had purchased a quart of oil the night before and had left it sitting near the radiator in the hotel room overnight. Standing before the plane, he removed the tarp from the lower cowling on the engine and lit a fire pot that was often used to heat the engines of large trucks. He placed it so that the heat would reach the plane engine and warm it up. He then poured the warm oil into the engine, replaced the cowling and removed the tarp from the rest of the plane.

As he had expected, the thin sheet of ice that rimed the plane's horizontal surfaces easily slid off the wings and struts. Sture paid the farmer the five dollars he demanded for taking down five fence posts and laying his wire netting flat on the ground to lengthen the path available for the plane to take off. Sture then removed his arctics and overcoat and gave them to Mr. Comstock to take back to the hotel where he was to pick up Mildred. From there, he would take her to another field that had previously been used as a landing strip but was also much closer to town.

To give Mr. Comstock enough time to get back to the hotel, Sture warmed the plane for about ten minutes, then revved the engine and forced the throttle to full open as he prepared to take off from the small field. He used the entire length of the field to take off, gaining the air only when he had reached the spot where the wire netting lay and beyond which the sharp rise of the railroad track stood. The five dollars, he thought, had been money well spent.

Route of Sture's and Mildred's return trip after purchasing the Stinson, February 1940.

At the field in town, he offered to pay Mr. Comstock for the use of the tarpaulin, but the scoutmaster and postmaster would hear nothing of it. "The whole town enjoyed the movies, and everybody was grateful for a pleasant and surprising evening. It's the least I can offer for the enjoyment."

Sture put his arctics, overcoat and gloves back on, helped Mildred into the plane and took off. He circled around the town twice to say "Thank You," before pointing the nose of the Stinson away from the morning sun and resuming his trek to California.

From Lakefield, Sture and Mildred flew toward Lincoln, Nebraska. Because they had been unable to obtain aviation strip maps for the area, Mildred was following their flight on a roadmap. They flew low enough to follow the path of dark roads inching their way through the blinding snow. The sky was bitter cold and the ground merely a reflection of the sky, but the dense air and lack of wind made for smooth flying. In order to be sure of their location, each time the road they followed entered a town, they searched the map and the skyline hoping to find the name of the town. For the sake of aviators, the name was usually painted across the face of a large building or a water tower.

At one particular town, however, they could see no name. The skyline was barren of a water tower, and none of the taller buildings at its outskirts bore the name of the village. The town was small enough that they easily located the railroad station where they knew the name of the town was always painted. Sture flew low over the station, but neither he nor Mildred could find the name. He made another pass over the station, and still they could find no trace of where they were. On his third pass, Sture side-slipped toward the station low enough to read the town name painted under the eave of the building. Without turning toward Mildred, he announced "It's Bancroft. Mark it on your map."

Mildred was silent.

"It's Bancroft," he said again louder. "Mark it on the map."

Still Mildred was silent.

Finally, he turned toward her seat and saw that Mildred had passed out. His daring in pulling the plane low enough and close enough to read the town name had simply proven too much. Sture quickly lit a cigarette, since the smell always seemed to soothe Mildred's stomach when she became airsick. The cigarette worked to revive her, but as soon as she awoke, she became nauseated. She didn't want to soil the inside of their new plane, so she slid back the window to her right and stuck her head outside the plane and threw up. The backwash from the propeller blew the warm semi-liquid into the hood of her flight jacket. The cold wind rushing past the plane quickly froze the liquid in the hood so that when she pulled her head back into the cockpit, she had a frozen helmet haloing her head, and a thin sliver of moisture clinging to her lips.

Sture looked at her and could not help laughing. Soon Mildred joined in his laughter.

"I guess the navigator is a real mess," she said, wiping her mouth with a tissue. "I have some nuisance value, at least. Whether I can read a map to your liking or not, I am certainly good for a laugh."

Looking around her at the empty sky, she added, "I guess we can use that now more than anything."

The couple landed in Lincoln, Nebraska shortly after 2:00 in the afternoon, and immediately became mired in the mud on the airfield.

After freeing the plane from the mud, a strong gust of wind blew the plane into a snow bank from which they could not free themselves. Since no one at the airfield made an effort to help, they climbed from the plane and walked disgustedly to the administration building. Once inside the warm confines of the building, they were informed that there would be no gas available until 6:00 that evening. The airfield had only one key to the gasoline tanks, and it was in the possession of the owner who was off enjoying the winter afternoon. Only half believing their luck, they walked back to the plane to pull it into a hangar for the night. This time, one of the men at the airfield went along to help. What they thought was the last straw of their visit to Lincoln occurred when the man tried to turn the propeller in the wrong direction. Sture and Mildred wondered aloud how so many things could happen to the same two people in only two days as they walked back to the administration building to obtain maps for their continued flight west. They were informed that no strip maps were available, and they would have to navigate the next 200 miles, as they had the previous two hundred, by road map.

Frustrated and rapidly approaching exhaustion, they decided that a good stiff drink would help them recover from Lincoln. They hurried to a hotel with a restaurant, but quickly discovered that there was just one thing money could not buy in Lincoln, Nebraska on a Sunday afternoon - a drink. Sture counted to ten and ordered a good dinner for the two of them. When the meal arrived, they found it to be exceptionally good, and rather than testing their luck any further, they paid the waitress, and went to their room to recover from the Midwestern day.

They started early the following morning. Still bitterly cold, snow and ice covered every inch of land over which they flew. Still navigating by road maps, the two flew close to the ground, and Sture quickly developed a headache from squinting into the glare of the sun upon the snow. Arriving in Wichita, Kansas, they landed on a smooth concrete runway and felt as though things were beginning to look up. They left the plane on the runway and walked into the administration building, where the airport manager Mr. Patterson gave them a far more cordial greeting than their reception in Lincoln. Mr. Patterson admitted that Sture was the first "ocean flying" pilot he had ever met, and the sky was the limit in making the couple feel welcome in Wichita. He took Sture and Mildred to lunch, but as they dined, they learned that they had to hurry out of Wichita in order to stay ahead of a storm coming in just north and east of city.

They hurried back to the airport and quickly sought the solace of the air as they headed for Wichita Falls. Aided by a steady tailwind, they made good time and often approached 115 mph. They refueled in Wichita Falls, and reached Abilene, Texas by nightfall. With the exception of snow on the mountaintops over which they would fly, they finally left the snow behind them for this trip. In Abilene, they ran out of what money they had brought with them, and Sture had to wire the Bank of America in Alameda, California, to send him $50.00 by Western Union. He asked for the money to be delivered the following day to the airport in El Paso, and he and Mildred prayed that their good fortune would last until they landed on the western border of Texas to collect their bounty.

The following morning, they left Abilene and followed a railroad track into Wink, Texas where they refueled before taking off again and following an above ground pipeline into El Paso. To their delight, their money had arrived. Though the airport had strip maps for the area, they discovered near El Paso that there was an area about 50 miles across for which the airport had no maps. The airport manager in El Paso assured them they would need no map since their course lay directly above a railroad that would lead them straight to the location where one of their strip maps would pick up. They flew for several hours toward Tucson, and about halfway there, passed over Rodeo, New Mexico. Off to the northwest, they could see the first high ridge of mountains between them and their destination, the Chiricahua Mountains, averaging about 8000 feet above sea level. Beyond Rodeo, they reached the area for which they had no charts. So they headed due west, continually trying to find their location on the strip chart for the area beyond.

After about an hour, they were still not able to find their location on the strip map. They turned around and headed back to Rodeo. In Rodeo, they discovered that the railroad they had been following had turned south. They had turned along with it. When they finally turned around to head back to Rodeo, they realized that they had almost been south of the border. They refueled in Rodeo and decided to fly a compass course over the tip of the Chiricahua Mountains. The range appeared to be only about five miles away from the airport, but was, in fact, 25 miles away; they would easily be able to gain sufficient altitude to clear the mountains before they were even near the crest.

Shortly after their takeoff from Rodeo, they discovered they had a third passenger - a fly they had picked up in Rodeo. At 7000 feet, the air became so thin that the fly kept falling down on the instrument panel. The fly, though lethargic, proved a great distraction as Sture kept swinging at it and missing. Finally, he turned to Mildred and told her to get rid of it. Though she had no love for insects, as she watched the fly buzzing about the instrument panel and trying in vain to gain flight in the thin air, she became very aware of how dependent upon the plane she and Sture actually were to make it safely over the mountains. For a reason she refused to explain afterward, she refused to kill the fly.

The Chiricahua Mountains rose directly from a vast flatland that stretched as far as the horizon. About 25 miles across, the range stretched from the northern to the southern extremes of the small plane's field of view. Sture and Mildred found the range breathtaking and were surprised at their own swaggers when the danger of crossing the range lay far behind them.

They over-nighted in Tucson, Arizona, and planned to get an early start for San Jose the following morning. But when they awoke, both felt poorly. A combination of nervous tension, the change in water, and the climate had taken its toll, and they did not hit the sky until 8:00 AM.

After leaving Tucson, they flew over Salton Sea and the vast water works that irrigated the rich Imperial Valley. They had reached a speed of 120 mph over Salton Sea when they realized they were flying below sea level.[20]

"Sounds like a pretty good place to me," Mildred smirked, "not too far to fall."

Her wise cracks seemed to help their spirits as the dessert stretched before them. In Yuma, they stopped and refueled and quickly took again to the sky. They were charted to fly to Palm Springs through the San Gorgornias Pass, and then to San Bernadino. They had been assured that, while it would be a rough ride, it would not be dangerous. The pass lay between two snow-covered mountains,

---

[20] Salton Sea, located in extreme southern California, is now a lake that sits at an elevation of 210 feet below sea level.

one whose peak reached 9000 feet and the other 11000 feet. The air was smooth as they entered the pass, and they began to suspect that there would be no rough wind, when out of nowhere a gust shook the plane and nearly rolled it tail over nose. Sture regained control of the plane, but had to fight the controls the rest of the way into San Bernadino as the wind slapped and dragged at the plane.

They landed in San Bernadino, refueled, changed the oil and ate lunch, then took off for Bakersfield. Again, the ride was rough all the way into Bakersfield as they faced yet another range of mountains, the Sierra Nevadas. By this time, Mildred had learned how to use the sectional charts, map a course, and determine their position at every landmark. They spent the night in Bakersfield.

The following day, they headed for San Jose. Rain and fog led them as they left the airport in Bakersfield and headed toward the mountains. They stopped in Fresno and refueled, and took off again heading for the mountains. Before they reached them, however, the fog grew so thick, they were forced to turn around and return to Fresno to await a later weather report that they hoped would promise clearer skies. As they gained altitude, they noted a very good ceiling at 9000 feet, so they started up the valley. The rain began to fall more heavily as they forged their way north, and they were forced to land as soon as they spotted the Modesto airport. The weather report forecast scattered clouds at 3500 feet, and Sture felt that they would be safer if they flew above the clouds. The weather report also noted several breaks in the clouds through which he believed they could navigate. When they were 45 minutes from Livermore, the clouds rolled together and they could see no breaks whatsoever. Though they had no instruments in the plane, Sture turned to Mildred and smiled.

"It looks like we're on instruments."

Mildred turned pale.

Sture told Mildred to take out their compass. Using his watch, he determined his airspeed and calculated their distance from Livermore. Flying sufficiently high to clear any mountains he could not see, he navigated by the compass and timed his flight to coincide with the precise moment he expected to pass over Livermore. Just one minute before he was planning to make his descent, Mildred noticed a Richfield Gas Station through a hole in the clouds. Sture recognized the station as one on the highway just outside Livermore.

He made his descent and set his course by following a set of rail tracks that he knew followed a canyon into San Jose. At one point on the map, Mildred noticed that the tracks made a sharp turn. Since the tracks seemed to fall between the mountains on level land, Sture planned to follow the turn in the tracks as well. When they made the turn, however, they faced a wall of mountain. It seemed that the railroad had dug a thousand foot ditch for the rail track, and nothing as wide as the Stinson could make it through the long, narrow gorge.

Sture immediately pulled back on the half-wheel and forced the plane into a steep climb. Leaning forward in his seat, he coaxed the plane higher as he rapidly lost airspeed. Finally, he glimpsed clouds instead of mountain and lowered the nose of the plane. They made it over the crest of the mountain with less than fifty feet to spare. Shaken and more than ready to get home, Sture flew directly toward San Jose, descending as the ceiling of clouds lowered rapidly around him. Rain and fog fought to swallow the small plane.

After several minutes, Sture spotted a lake. Thinking they were off course, he passed over the lake and decided to turn around to try and make a landing beside the lake. By this time, the ceiling was around 100 feet, and the clouds forced him closer and closer to the ground to be able to see. Somewhat confused that he had entirely missed the airport and worried about the foothills of the mountains that he knew must lay dangerously close, he turned back toward the lake and was surprised to see two yellow planes sitting in the center of the water.

As he would learn when he landed, the airport he expected to find lay under four inches of water and looked like a small lake from the sky. When his plane had flown over what he thought was the lake, several Civil Air Patrol pilots out for their Sunday flying heard him from the hangar in which they huddled, and realized that he must be searching for a runway. Knowing the pilot would not be able to see the runway under the water, they dragged two yellow planes from the hangar, hoping that their color would stand out for the passing pilot, and placed them in the center of the runway. Thanking whoever was responsible for placing the planes where he could see them, Sture landed his plane. He pulled to a stop just past the two quiet planes, and saw the hangar that had previously been obscured by the weather. Several men were working inside, already oblivious to the plane they had guided safely to the field.

Sture stopped the engine and turned to Mildred. "Thanks to them, we're home."

Mildred looked out over the soggy airfield. "Finally," was all she could think to say.

Traffic

1940 - 1941

During the summer of 1940, Sture was once again on vacation, this time to visit his family and drop Mildred off in Baltimore where she would remain with her parents until her divorce became final. The trip began in Oakland, California, and ended in Baltimore, with a long stop in Parkers Prairie. Sture and Mildred headed up the northern California coast and through Oregon. Roughly following the path taken by Lewis and Clark, they turned to the east in Washington, relishing breathtaking vistas over the Columbia River.

Sture with Dickey Johnson, son of a former classmate from the Parkers prairie School, San Francisco, 1940. Sigfred collection.

On the second and final day of their flight to Parkers Prairie, they left Missoula, Montana at 4:00 AM, flew over the eastern ridge of the Rockies at 12,000 feet and ran into rain. They landed in Butte just after daybreak. After departing Butte, they flew on instruments and followed a strong beam on their portable receiver through Bosman, Montana, and Bismark, North Dakota and into Fargo, North Dakota where they encountered twilight fast approaching darkness. They ran out of money in Fargo and hurriedly bargained to have their gas tanks filled, leaving Sture's gold watch as security. They desperately needed to get to the Alexandria Airport, twenty miles south of Parkers Prairie, before dark. They left Fargo and flew southeast following beacons flashing letters by Morse code. The beacons were stationed ten miles apart, and each successive beacon was visible from the one immediately preceding it. They determined that by turning east at beacon H, they would fly right over Parkers Prairie. Sture had never seen Parkers Prairie from the air at night, so he decided to circle the city and somehow signal his brothers Ed and Tony that he was almost to Alexandria where they planned to meet him.

After passing over the village, they were just about to turn south toward Alexandria when they noticed people flocking out of the downtown theatre, getting into their cars and forming a slow moving eastward procession on the highway. Approximately a half-mile east of town, the cars turned right and headed into a field where they formed into a fan and shone their headlights on the center of the field. There a man gestured to the sky with a flashlight.

Sture turned to his wife. "Mildred, that's Ed. He expects us to land here. Now what do we do?"

Dead tired and ready to set down anywhere, Mildred replied, "I'd really hate to disappoint Ed and Tony and all their friends. Just land."

Sture smiled. "I've never landed a plane at night, but here goes. You sit on or hold everything loose in the cockpit. I'm going down."

Sture and Mildred outside
Baltimore, summer 1940.
Sigfred collection.

Sture approached the field from the east, behind the cars, with the flap down and more than a little power in a power stall. He passed over the cars at only ten or fifteen feet. The light shone by the cars was so limited that he landed in the dark, hitting the ground on top of a knoll and rolling scarcely twenty feet before stopping. The left wheel landed at the edge of a plowed furrow and stopped immediately. When Sture entered in his

Stinson 105 in a field
outside Baltimore, summer
1940. Sigfred collection.

logbook that he had thirteen hours and twenty-five minutes of airtime when he landed, he suddenly realized why he was tired.

Almost an hour later, it occurred to him that he had "PX'ed" to Alexandria, so he rushed to the phone and called the airport. "I had a little trouble getting to a phone," he explained, "but I have landed safely in Parkers Prairie."

Sture and Mildred glanced dejectedly at their map. The Stinson shook around them, and the landscape stretched flat and vacant, even in its vacancy offering no place to land. With Parkers Prairie long behind them, they looked forward to finally arriving and landing in Baltimore. Mildred had planned the trip for weeks prior to her departure and thought she had covered every detail, including several telephone calls home to ensure that her family understood all of the details. But when she and Sture arrived over Baltimore, they discovered a grand surprise. They could not execute their plan. They had expected throughout their trip to land at the Martin airplane factory outside Baltimore, but as they approached the city, Sture noticed that the landing field shown on the map was a restricted area. Though the United States had not entered the war, tensions had mounted sufficiently that access to manufacturing facilities throughout the country had been restricted. Rather than risk losing his license, or worse, he quickly determined that he would not land at the Martin field and told Mildred "How are we going to let my Mom and Dad know where we are," Mildred asked him. "I would rather not wait around at Curtiss Wright Field until we can find a phone and, hopefully, catch them at home, if they haven't already left for the Martin field."

Sture looked around the plane. "We'll drop them a note."

He had Mildred compose a note explaining that they would land at Curtiss Wright Field. She then attached the note around the neck of a stuffed dog she had carried with her from California. Sture circled over the Krastel farmhouse where Mildred's

Will Krastel, Mildred's brother, relaxing in El Paso, Texas, prior to shipping out to support Allied forces in the battle for Sicily. 1943.
Sigfred Collection.

parents lived and, when he could fly no lower because of power lines strung across the fields, dropped the small black dog from his window. Pulling back on the control wheel, he flew the plane higher while Mildred peered out the window to be sure it landed near her parents' home. Sure that it had landed near enough and that waiting would accomplish nothing, Sture flew on to Curtiss Wright Field. After he landed the plane and completed his check in with the airfield, Mildred's brother Will[21] walked up to the couple, smiling.

"Son of a gun! You'll never guess what dropped out of the sky like a message from God into the neighbor's yard?"

Sture winked at Will. "Not a black dog with a note around its neck?"

"Nothing but," Will answered, gathering his sister into a bear hug and slapping Sture on the shoulder.[22]

While Mildred remained with her parents until her divorce was finalized, Sture flew back to California alone. Flying over Tennessee, he noticed one of his propeller blades fluttering and knowing that the Stinson factory had moved from Wayne, Michigan to Nashville, he landed at the factory on June 20, 1940, and had the propeller replaced free of charge. He left Nashville immediately after the propeller was repaired and flew to Memphis where he spent the night. The following morning, with poor weather looming in the west, he took off from Memphis. He fought poor weather the rest of his way west. Struggling into Amarillo, Texas where fifty mph winds blew across the runway, he wasted little time in turning his plane around and refueling. When he went into the administration building to purchase a map for the Albuquerque area, he was told that they were out of

---

[21] Mildred's brother Will Krastel and Sture became very close friends. Though they could go years without seeing each other, each reunion found them sitting under a tree, laughing and talking about aviation. His imminent departure for Europe at the beginning of 1942 convinced Sture and Mildred to keep Mildred's pregnancy a secret from her mother who had more than enough to worry about. A member of a chemical battalion during World War II, Will was offered a commission but declined it in favor of remaining with his men. While a sergeant in the Army during the battle for Sicily, he stepped on a land mine and was severely injured. He survived his injuries but was plagued with pain for the rest of his life.

[22] Sture carried the stuffed black dog with him on all future flights, as both a reminder of his wife and a good luck charm.

maps. Worried that he should not fly in inclement weather without a map, he reconsidered whether he should leave Amarillo until the winds calmed.

Among other memorabilia of flight, the stuffed dog that Mildred dropped from the Stinson with a note to inform her family to meet her and Sture at Curtiss Wright field. Sture carried the dog with him on all future flights. Sigfred collection.

As he pondered what he should do, he struck up a conversation with two Second Lieutenants from the Army Air Corps near him on the runway. Upon learning that the two were making their first cross-country flight together and that both of them had maps, he asked if he could borrow one of their maps of the flight area to Albuquerque. Both pilots were hesitant. He explained the urgency of his returning to San Francisco and promised that he would leave the map at the airport in Albuquerque. They could pick it up the next day, he assured them. After a couple of minutes, the pilots agreed and gave Sture one the maps. Thanking them profusely, he climbed into his plane and started the engine. Applying full throttle against a battering headwind, he was soon in the air, being buffeted like a leaf in a windstorm.

After taking off, Sture quickly reached 8000 feet where a 100 mph wind blew from the south. Though the plane was pointed due west, the wind drove it at a forty-five degree angle off his intended course. To compensate for the wind, Sture pointed the plane toward the southwest, expecting the combined effect to be a course roughly due west. While his posture prevented him from being blown too far off course, it also gave him little ground speed, and he noted with a sinking feeling in his stomach that he was consuming a large amount of fuel for very little distance. It was well over an hour before he approached Tucamcari, New Mexico, only seventy-five miles away. As he approached the small town, seven miles west of a small emergency airfield, a voice crackled to life over his receiver.

Dr. Cliff Wagner and his Fonck in San Jose, Costa Rica. 1942.
Sigfred collection.

"This is Tucamcari. We have you in sight. Do you read?"

Because he had no transmitter, Sture dipped his wings to acknowledge the report.

"We have winds at fifty-five gusting to sixty-five on the surface. Winds gusting to 105 at 9000 feet." The voice crackled again. "Do you have enough fuel to fly through?"

Sture looked at his fuel gage. Though he had flown only seventy-five miles, the needle rested below a quarter of a tank. He maintained his wings level as a negative response to the radioman's question.

"Will you land?"

Sture dipped his wings.

"Will you overnight?"

Sture dipped his wings.

"Very well. Land straight south at the small hangar on the field just east of town. You will have trouble staying down until you get within the lee of the hangar, but I'll be out there to help hold you down."

Sture dipped his wings for the final time before turning to make his approach to the field. As he got closer to the ground, the wind whipped him more furiously, and as he approached the field he fought to keep the plane near the ground without crashing. In a split second, he would go from two feet off the ground to ten. When he finally got downwind of the hangar, he was able to land the plane, and as promised, the man from the radio station rushed out to help hold the plane in place until Sture could tie her down. When the plane was secured, the two men walked into the hangar where a wrecked Fonck lay in a pile on the floor.

The radioman nodded toward the pile of bent and twisted metal. "Belongs to the doctor. He wrecked her a few months back while taking off from Albuquerque after performing surgery all night. Had the plane carried back here by truck. He's a nice enough man, nice looking, but his face is scarred up a little from the crack up. Left orders that anyone landing here is to be his guest at the hospital in town. I called him just before you landed. He's only seven miles from here, in town, so he should arrive shortly."

No sooner had Sture and the radioman sat down than the doctor drove up and jumped from the car. Smiling broadly, he pumped Sture's hand and introduced himself as Cliff Wagner. Without further conversation, he helped Sture into the car and drove him to the small hospital in town. He apologized that he had a date that evening and would be unable to take Sture to dinner, and began explaining his plans for a trip through Central America he had been planning for several months.

Sture mentioned that he worked for Pan Am and that he had once worked with Johnny Forbes, the man Pan Am had recently assigned as the comptroller for the Brownsville Pan Am facilities. The two had worked together in Brazil for over seven years. The doctor listened intently to Sture's conversation and, as the car pulled in front of the white stucco building that served as Tucamcari's hospital, apologized again for being unable to keep him company for the evening. "But," he assured Sture, "I will provide you with a comfortable and very clean room and will awaken you early in the morning so we may talk and you can have a warm breakfast before leaving."

True to his word, the doctor woke Sture at 4:00 the following morning. After dressing and making his bed, Sture met him in the kitchen of the hospital. The doctor stood at a large stove frying ham and eggs and potatoes.

"I hope you slept well," he called over his shoulder.

"Quite well, thank you." Sture sat at a small table in the corner.

The doctor placed a heaping plate of food in front of Sture and sat down opposite him. "I suppose you saw my plane at the hangar."

Sture nodded.

"I split my time between here and Albuquerque. Bad luck to have wrecked the plane like that. But I'm going to get another. I sold the hospital to the city of Tucamcari, and I'm going to buy a new Fonck - I've already ordered it - and take it and the money south before the little man with the moustache can get it."

The Boeing B-314 *Yankee Clipper*. Sigfred collection.

At the mention of Hitler, Sture stopped, his fork halfway to his mouth.

"I know that Pan Am has facilities throughout Central and South America, and I have been thinking that I might persuade you to put in a good word for me. Perhaps I can use your facilities on my way down. I understand that's a common practice among unaffiliated pilots."

Sture sat his fork on the edge of his plate and pushed himself away from the table. Leaning back in his chair, he eyed the doctor carefully. "From what I understand, we often let pilots land and use the facilities. As I explained last evening, an acquaintance of mine is the airport comptroller in Brownsville. I could write you a letter of introduction."

From a drawer beside the table, the doctor produced paper and a fountain pen. Sture pushed his plate aside and wrote that the doctor had treated him kindly when he was his guest after being forced to land in Tucamcari. Explaining that the doctor planned to fly south using Pan Am's facilities, he asked that Johnny return the kindness. He signed the letter, folded it into thirds and placed it in an envelope. He then handed the unsealed envelope to the doctor. "You can read it if you'd like."

Sture finished his breakfast with occasional sparks of polite conversation breaking the silence, and the doctor drove him back to the emergency field where his plane was located. Before sunrise on June 22, 1940, Sture was back in the air and on his way home.

Boeing B-314 over Oakland Bay Bridge, early 1940s. Sigfred collection.

In Mildred's absence, Sture soon added a stack of long distance telephone bills to the many other stacks of paper and books on his desk. The stacks included his preciously maintained and protected flight logs. For him, 1940 passed in a string of entries in his log, Pan

Am flights to the west, and solo flights up and down the coast of California amassing hours for his eventual promotion to captain.

In early 1941, Mildred's divorce was finalized, and she returned to California by train. She and Sture planned to marry as soon as Sture returned from one of his scheduled flights to China, but when Mildred had been back in San Francisco for only a few days, Sture was notified that his father had died. The two returned to Parkers Prairie for the funeral, and when they arrived back in San Francisco, a series of back-to-back flights prevented their marrying for several more months. Finally, on July 26, 1941, with a break in Sture's schedule, they stole away from the bustle of the Bay area, and were married at a small chapel in Reno, Nevada. Their cab driver and the presiding minister's wife served as witnesses.

It had taken several years and what seemed to Sture a small fortune, but he had finally achieved his personal and professional goals, had melded his personal and professional lives into one. His wife and his plane were in the same location, and when he was not away on scheduled trips to the Orient, he paid equal attention to both. Life was looking up. Still needing command time and instrument flying to qualify as a Master Pilot, he set up a small workshop in the living room of their apartment and installed an instrument panel in the dash of the Stinson. After reinstalling the dashboard and assembling a Bakelite spool for trailing his antenna from the bottom of the plane, he enlisted Mildred's assistance in honing his skills. With a makeshift blind drawn before him in the cockpit, he flew blind, relying only on his instruments, on dozens of jaunts around northern California and Oregon. For safety, Mildred watched the skies. As imperfect as the arrangement was, it worked. Sture was able to get his command time, and Mildred was able to spend time with her new husband, and the two took every available opportunity for their flights together.[23]

---

[23] In early 1942, after Sture had mastered instrument flying and met all qualifications for promotion, they sold the Stinson to an airline company that planned to use the plane to train its own pilots in instrument flying.

Pan Am promotional poster
showing clipper ship, after which
its fleet was named, and plane,
early 1940s. PAA.

His work, a profession that had always been dear to him, the most important aspect of his life, continually took on new meaning and new challenges where he least expected. The most challenging aspect of his duties as first officer had surprisingly little to do with flying. It was determining the weight of the plane and the appropriate combination of fuel and cargo loading. This above all other characteristics would make the difference between a safe flight and disaster. The crew could not exceed the maximum weight of the plane under any circumstances, and before each flight, the first officer had to calculate the weight of the passengers and cargo and the fuel load. He would then determine, based upon the best available weather reports, if the fuel load was sufficient to carry the plane to Hawaii. During the summer, tail winds helped the planes make the flight from San Francisco to Pearl Harbor in approximately nineteen hours. During the winter, however, prevailing westerlies increased the flying time to as much as thirty hours. If necessary, the number of passengers was reduced to accommodate a greater fuel load for the increased flight time.

Since 1935, when the first load of airmail was flown to Manila, control of the cargo and fuel loading west of Honolulu had never been solved. In order to solve the problem with load and to help the crews understand the appropriate procedures for ensuring sufficient fuel loading, Pan Am furnished the crew with seven pages of instructions. Unfortunately, the instructions were so complex that few in the crew entirely understood them, and filling them out became more a formality than an integral part of maintaining the plane. By 1940, when Sture was promoted to first officer, the length of the instructions had been reduced to three pages, but still, few understood the three pages. So after dinner at Midway one evening, while the plane sat moored to the dock, and the ground crews serviced the engines, Sture found himself heaving bags of airmail onto the dock, checking their weights, and trying to make sense of what seemed the senseless records no one had satisfactorily put into black and white.

During his first trip as first officer, after departing Honolulu, Sture thought long and hard about the process of properly loading the plane and came up with an idea about how the problem could be solved. By the time the plane landed at Midway, he had completed a rough sketch of a form consisting of a series of blocks and squares on a large sheet of paper to be placed in the Navigation Log.

The "half-wings" emblem that Pan Am used on promotional materials. 1930s. PAA.

Upon his return to San Francisco, he submitted the form to the Operations Manager. The manager carefully scrutinized the form and finally told Sture that it was so simple he was surprised no one had thought of the method before. At the next pilot's meeting, the manager demonstrated use of the form to the other pilots who congratulated Sture on his ingenuity. The most favorable and lasting recognition, however, came when the engineering department was required to make blueprints of the blank form carrying the inscription "drawn by Sture Sigfred." From then on, each printed form bore his name.

With a growing sense of challenge, determination and accomplishment, he settled gracefully into his career, as though into the comfortable cushions of a favorite chair. With excitement he faced his flights to the Orient, and with determination he faced his training in and around San Francisco. And like most other Pan Am employees, though he would never be able to consider himself a hero, he grew to relish the attention he received amidst the pomp and ceremony of the seaplane takeoffs from the Pan Am air base. Standing tall and proud, the insignia of Pan Am glistening above the breast pocket of his uniform jacket, he marched with his crew from the Pan Am terminal at Treasure Island, down the long dock to whatever plane awaited him for his impending journey. Accompanied by traditional Hawaiian music, with eyes straight ahead, he crisply embarked upon the plane and removed his hat, a gesture of respect and admiration for the beautiful and powerful ships that like God and nature both protected and threatened his life. Beyond the rope barrier erected to hold back excited crowds, audiences cheered and applauded him and his fellow crewmen, heroes of ocean and sky, and he was humbled at their admiration, wondering why he had been chosen to live this dream.

On several occasions, he saw in the crowd people he knew. The most surprising for him occurred late one summer afternoon as motion picture cameras whirred and still cameras clicked in time with the music. From a distance, he heard a woman call his name from the crowd. Though he normally ignored the cheers from the crowd, the woman's voice sounded familiar, and he turned toward the sound. Behind the red rope stood an older woman, frantically waving her arms. Sture recognized Helen Weiberg, who as a seventeen-year-old girl had helped his mother deliver him and who at fifty-six attended the San Francisco International Exposition. Carried along by the

Sture beside the *China Clipper*, 1941. Sigfred collection.

forward progression of his fellow crewmembers, all he could offer was a slight wave and a smile to acknowledge the presence of his family friend.

While no two flights were ever alike, Sture had grown to expect the unexpected. In June of 1938, a typhoon forced the *China Clipper* to return to Manila after more than three hours of fight. In April of 1939, severe rains and winds forced the *Honolulu Clipper* back to

Macao after only forty-nine minutes. After having been delayed in Hong Kong because of poor weather, engine trouble in August of 1939 forced the *California Clipper* to abort her run from Guam to Wake. And on June 28, 1940, after dozens of successful takeoffs and landings in the shallow atoll surrounding Midway, the *California Clipper* struck a submerged coral head, tearing a hole in the hull that almost sank the plane. She was forced to remain in Midway for six days while workers unfamiliar with the work effected emergency repairs to her hull.

Delays were part and parcel of Pan Am's Pacific routes, but one particular flight, delayed for weeks because of engine trouble, remained a continual reminder for Sture of how vulnerable to the forces of nature the Clippers really were. On June 29, 1938, as Pan Am struggled to maintain its schedules in the face of mounting losses and increasing demand, the *China Clipper* was forced by bad weather to return to Manila shortly after takeoff. In Manila, the ground crew discovered that one of her engines had sustained sufficient damage to warrant replacement. With no replacement engine on hand, one had to be ordered from San Francisco, and her passengers were provided two additional nights in the Manila Hotel.

Pan Am logo featuring the familiar "half-wings."
1930s and 1940s. PAA.

The *Philippine Clipper* was ordered to Manila to replace the damaged plane, and arrived on July 1 with bad weather right behind her. With her crew standing by to depart, the flight to Macao was canceled. The poor weather that had arrived with the plane had turned into a typhoon that lingered over Manila. The passengers, their patience already stretched to the limits of human endurance, were instructed to stay a while longer at the Manila Hotel until the weather cleared. Some decided not to return to San Francisco on the Clipper and canceled their reservations. Each day, the passenger list grew shorter. Finally, late in the afternoon on July 2, the weather department at Cavite, approximately twenty miles from the hotel, called the crew and informed them that it looked as though the storm were starting to move. If it continued, they said, the *Philippine Clipper* would be able to leave the following day. The crew, anxious to depart but taking the news with a grain of salt, called the traffic office at the Manila Hotel and asked how many passengers remained for the return flight. The traffic manager responded, rather quietly, that he had "fourteen angry gentlemen and one mad son of a bitch."

The weather did clear, and the flight departed Manila on July 3, only four days behind schedule. Poor weather and schedule problems, however, delayed arrival of the new engine for the *China Clipper* for several weeks, and when she finally departed Manila, her normal three-week journey had lasted fifty-five days.

This, of course, was the exception. Most of the flights were as routine as routine could be considered during the golden age of aviation. When the B-314's appeared the following year, many, though not all of Pan Am's schedule problems disappeared.

Sture and Mildred enroute to Parkers Prairie for John August Sigfrid's funeral. 1941. Sigfred collection.

Both the M-130 and the B-314 were so large that during normal flight, passengers and crew could easily forget they were flying. The crew could calmly track their position during the day by tracking ships on the surface of the sea or at night by shooting stars with an octant, a navigational aid developed by Admiral Byrd during his south pole ventures. More often than not, Clipper flights proceeded inevitably, almost boringly, smoothly.

When the weather turned bad, however, and the crews were forced to fly on the few instruments available in the cockpit, the planes, especially the M-130, had all of the flying qualities of a brick. During a January, 1940 flight between Honolulu and San Francisco, Sture and his crew on the *China Clipper* were caught in yet another typhoon. The storm, which had not been forecast, took them completely by surprise. Despite their best efforts, they could fly neither over nor around the storm. For several hours, the pilots fought the storm and the ship itself. But they were tossed about in winds that threatened at every moment to send the plane hurtling into the Pacific. The plane bucked beneath them, dropping erratically toward the sea only to gain altitude in the blink of an eye. The men were in a single breath weightless and straining against their seatbelts or falling like rocks against the cold steel deck below them. Not even their padded chairs could protect them from the bone-breaking anger of the storm. So violent was the typhoon, that when the plane finally returned safely to Hawaii, Captain Joe Chase and his First Officer, Sture, had to be examined by a doctor to determine if they had injured their backs during the flight.

Color rendering of the Boeing B-314. Boeing.

Yet even in the face inclement weather and engine troubles, Sture maintained his composure and exemplified what Pan Am had trained all of its pilots to show - bravery and professionalism, especially when matters seemed to fly out of control. His skill and demeanor earned him both within the company and the community several trusted friends and a reputation as a man for whom it was safe to take risks. He found that he was often able to get special favors when others could not. When his father died in January of 1941, Sture was on Canton Island in the south Pacific. As he made his way back to the United States, he had Mildred, back in San Francisco only a few days, get the Stinson serviced and ready for a flight to Parkers Prairie. The plane was ready when Sture arrived in San Francisco. Arriving with him, however, was one of the worst fog covers the airport had seen in several years, and the airport manager at Alameda and Oakland canceled all outgoing flights on January 12. Incoming flights that could be diverted were directed to other airports where visibility was better. When Sture explained his situation, however, the airport manager was moved. He personally cleared Sture through the control tower and walked along the yellow line that led to the takeoff position on the runway.

Sture lined up the plane on the yellow centerline. He ran up the engine until the tachometer was pegged at its maximum. Then he released the brakes and sped down the runway, quickly soaring into the sky and popping out of the fog at 800 feet. His was the only flight out of San Francisco that day. Yet despite the airport manager's assistance, the weather proved relentless. Sture and Mildred made it only as far Elko, Nevada before they were forced to take a train the rest of the way to Parkers Prairie.

Time and the Evening Sky

Midway Island, 1941

The afternoon sun inched its way across the sky, casting long, cool shadows along the eastern beach of Sand Island. Except for waves lapping gently against the shore and notes of a song drifting from the lobby of the Pan Am Hotel one-quarter mile inland, the afternoon was silent. A breeze stirred the tropical air, ruffling the feathers of gooney birds lazing on the fine sand of the beach and rustling the shuddering scrubs, dark beneath the crystal sky. Midway Island - actually two islands, Sand and Eastern - rose thirty-nine feet above sea level to expose two square miles of land at the southeastern

The *China Clipper* over San Francisco Bay. PAA.

edge of its six-mile diameter atoll. Surrounded by the teal waters of the central Pacific, it glistened in the late winter sun, a brief paradise on the vast expanse of ocean and time.

Dressed in khaki and almost hidden in the sand, Pan American Junior Pilot Sture Vivien Sigfred sat facing the lagoon between the two islands, knees drawn to his chest, elbows resting on his knees. His eyes, the steel-gray color of the morning sea, stared toward a seaplane moored in the lagoon and bobbing on the incoming tide. The *China Clipper* rested nose-high on her seawings; her aluminum hull shone brilliantly in the sun. Her four Pratt & Whitney engines were silent; her three-bladed propellers still. Her 130-foot wingspan darkened the sea around her, and she seemed to Sture to bask in the afternoon warmth, to doze in preparation for another journey across the sea.

Transfixed by the play of opposites that met in the Martin M-130 seaplane - sky touching sea, shadow caressing light, power greeting silence - Sture smiled and found himself thanking God, yet again, for blessing him with the realization of his dream. In a silent prayer in Swedish, the language of his ancestors, he thanked God for allowing him to be a pilot, for letting him explore and expand the boundaries of continents, oceans and time, and for granting him the taste of peace that land and air and sea brought to him.

To his right, as though conscious of his prayer, a gooney bird, white-breasted and hook-beaked, rose and prodded a chick beside her. The chick rose to its feet. Following its mother and tripping in the sand, the down-covered chick waddled on webbed feet to a dune several yards from the shore. Its mother already stood at the crest of the dune. Glancing back toward the chick as though to say, "follow me," the hen turned into the wind, spread her wings. She ran down the eastern face of the dune. Just before reaching level ground, she flapped her six-foot wings just once and lifted gracefully into the air. Catching a current of wind beneath her brown-feathered wings, the hen soared almost straight up into the sky, banked to the left and dove toward the lagoon's rippling surface. Then, as the surface of the water rushed up to greet her, she lifted the front edge of her wings to brake her descent and lowered her feet, front up, to the water. A white spray beside her and a wake from her feet behind, the hen pulled her wings against her body, softly fell into floating, and looked ashore where the chick now stood at the crest of the dune.

The chick, like its mother, turned into the wind, flapped its wings and waddled down the dune. Halfway down, it tripped and rolled to the bottom. In a flurry of flapping wings and blowing sand, the chick quickly uprighted itself and shook its head. As though dazed by the tumble, it glanced toward its mother, turned from the dune and hobbled a few feet away. Stopping in the shadow of a scrub, the chick dug a shallow hole in the sand and curled into the hole. Facing away from the shore, it lowered its head to the sand, beak almost touching the powdery coral, and closed it eyes.

As the chick drifted to sleep, Sture laughed and turned back toward the water. A metallic glint caught his gaze. Rising to get a better look, he waded into the foaming surf. The cool water lapped at his ankles as he bent down and lifted a small, round bulb from the water. Holding it to the sky and running his fingers across its smooth surface of translucent glass, he recognized the bulb as a float, one that natives of many of the Pacific islands used to weigh their fishing nets. He had noticed the natives many times, perspiration glowing on their bronze skin as they cast their heavy nets into the sea. He had watched as the nets filled with water and fish, and later relinquished the harvest that was the natives' sustenance, their livelihood, their life. The thick, woody fibers of the nets quickly absorbed water and gently sank into the sea, leaving visible only the multicolored floats glistening like gems on the ocean surface. Sture found the floats strangely beautiful, incongruous with the heaving muscles of the fishermen, the untamed power of the sea, and the dead weight of a prolific catch. It continually surprised him that the thin, fragile floats could survive the pounding surf and support the weight of the nets, that the floats could support generation after generation of island population. But that is what the world comes down to, he thought, strength in the most fragile artifact, complexity in the simplest creation.

Bleached mossy green by the sun and salt, the float weighed about a pound, fit easily in the palm of his hand, and formed an almost perfect sphere, hollow and watertight. Sture surveyed the horizon for its source but saw no fishing boats in the waning light. Knowing that Pan Am normally received its supplies from the mainland, he suspected that few of its station contingents were avid net fishermen. With a shrug, he concluded that the float must have made its way from one of the thousands of distant islands that dotted the Pacific, to rest like the gooney birds on this shore for a brief time before bobbing on the ancient currents to a more distant and isolated land. The thought that this fragile piece of glass could survive the storms and currents of the Pacific comforted him.

He glanced again toward his seaplane.

The setting sun cast a long shadow from her hull toward Eastern Island, and the pitch and pace of music from the hotel, hidden behind a wall of scrubs, reminded him of his professional duty to mingle with his passengers. He slipped the float into his pocket, bid good night to the *China Clipper*, and turned toward the west. As his steps kept beat with the music, he marveled at time and the evening sky, a palette of orange, plum and blue. At the International Date Line, only two degrees, thirty-seven minutes and fourteen seconds to the west, one hundred and twelve miles away, it was already another day. Already tomorrow: the day that when it caught him would mark his departure from Midway to Wake.

This evening, he thought, is still yesterday. He shook his head and stepped through the thicket onto the crisp, manicured grounds of the island hotel.

To the east, the *China Clipper* bobbed silently in the surf.

A single star appeared gradually in the violet sky.

Attack

1941 - 1942

On December 7, 1941, their enjoyable but uneventful vacation nearing its end, Sture and Mildred drove from Chicago to Minneapolis. On a rural Wisconsin road, Sture stopped to fill his station wagon with gas. When he entered the small white station to pay the attendant, a voice, clearly excited and insistent, crackled barely audibly from a radio in the corner.

Amid the interference and fading in and out of the voice, Sture made out words to the effect that the hangars at Hickham Field were burning. Picking the words Hickham Field out of the din, he thought he heard that battleships lay sinking in the harbor.

The station attendant ambled to the cash register and winked at Sture. "Some of these fellows, the way they announce a soap opera, they can almost make you think something terrible is really happening." He shook his head and reached for the volume dial on the radio.

"Wait," Sture said, more loudly than he expected. He caught his breath and spoke cautiously. "Something has happened. It's Sunday; there shouldn't be any soap operas on now. The announcer said Hickham Field. That's not in any soap opera I've heard of. I'm a pilot with Pan Am, and I was in Honolulu only four weeks ago. Can you turn it up?"

The attendant turned the volume up on the radio just as the announcer launched into another report.

"This is no test. This is no test," he repeated. "The Japanese have launched an unprovoked attack on military and civilian facilities in Pearl Harbor, on the island of Oahu in Hawaii. There is yet no count of personnel casualties, though the hangars at Hickham Field are burning and many of the battleships of the Pacific fleet lay stricken and sinking in the harbor."

As Sture stood with his money in his hand still poised above the counter, the attendant's face went pale. Then he calmly turned away from the counter and walked to the phone. As though a robot, he rang and waited for someone at the other end of the line to answer. All

Sture could do was stand at the counter and listen, his hand suspended as though disembodied from his arm.

Apparently remembering the sugar shortage that occurred during World War I, the attendant seemed somewhat agitated. "Rose," he said into the mouthpiece, "call Joe at the co-op and order 100 pounds of sugar."

The attendant paused, listening. The voice at the other end of the line spoke so loudly that even Sture could hear her across the room. At his distance, the voice sounded like the buzzing of an insect against his ear.

"Then turn the radio off and listen to me." The man spoke slowly and loudly into the phone.

After a moment, he spoke more quietly. "Don't ask questions, just call Joe at the co-op and order 100 pounds of sugar. I will be home soon." Without saying goodbye, he hung up the phone and stood facing the wall.

Sture cleared his throat. "Excuse me, I'd like to pay for the gas."

The man turned, a blank look on his face.

"I just got gas," Sture tilted his head toward the station wagon sitting under an awning in the driveway of the service station.

The attendant looked out the window. "Oh, yes. Sorry to keep you waiting. The last time we went to war, we couldn't get sugar until the damned thing was over. I hope this time we beat the rush."

The man's mention of the war shook Sture, and he realized that this could be the only reasonable course of action for his country. In an instant, the world had changed. The United States would surely go to war now. It had been coming for years, and now it was here. Suddenly, the Wisconsin country road seemed not nearly so peaceful, the countryside not nearly so safe.

The attendant walked slowly back to the counter and took the money from Sture's hand. Only then did Sture realize that his hand had been raised in the air for several minutes. Without paying attention, the man counted some change into Sture's palm. Sture too paid little attention. Then the man pushed the drawer of the cash register closed and looked toward the car outside.

"Not from here, huh? You have a nice trip. You have a safe trip; the roads are hell this time of year."

Sture nodded and walked into the brisk December morning. As he slid into the driver's seat of the car, he noticed that the attendant locked the door behind him and turned the sign on the glass to "Closed."

He started the car and pulled onto the highway. Only when he was several miles down the road did he tell Mildred what he had heard on the radio. She remained quiet and stared at the fields of snow slowly gliding past, their reflections like ghosts in the thick glass of her window.

When they returned from vacation, Sture heard the stories of that fateful morning. With a silent prayer of thanksgiving playing in the back of his mind and a nagging dissatisfaction that he had not been a part of the action, he listened to how Lanier Turner had safely landed the *Anzac Clipper*, en route to Pearl Harbor from San Francisco, in Hilo after learning of the Japanese attack. He marveled at the courage of Fred Ralph who lost his *Hong Kong Clipper* in the Japanese strafing of the British colony whose name the Clipper bore, and who with his crew escaped Hong Kong in the dead of night aboard a DC-2. He had picked his way across Asia and Europe before arriving in the United States in January of 1942. He was awestruck with the resourcefulness of Robert Ford who foraged halfway around the world, from Auckland, New Zealand to New York, in his *Pacific Clipper*. But none of the stories interested him more, moved or stirred him more than that of his beloved *Philippine Clipper*.

The captain of the *Philippine Clipper*, John Hamilton, departed Wake Island for Guam as scheduled on the morning of December 7, 1941. He had been in the air for only thirty minutes when the radio station at Wake ordered him back with the news that the Japanese had attacked Pearl Harbor. As he had been instructed to do, Hamilton ripped open the contingency orders that all planes had carried since relations between the United States and Japan had begun to degrade. The orders instructed him to return to the last point of takeoff and evacuate Pan Am personnel. He returned to Wake, landed on the lagoon and quickly conferred with the commanding officer of the Marine contingent on the island. The commander convinced Hamilton to lead a patrol of Marine fighters far enough away from the island that the patrol might find some Japanese warships. Hamilton agreed so long as he would be able to obtain sufficient fuel for a four-hour flight with the fighters and a return flight to Midway.

As Hamilton supervised the refueling, two formations of Japanese planes, appeared on the horizon. The *Philippine Clipper*, her fuel tanks completely filled, languished in the water as the planes flew overhead. Hamilton dove into a drainage culvert. One line of planes approached the Marine landing strip and the other headed straight to the Pan Am landing strip. Two gas dumps and the hotel were hit as the planes made three passes over the island. All Hamilton could do was lie in the ditch. When the drone of the planes finally faded in the distance, he emerged to an inferno. Strangely, however, the *Philippine Clipper* bobbed quietly on the lagoon.

Hamilton jumped aboard the clipper and performed a quick inspection. Though there were more than sixty holes in her fuselage, the plane appeared to be air worthy. He ordered his crew to strip the plane of all of its cargo and comforts and turned the mail over to the Marines. Three hours after the Japanese had launched their attack, he taxied the clipper with sixty passengers into the shallow and short lagoon. Grossly overloaded, the planed responded sluggishly to Hamilton's acceleration of all four engines. The plane failed to gain the sky on her first pass. Hamilton made a second attempt, and again the plane failed to take off. Desperate and frustrated, Hamilton made a third attempt. The plane gradually lifted from the water, leveled off barely above its surface and, finally, began to gain altitude. Hamilton pointed the plane toward Midway and prayed that the plane and fuel would last.

Hamilton remained twenty-five feet above the water as he flew toward Midway. Unfortunately, the Japanese had also attacked Midway. Her direction finder and radio station were destroyed. Hamilton, though he could not at the time know it, was truly flying blind. Because most of the island's facilities were afire, Hamilton was able to spot the island from several miles away. Making a pass over the island, he noted that the lagoon was littered with small craft and debris. Pulling the plane to the edge of the lagoon, he guided the plane to the water and taxied to the Pan Am barge. He tied up to it, and ordered his plane refueled. Within an hour and a half, he and his passengers were back in the air, heading toward Hawaii.

After several hours, Hamilton spotted Oahu and transmitted his request for landing instructions. To his surprise, he was directed to land at Pearl Harbor. The Pan Am side of the harbor had been untouched by the Japanese attack, and on the morning of December 8,

1941, Hamilton landed and taxied to the Pan Am pier. Two days later, after a much needed rest - he had been on duty for over thirty-six hours - Hamilton flew the *Philippine Clipper* back to Alameda. The plane was shortly transferred to military service, as was most of Pan Am's fleet, but the *Philippine Clipper* alone would wear a stripe for the fire she had taken at Wake.

On the day following the bombing of Pearl Harbor, as Sture readied for his return to San Francisco, the United States declared war on the Axis powers. They, in turn, declared war on the United States. The celebrations that had once accompanied each takeoff of a Clipper Ship from San Francisco for Honolulu gave way to secrecy and silence. No longer were scheduled flights announced in newspapers and on the radio. The crew no longer marched as a group to the plane. Instead, they drifted one at a time and in civilian clothes to the dock. No longer did Pan Am's emblem glitter in the northern California sun. Not surprisingly, Pan Am quickly cancelled all passenger flights to the Orient. All that filled the hulls of the Clippers were mail and military supplies. And, as though inevitable, as their mission gradually became nothing more than military support flights, Pan Am's planes were officially appropriated for the military, with most of the seaplanes in San Francisco and Hawaii going to the Navy.

As the planes were reassigned to wartime duty, so were their crews. Gone were the luxuries within the planes and the leisure to which the crews had grown accustomed. Sture made no more trips to the Orient, now besieged by a skillful and ferocious enemy. Instead, he flew frequent hops between San Francisco and Honolulu and quickly completed his training. In June of 1942, he was transferred back to the Eastern Division of Pan Am in Miami, where he would soon serve with the Air Transport Command.

Between his first transpacific crossing in November of 1937 and his transfer from San Francisco, Sture had flown more than twenty-five crossings of the Pacific between San Francisco and Manila or San Francisco and Aukland. He had also flown seventeen shuttle flights between San Francisco or Los Angeles and Honolulu. He had flown all three of the Martin M-130 Clippers: the *Hawaii Clipper (NC-14714)*, the *Philippine Clipper (NC-14715)*, and the *China Clipper (NC-14716)*, and six of the twelve Boeing B-314 Clippers assigned to the Pacific Division: the *Honolulu Clipper (NC-18601)*, the

279

Boeing B-314 *Dixie Clipper*. PAA.

California Clipper (NC-18602), the *American Clipper (NC-18606)*, the *Pacific Clipper (NC-18609)*, the *Anzac Clipper(NC-18611)* and the *Capetown Clipper (NC-18612)*. Between his arrival in San Francisco and his departure to Miami, he collected 1090 hours and five minutes of flight time, and flew on 565 of his 1417 days assigned to the Division. In that time, he was forced to land or to turn in mid-flight ten times because of bad weather and nine times for engine trouble. His luck – and he was keenly aware that it was just that - had been and would continue to be better than most others'.

Though he had been fond of the Boeing B-314, his favorite seaplane remained the Martin M-130. He had known and trusted the planes as friends, and in July of 1940, he mourned the loss of the *Hawaii Clipper* just as deeply as he mourned the loss of her Captain Leo Terletzky and her crew. By the end of the war, he would also mourn the loss of the last two M-130's.

On the morning of January 21, 1943, the *Philippine Clipper*, the ship on which he had spent more hours than any other and with which he had grown so familiar, crashed into a mountain near the Russian River, a few miles west of Ukiah, California. Lost 100 miles north of San Francisco with all onboard, including Rear Admiral R.R. English, commander of the Pacific submarine force and his staff, the

Philippine Clipper was presumed to have crashed when her pilot, Captain Robert Elzay, descended from a thick ceiling at 900 feet for what should have been a visual approach to the Pan Am air base. Because the plane was so far off course, his descent proved disastrous.

The *China Clipper* was lost in a nighttime crash while trying to land at Port of Spain in Trinidad on January 8, 1945. The ship was on a normal, nighttime approach - always a difficult and often a dangerous undertaking - with an airspeed of one hundred knots. Flares lit her landing path when she tore into the black water and was ripped apart. With nine of her twelve crewmembers and fourteen of her eighteen passengers dead, she sank in thirty feet of water, the last of the great Martin Flying Boats.

Yet these losses remained in the future as the summer of 1942 spread in a glaring haze across the country. As the war quickly overheated in the semi-tropical waters of the Pacific, and cities up and down both coasts blacked themselves against the night to hide from enemy submarines, Sture placed his new wife and all of their belonging into his station wagon and began the long trek to the east.

The Boeing B-314 *California Clipper*. PAA.

In Command

1942-1945

In June of 1942, Mildred and Sture began the drive back to Miami. Mildred, six months pregnant, divided her time in the station wagon between the vinyl front seat that stuck to her skin on hot afternoons, and a soft bed that Sture had made in the back of the car. For five days, they pushed across the country, making 700 miles a day, Sture bending low in the mornings over the steering wheel, squinting into the sun, or chasing in the evenings the shadow that stretched for miles before them across the flatlands of the southwest, at once leading and beckoning them east.

As though mutually conspiring to protect the other, they refused to speak of the worry for their safety that had punctuated their days since the previous December. Before they left San Francisco, rumors had circulated throughout the Bay area that Japanese submarines skirted the California coast. No sooner had they begun their trek to Miami than rumors surfaced of German submarines within sight of major cities up and down the east coast. Having just left a city blackened at night against an inimical sky, they trudged toward another that was also forced to extinguish its lights under a sky of peering and probing stars. For the first time in as long as they could remember, darkness was safety, and light was danger. When the Japanese descended upon the small, green islands of the Pacific, islands that Sture had once explored with childlike eyes and innocence, their world turned suddenly inside out. And as they drove through the still, cool nights of early summer, they wondered if somewhere above, like a cloud of gas rolling across the horizon, an unseen enemy lurked, tracking the lights of their car that stole across the plains.

Perhaps to forget or to deny for a time the threat that followed and lay before them, Mildred pointed out the changing flora as they drove east, vegetation that became more green and dense as they left the windblown west and forged their way toward the Mississippi River. During their days, Mildred thumbed through the most recent *Time* magazine and shared its stories with Sture, who nodded silently, as though only half-aware of her words. Yet within his preoccupation, he heard each syllable, as though an incantation, but avoided looking too closely at his young wife. He worried that his fears might become palpable in the close quarters and stifling heat of the station wagon. He worried that the palpability of his fear might prove contagious, worried that the woman whose ankles swelled as the day progressed, whose belly grew sore from a kicking child might herself worry all the more. He listened silently to news he already knew and stared at the dashes of white lines evenly splitting his view.

In the evenings, Mildred counted the license plates of cars they passed in countless numbers across the south, while Sture searched for the black and whites signs of merging and diverging highways that marked his progress. Each wore a smile of preoccupation, trying to hide from the other an insidious fear. Miles of highway passed below the tires of their station wagon in a dull hum, lulling them into the belief that when the baby arrived, when the war was over, when they settled in Miami, everything would return to normal. Yet they also realized that change was the nature of normalcy. As the country clicked past their windows like the frames of a silent motion picture, they wondered what would come next.

Sikorsky S-43, Sture's first command and the last flying boat he would fly. 1942.
Sigfred collection.

After settling his wife comfortably into their new home in Miami, Sture characteristically threw himself back into work. On June 27, he checked out as captain on the S-43 flying boat and finally achieved his long awaited dream of becoming a Master Pilot. Though not unnoticed, the day passed quietly, and only a single line of neatly blocked letters appeared in his log: "check for solo." On July 31, he began training on the DC-3, the first commercial land plane he flew.

And on August 8, the day before his first child, Joanna, was born, he completed his check out on the plane. During July, he flew a total of 107 hours, including his checkout on the S-43, his training on the DC-3, and his first flight as captain of a flying boat.

When it finally arrived on July 23, 1942, Sture was emotionally and physically primed for his first flight as the Captain of his own seaplane, a Sikorsky S-43. With eighteen seats and a cruising speed of 165 mph, the S-43 was an amphibian, a scaled down version of her larger sister, the S-42. She was used throughout the Caribbean where passenger loads seldom justified the use of the larger S-42, and Sture was as comfortable with the smaller plane as he was with the larger. His trip was expected to last six days, with several stops in various locations each day. On the first day, he was scheduled to depart from Miami and to stop in Antilla, Port au Prince, Haiti, and San Juan, Puerto Rico. On the second day, his plane would leave San Juan and return to Port au Prince before continuing on to Santiago, Cuba. From Santiago, he would fly to Kingston, Jamaica, back to Santiago, to Port au Prince and, once again, back to Santiago for an overnight stay. On the third day, he would again depart Santiago and fly to Port au Prince, before returning to Santiago and continuing on to San Juan. One the fourth day, after leaving San Juan, his plane would make stops in St. Thomas and St. John in the Virgin Islands, Guadeloupe in the French West Indies, Fort de France on Martinique in the Windwards, and Port au Spain in Trinidad. On the fifth day, the flight would progress to Georgetown, British Guyana, before returning to Port au Spain, Martinique, Guadeloupe and St. John. Finally on the sixth day, the plane would leave St. John and fly to St. Thomas, San Juan, Port au Prince, Antilla and, finally, back to Miami.

As expected, the trip lasted six days, though it did not pass as painlessly as Sture had hoped for his "Baby Clipper." The flight progressed smoothly, as Sture had expected, up to the fourth day of hops between the islands. As Sture landed at Guadeloupe to deliver his cargo of airmail, however, a heavy rain began to fall and heavy ground swells pummeled the small seaplane. The bobbing of the plane on the swells made it difficult to pick up the float line and pull the plane to the barge from which Pan Am operated. Because he was required only to drop off the mail and needed no fuel, Sture anticipated a very short stop on the island, but as he taxied away from the island and out into open water to gain his takeoff position, a heavy

Havana, Cuba from the air, 1942. Sigfred collection.

squall approached from the northeast. Hoping to be airborne before the storm and its zero visibility hit, he opened his throttle fully. After taking two large waves over the bow, the S-43 shuddered before she slowly gained speed. Almost groaning with the effort, her engines had almost lifted the plane onto the step when a man ran, screaming wildly, from the passenger cabin and threw his arms around Sture's neck.

By reflex, Sture jerked back on the throttle. One of the stewards ran into the cockpit and grabbed the screaming man. By the time Sture had throttled the engines back, the steward had pinned the distraught passenger to the deck. As the plane weather-vaned in the wind, Sture noticed that the passenger was soaking wet. He asked the steward if the man had fallen overboard.

Inactive volcano in the Caribbean, 1942. Sigfred collection.

"No," the steward answered. "He is just scared and in a bad sweat and screaming to get off."

285

By this time, rain had enveloped the plane, and the crew experienced difficulty tying up to the barge. Sture directed the radio officer to send a message to Miami that the plane was returning to the float to unload the problem passenger. Shortly, headquarters replied to the message and advised that no one be allowed to leave the plane, not even the captain. Guadeloupe, the message explained, was a Vichy French possession, and the legalities of an unplanned debarkation of passengers were too numerous to detail. The message suggested that Sture try to reach the next large island where the passenger could be more easily unloaded. Though it would result in a significant delay while he was cleared through security, the action offered fewer problems than leaving the passenger in Guadeloupe. Sture complied with the company's directions.

The Pan Am agent in Martinique, the next planned stop, proved to be quite a diplomat. After receiving a radio message from Pan Am's facilities in Miami, he quickly succeeded in persuading the local officials to allow all of the passengers and crew to disembark from the bobbing seaplane onto a more stable barge.

So Sture transported his passengers and crew to Martinique, dashing off a radio message to Miami en transit detailing the status of the trouble he had encountered with the passenger. Then, in a more personal note, he noted that this was his first trip as Captain and that his wife was alone in Miami, expecting a child. "If this message gets through all of these islands," he added, "please call Victoria Hospital in Miami and see if my firstborn has arrived."

When the plane finally arrived in Martinique, conditions had drastically changed. The rains had abated, and the passenger had calmed down enough to decide that he could remain aboard all the way to Trinidad. He apologized profusely to passengers and crew for the delay he had caused, then settled himself quietly into his seat for the gentle and uneventful flight to Trinidad.

Sture's first flight as a Captain was also his last flight on a seaplane. Technological advances, wartime realities, and the net of landing strips Pan Am had carved for the Air Corps throughout Central and South America, Africa, the Indian subcontinent, and the Far East had rendered the land plane increasingly important and the seaplane increasingly obsolete. Though only their absence at the end of the war would make him realize it, Sture's beloved seaplanes were quickly becoming just a footnote in the history of World War II.

Miami's 36th street airport for land planes. Early 1940s. PAA.

Exactly a week before Sture checked out as the Captain of the S-43 and qualified as a Master Pilot, General Henry H. Arnold, Chief of Staff of the Army Air Forces officially established the Air Transport Command. Since the summer of 1941, Pan Am had been taxiing U.S. built airplanes from Miami to British forces in Khartoum, Sudan, as part of the lend lease program. Shortly after the Japanese bombed Pearl Harbor and the U.S. entered the war, the route had been extended to Cairo, Egypt, and Teheran, Iran, and Eastern Airlines began in May of 1942 to assist Pan Am's efforts. In February of 1942, Northwest Airlines had begun similar services to Alaska, supported by Western and United Airlines. During late 1941 and early 1942, thousands of contracts were awarded to various airlines by all of the military branches to support logistical operations, and quickly the programs became almost unmanageable. As a result, L.W. Pogue, Chairman of the Civil Aeronautics Board, suggested that all military support operations be united under a single command. General Arnold's formation of the ATC, though an operational formality, militarized essentially all of the civilian airlines in the United States and tasked the command with three primary duties: to ferry all aircraft within the U.S. and to destinations outside the U.S. as ordered by the

Commanding General of the Army Air Forces, to provide air transport of mail, material and personnel for all but a few specific War Department agencies, and to control, operate and maintain support facilities on air routes outside the U.S. under the control of the Commanding General of the Army Air Forces.

Air Transport Command pilots, 1942. Sture stands in the back row, second from left. Sigfred collection.

Though many of the pilots with the ATC remained in the employ of their civilian airlines, the airlines were in turn under contract to the ATC. The effect was that they became *de facto* military pilots, wearing military uniforms and enjoying most of the responsibilities and privileges of commissioned military officers. Their service also exempted them from the draft, though as the war dragged on, many would find themselves subjected to the same dangers experienced by their military counterparts, including taking enemy fire. While most of the missions Sture flew with Pan Am's Eastern Division after June of 1942 were military support operations, civilian travel having all but dried up after the U.S. entry into the war, he was officially transferred to the Africa-Orient Division in May of 1943 where all of his flying directly supported military operations.

On August 9, 1942, the day after successfully checking out as a captain on the DC-3, Sture was again in the cockpit. This time, his flight was uneventful except for a short message he received while in the air, a message he documented in his flight log with a one-word note: "Girl." Sture had taken Mildred, already overdue, to the hospital the day before to deliver the baby. Her doctor had been patient as the days beyond Mildred's due date dragged into weeks, but he finally insisted that they induce labor so that his joining the Army would be delayed no longer. The war could hardly wait on a reticent child. As most fathers in the early 1940s were expected to do, Sture had gone to work to await word that he was a father. When he finally touched down on the tarmac in

Sture with Joey, Miami, 1943.
Sigfred collection.

Miami, after what seemed the longest flight of his career, he rushed to the hospital, the proud father of his baby daughter Joanna Kathleen Sigfred, named after her maternal grandparents Joseph and Anna Krastel.

Neither Sture nor Mildred in the months preceding Joanna's birth had told Mildred's mother Anna that Mildred was pregnant. Mildred's brother Will was preparing to go overseas with the Army, and his wife Helen had delivered Anna's first grandchild only two weeks before. Both Sture and Mildred felt that Anna had enough to worry about with a newborn grandson to care for and a son about to fight a war. Rather than add to her concerns, they decided to keep Mildred's pregnancy a secret.

But on the morning of Sunday, August 10, with the baby kicking and screaming behind the thick glass of the Victoria Hospital nursery, it was clear that the time had come to tell her. There was no longer any need for secrecy. For years, Mildred and Sture had only half jokingly told Anna about Sture's penchant for sharing a bottle of Four Roses whiskey with a friend and writing silly poetry late into the night. If she were to receive a silly poem through Western Union, they had told her more than once, she should simply disregard the message as one of Sture's less sober ventures into the literary arts. Surprisingly, when Western Union phoned on Sunday morning and read her a barely decipherable poem, she politely thanked them and hung up. When her husband Joseph asked who had called, she responded that it had simply been Western Union with one of Sture's silly poems, something about dolls and taxes and a mother doing nicely. Yet even as she recited the nonsensical contents of the message, she began to wonder if, in fact, it had not been a hoax. She looked at her husband and, arching an eyebrow, stated matter-of-factly: "Something's up in Miami."

She went back to the phone and had the operator ring Western Union. When the clerk answered, she asked him to repeat the message she had been read only minutes before. He willingly responded.

"She'll play with ribbons and dolls of wax.

"She'll help us lower the income tax.

"She tipped the scale at nine precisely.

"Mother and daughter are doing nicely."

Barely stopping to acknowledge the message, she hung up the telephone and called to her husband, "Joseph, Mildred's had a baby."

Mildred remained in the hospital from August 8 until August 22, with Sture at her side every evening, recounting the journeys of his day. On August 23, 1942, with his wife and daughter safely at home, Sture left Miami on his first flight as the Captain of a DC-3. Prior to this flight, he had performed various daytime checkout flights between Miami and Nassau, Miami and Havana, and Miami and Merida. After the 23rd, however, he made the flights as a captain. From August 23 until September 22, he served as the pilot on the regularly scheduled island jaunts, dutifully reporting to work each day and equally dutifully reporting home in the evenings to care for his wife and young daughter.

His weeks of flying the DC-3 convinced Sture of what many in the aviation industry had known for several years. It was one of the best-designed and manufactured airplanes in the short but intense history of aviation. With a takeoff weight of 24,400 pounds, a length of sixty-four feet, a height of seventeen feet, and a wingspan of ninety-five feet, the plane was one of the largest in the world. But the plane's two Pratt & Whitney Double Wasp engines could propel her at 180 mph for a range of 1000 miles. She was the first plane to prove without question that commercial passenger service could be economically viable, without subsidies or large airmail contracts. She was also the plane that opened up the half of the world Sture had not already seen.

His journey started on familiar territory. On September 25, 1942, after an absence of five years, he flew his DC-3 into Brazil and was overcome with the same emotions he had experienced when he returned to Parkers Prairie on leave from the Navy during the Christmas holidays of 1919. A bittersweet sense of loss accompanied the exhilaration of familiarity as he flew low over the lush jungles and forests of the eternally green landscape. The feeling grew more intense when he ventured into the cities that had been so familiar to him before he went to California. But especially at the Grande Hotel in Belem, where it seemed that scores of people he had previously known poured into the lobby to greet him, he felt the haunting presence of time.

The old waiters who had worked in the hotel before he left in July of 1937 were not only still working at the hotel, they were also enthusiastic in welcoming back the man who seemed their long lost friend. One of the waiters in particular, whom the pilots had dubbed Tom Mix because he resembled the actor, used to keep tabs on the pilots and their card games at the slate-topped tables of the game room. When Sture returned to the tables, as when any other pilot returned, the waiter reminisced long and loudly about the good old days less than a decade before. His memory proved remarkable to all of the pilots, especially so in the morning hours when he shared details of the pilots' pasts that many of the men had forgotten and preferred not to remember. Like the other pilots, Sture was impressed with Tom Mix's memory, but he knew it could never rival the memory of his old friend Brooklyn, the shoeshine man who had been born in Brooklyn but moved to Brazil when he was still a child.

Douglas DC-3, among the planes Sture flew in the Air Transport
Command. Sigfred collection.

Though Sture remembered the shoeshine man from his previous
years in Brazil, he did not run into him until 1943, after Pan Am had
been officially contracted by the Army for the war effort and become
part of the Air Transport Command. Instead of the blue serge
uniforms from their Pan Am incarnation, the pilots wore khaki, and
rather than staying at the Grande Hotel in Belem - a security risk at
the height of the war, even in Brazil - they stayed at the Staff House,
about a half mile away from the hotel. Late one evening, Sture sat
with several of the pilots on a long bench outside the Staff House.
They were speaking quietly and enjoying the cool breeze when they
heard the tapping of a cane against the sidewalk. Glancing lazily
toward the tapping, one of the pilots said: "There's Brooklyn, the
blind shoeshine boy."

Sture, too, glanced toward the sound and recognized his friend
from 1937, but rather than speak to him, he remained silent, struck by
the changes that only seven years had made. Though he had also been
a shoeshine boy in 1937, Brooklyn had been blind in only one eye.
Now, as evidenced by the palsied motion of his cane against the
ground, confident but seemingly unfamiliar, he was totally blind.
With painstaking effort and forced cheerfulness, he walked until he

stood directly in front of the gathered pilots. Pointing his face in the direction of each of their faces, he launched into the routine that had long ago become a ritual both for the pilots and for Brooklyn. He politely asked the color of their shoes. When they answered, he held up a box of wax from his bag of supplies and, smiling, asked the pilot in question the color of the wax he held. When the colors matched, as it seemed to Sture they always did, he lowered himself to his knees and set about polishing the shoes as though he could still see.

Dinner Key, 1942. Sigfred collection.

The routine seldom varied, and each of the pilots respected its sanctity, speaking softly and respectfully to the blind man bent double before him. On the evening that Brooklyn appeared before Sture, the ritual continued as always before, and when Brooklyn got to Sture's position, as he had with each previous pilot, he asked Sture what color his shoes were.

"They are brown, Brooklyn," Sture answered.

With recognition gleaming in his sightless eyes, Brooklyn jumped to his feet and cried, "Mr. Sigfred, I have not heard your voice since October of 1937."

"No, Brooklyn," Sture answered. "It was September 1937. But you were close."

His eyes fully open and his hands grasping Sture's, Brooklyn seemed to stare with wonder into the pilot's face. "I still remember," he said, "what you looked like. You were quite thin with light hair."

Dinner Key from the air, 1943. PAA.

"And so I am still," Sture answered, not mentioning that his hair was now somewhat thinner. He pulled Brooklyn to the bench beside him, and the two spoke quietly and happily for several minutes. Talking to Brooklyn again brought back to Sture the sweet days from so many years before, before NYRBA had been smothered by Pan Am, before Pan Am had grown into the largest international airline in the world. Before war had once again split the world in two. Only when the two had finished their conversation, only when the shoeshine man had packed his horsehair brushes and chamois cloths neatly into his bag and hoisted it over his shoulder, only when he had walked slowly away, the sound of his tapping cane fading with his image into the Brazilian night, did Sture finally appreciate just how much the world had changed.

Yet even as it changed, Sture was reminded every day of how much it remained the same. Late in the summer of 1942 during which most of the male journalists who had not become soldiers covered the European and Pacific theatres of war, women journalists flew individually and in small groups down the west coast of South America, across the Andes and up the east coast to Rio to finish their sojourn at Belem. As a decade before a generation of male journalists had swaggered about the bars of Belem, so too did the women spend much of their time at the bar of the Grande Hotel. There they learned the real geography of the world, the real sociology of people clinging day in and day out to an earth that provided plenty, but only to the hardest working. Over shots of whiskey and an occasional glass of wine, they were force-fed many of the lessons they should have studied and mastered in grade school, and like children, they relished those lessons, never sated, always asking for more. Though some held Ph.D.s in geography, and others were internationally known writers, many had not known before their arrival in South America that Santiago, Chile and the west coast of South America were east of New York City, or that the mouth of the Amazon River is actually 200 miles wide.

They discovered a wealth of information in the bright and lively bar of the Grande Hotel, and produced dozens of articles about the exotic places in which the aviation pioneers lived and to which they traveled. As often as not, without interviewing their subjects or leaving the cool, dimness of the bar, they created a mythology that the pilots themselves encouraged with their stories and their silences. They wrote of a breed separate and above the rest, heroic in their exploits and patriotism. Flipping silently through the magazines that bore the by-lines of the women with whom they had shared drinks and dreams, the pilots smiled knowingly to themselves, willing to admit that they were, in fact, only human, but just as willing to believe that they were also heroes, still unsure they could be both at once.

On September 4, 1942, under the cover of darkness, Sture guided his DC-3 into Miami with a full load of allied seamen from a merchant steamer that had been torpedoed and sunk off the coast of Cuba. A strong wind howled from the southwest as he guided the plane toward the airfield. Beside him, Tony Rush, the check pilot, watched his every move, certifying Sture for flying the DC-3 at night. With Tony's eyes darting alternately between the instrument panel and Sture's face, Sture surveyed his indications, peered through the cockpit window into the void before him and opted to land on the short northwest runway. The control tower radioed the current barometric pressure for his altimeter setting, and Sture leaned forward to dial in the newly reported pressure. He then verified that he had permission to land on the northwest runway and aligned the plane for his descent to the field.

C-47, military equivalent of the DC-3. Sigfred collection.

As he gradually decreased his altitude and neared the airfield, he almost unconsciously shifted from instrument flying to visual flying while Tony continued to scan the wall of instruments before him. With only an occasional glance across his panel, Sture aligned the plane with the runway and throttled back his engines. As he verified his level and stable approach, Tony suddenly grabbed the wheel and pulled it back, trying to force the plane into a climb. For a split second, Sture thought Tony was playing games with him, trying to see what his reaction would be, but one glance at Tony's face told him that the man was deadly serious and desperately wanted the airplane to climb. For several tense seconds, Tony and Sture fought for control of the aircraft as it rose and dove in darkness over the landing field. Finally Sture had his way.

He eased the plane onto the runway, but when his landing gear touched earth, it became clear that the plane was traveling too fast and would overshoot the runway into the turn area. As he had been trained to do, he applied hard left rudder and forced the plane into a spin across the runway. Fighting to keep the plane under control, he guided it to a complete stop and leaned back in his chair, exhausted and sweating profusely. Though his first concern was for the twenty-one shipwrecked sailors who had experienced their second life-threatening adventure in as many days, he could not ignore his anger.

Fighting for self-control, he turned to Tony. For several minutes, the two simply stared at each other. Then Tony blinked and burst into a belly laugh that shook the cockpit. Wiping tears from his eyes, he pointed to the instrument panel and explained to Sture what had happened.

"It just dawned on me that it is 7:00 PM. Zero hours Greenwich Mean Time. The code has changed, hasn't it? When the tower gave you the altimeter pressure, it was in the new code, but you dialed it in under the old code. When I saw our altitude dip below sea level, I panicked. That's why I took the controls."

Looking at the check pilot, Sture shook his head and exhaled loudly. Without speaking, he realized that Tony was right and chalked up a new lesson to experience. Don't change the code in the middle of a maneuver. He replayed the landing in his mind and silently thanked God that he had been approaching the runway visually. Had he too been monitoring the instrument panel, the result would almost certainly have been the death of his twenty-one passengers and himself.

He unbuckled the belt across his hips, and heard behind him the sailors filing quietly but quickly from the plane. Though he could not be sure, he thought he saw one of the sailors dropping to his knees and kissing the ground.

I Needed Your Hands Too

1943 - 1944

On the morning of November 12, 1943, Sture received a call from a Pan Am official in Miami, instructing him that he had received orders for a secret mission. He was advised to pack warm clothes and to report for his assignment to Washington D.C. where he would receive more detailed instructions. The assignment, he was promised, would be a lengthy mission.

Sture in his ATC uniform, 1943.
Sigfred collection.

As ordered, Sture flew to Washington that afternoon. When he landed, he received specific instructions on where to park the plane and was ordered to allow no one to disembark. He was then told to open the cabin hatch and to wait as stairs were pushed up from outside. When the stairs were rolled into place, he was again cautioned that no one should leave the plane. A Lieutenant Colonel in a Jeep stopped at the foot of the stairs and requested that Captain Sigfred come down and identify himself. Sture did as he was directed and showed the colonel both his pilot's license and his driver's license. Captain McGlohn, Sture's copilot for the flight from Miami to Washington, was also ordered to disembark, to identify himself, and to identify Sture. When the Colonel seemed satisfied that he had the right men, he asked McGlohn and Sture to board the jeep while he assigned a special escort to the rest of Sture's crew. The Colonel then drove the two pilots a short distance from the airstrip to a small building, isolated in the center of a large field and surrounded by brush.

Before speaking, the Colonel led the two pilots from the Jeep and into a small room approximately twelve feet square with no windows. As the Colonel shut and locked the door behind him, Sture surveyed the briefing room, surprised that it was so sparsely furnished. The room took up the entire building in which they stood, and the only furniture it contained were several chairs arranged haphazardly across the floor. Maps covered all four walls. Without offering either of the men a chair or asking for their comments, the Colonel began to relay Sture's orders. He spoke for several minutes without stopping, not once saying aloud Sture's destination. Familiar with the rules of security, Sture was not surprised at his silence. Finally, the colonel paused and pointed to one of the maps on the wall. "You are going here."

Sture followed an imaginary line from the tip of the Colonel's finger to the map of northern Africa hanging on the wall. Cairo, Egypt, was his destination. The Colonel then produced an envelope containing Sture's Secret orders and handed them to him, explaining that the details of his route were enclosed. Sture quickly opened the envelope and removed its contents: a single copy of the orders. No orders were presented to McGlohn. The officer, visibly more relaxed after briefing Sture on his orders, explained that the mission would commence the following Sunday. Its immediate destination was West Palm Beach, Florida.

Sture glanced again at the orders in his hand. They appeared no different from countless others he had received in the past, but for some reason unknown to or unexplained by the officer in front of him, this mission seemed somehow different. As the officer paused, Sture reread his orders from the Headquarters of the Air Transport Command in Washington, D.C.

Operations Authorization No, 25

Sture V. Sigfred - Pan American Civilian

You will proceed with aircraft C-54v (PAA) No. 138 from Washington D.C. to Morrison Field, West Palm Beach, Florida, remaining over night at Morrison Field, thence via the Caribbean Wing to Atkinson Field, British Guyana, departing the second day via the Caribbean Wing and South Atlantic Wing to Natal, departing the third day from Natal via the South Atlantic Wing and Africa Middle East Wing to Ascension Island and Accra, departing the fourth day from Accra to Maiduguri and Khartoum, departing the fifth day for Cairo, to arrive at Cairo by November 20 where further instructions will be received. You are authorized to proceed from that point to any point so directed by the passengers or the designated officer so charged with this responsibility. The return flight will be via the South Atlantic Wing to Miami or Washington on regular schedule. Armed guards will be provided for aircraft while on ground.

Substantial variation from the above itinerary is authorized if directed by the person or persons so designated. Aircraft will at all times operate according to ATC operational procedures in effect in each Wing through which this aircraft passes. Cargo or passengers aboard this aircraft will not be removed or adjusted prior to their destination.

The pilot will report daily the position of the aircraft to the Commanding General, Air Transport Command, Washington, D.C. by priority cable.

The orders were signed by Lieutenant Colonel James C. Flynn, Jr. the Acting Assistant Chief of Staff for Operations of the ATC, by order of the Commanding General.

"It's not necessary for me to emphasize," the Colonel added, "the secrecy of the mission you and other ships from different parts of the world will carry out." He closed the file from which he had briefed Sture. The snap of the pages against each other was the only sound in the room. "Be sure to see that your navigator has the proper maps every day before departure. At every airport along your route, access to the area where your plane is secured will be restricted, and tight security will be enforced. Only when you reach this body of water," he said, pointing to the Nile River, "can you advise the rest of your crew of your destination.

"Now," he said, "are there any questions?"

Sture read the orders a final time before shaking his head and telling the Colonel that he understood his mission. Then he informed the Colonel that his wife's family lived near Baltimore and asked if the Colonel would object to his spending some time with them.

The officer thought for a moment before telling Sture that it would be acceptable for him to visit. "You will probably be asked for information by your crew, so visiting Baltimore will be a plus for you. It will keep you away from them for as long as possible. I must remind you that all of this information must be closely guarded, even from your crew. I apologize for that. I never liked to keep secrets from my men, and I'm sure you don't either. But I assure you, it is for reasons that could have a profound effect on our national security and the war that we must keep the lid on this."

Sture nodded, and without further conversation, the Colonel opened the door to the room. The three men exited without a word. Sture explained to his crew that they would stay in Washington for a couple of days and ensured that each man had appropriate accommodations. Then, without discussing his orders with McGlohn or mentioning their mission to his crew, he left for Baltimore.

Mildred's mother Anna Krastel, right, with her youngest daughter Dorothy. Approximately 1956. Sigfred collection.

Sture visited with the Krastels for two days, and on Saturday evening, November 13, returned to Washington. As his orders specified, he departed for West Palm Beach about 1:00 PM on Sunday. He had approximately twenty passengers on board for the flight to Florida, though Captain McGlohn remained in Washington. A Navy Captain who had been one of his passengers only a week before was the only person Sture recognized. Glancing across the plane and recognizing Sture from the previous flight, the Captain smiled and remarked that the only two long flights he had ever taken were with Sture. "I hope to make many more."

The Cairo Conference, as it would later be called, was Sture's destination. Preceding the Malta Conference, the dessert summit proved just as important to history as its follower, for it was here, without Stalin, that Franklin Roosevelt and Winston Churchill

TO EVERY NOBLE ARAB

Greetings and peace of Allah be upon you. The bearer of this letter is an
officer of the United States of America, assisting the British Government and a
faithful friend to all Arab Nations. We beg of you to treat him well, guard his
life from every harm and supply his needs of food and drinks, and guide him to the
nearest British encampment. You will be rewarded generously in money for all your
services. Peace and mercy of Allah be upon you.

By a permit of the British High Command of the East.

USEFUL WORDS

English	Arabic		English	Arabic
American	Amrika-ni		Water	Moyah
American Flying Officer	Za-bit Amrika-ni Tyo-yar		Food	A'-kl
Friend	Sa-hib, Sa-deek		Sick	Ma-reed

Take me to the English and you will be rewarded.
Khud-nee eind el-Ingleez, Ta-khud mu-ka-fa-a.

Front and back of card Allied pilots were required to carry with them when
flying in Arab countries. 1943. Sigfred collection.

determined plans that would change the course of the war and the face
of an emerging Europe. It marked the beginning of the concerted
Allied strategy that would ultimately result in victory, and every
aspect of the conference was shrouded in secrecy.

The route was one with which Sture had already become familiar.
On June 15, 1943, he had made his first transatlantic crossing over the
"hump" between Natal on Brazil's eastern coast, Ascension Island
approximately midway between the South American and African
coasts, and Accra, the capital of the Gold Coast in Africa. On July 29,
1943 he made the complete, nonstop jump between Natal and Dakar,
a former French dependency occupied by the Allies in 1942, on the
extreme western coast of Africa.

The route for the flight to Cairo, while it would take him to places he had not been before, would largely track routes he had already flown. On Sunday, November 14, 1943, he landed at Borinquen field in Puerto Rico, a pre-war installation under the jurisdiction of the Antilles Department, Caribbean Defense Command. The hub of air operations in the Caribbean, the field offered bulk supplies of 100-octane fuel, extensive overnight accommodations, and a hospital. The field was a half-mile inland from the coast, with its buildings camouflaged on the ocean side.

On November 15, he departed for Atkinson Field. Also a part of the Caribbean Defense Command, the field was located approximately twenty-two miles south of Georgetown in British Guiana, on the Demerara River. The base was located only a mile away from a seaplane base previously used by NYRBA.

After staying the night at Atkinson, the flight departed on Tuesday morning for Natal, bypassing Belem where it would have been forced to land for refueling in previous years on less efficient planes. The airbase in Natal was larger than LaGuardia Field in New York and built in less than twelve months. Near many of Brazil's largest cities and on the extreme eastern coast of South America, the base was the envy of Hitler's Air Force. It was also one of the most highly fortified and defended allied bases. Only weeks before Sture's arrival, while on his way to the Cairo Conference, had the name of the base, Parnamirim, been published in an American newspaper.

On November 17, the flight departed Natal for Ascension Island in the Atlantic. A small island, it bore an importance far greater than its size. It was high on the secret list of U.S. military installations, and any pilot who did not demonstrate complete familiarity with its landing procedures could expect to immediately draw fire. While many flights crossed regularly between Natal and Dakar, Ascension was a required refueling stop for those on the longer Natal to Accra route. It was a stop for all fighter planes en route to the war zone and the hub of South Atlantic anti-submarine operations. Wideawake Field, named for the wideawake bird, a tern that like the gooney at Midway migrated to the island in such numbers that they made night landings hazardous, stood 279 feet above sea level, was one of the busiest airfields of the war, and was the pride of the U.S. Army Corps of Engineers.

On November 18, Sture's C-54 departed Ascension for Accra. On the 19th, they flew from Accra to Maiduguri and finally to Khartoum, and on November 20, 1943 made the final hop from Khartoum to Cairo, Egypt.

At every location in which Sture's C-54 landed, he and his crew were ushered into a roped off and secured area. Security remained tight, even after landing. Before he could leave the cockpit, a high ranking officer of the host base, often a general, would inevitably approach the plane from the ground, cup his hands around his mouth, and call out to Sture in the cockpit, "Is F.D.R. aboard?"

And just as inevitably, Sture would tell him that he was not.

When the officer received a negative response, he would relax and an apparent reduction in tension would pass through the assembled troops. The same procedure recurred at each destination listed in the Secret orders until Sture and his crew arrived in Cairo.

Sture, on the second camel from the left, visits the Sphinx and Great Pyramids at Giza. 1943. Sigfred collection.

Despite the tight security, the crew did get an opportunity for occasional relaxation. While departing Accra, Sture experienced engine troubles that necessitated a late start. The delay forced the crew to land in Maiduguri for the night, and in celebration of the fates that brought them heroic visitors, the citizens of the town treated Sture and his crew to gazelle steaks and sweet corn for dinner. The meat was piled high on large platters, and corn was stacked like cordwood on dozens of other platters. Sture was amazed that such delicacies could be found in what he had always read were the wilds of Africa, but he soon discovered that Maiduguri and the rest of the continent were very little different from the world he had always known. The people were of different shades and religions than those he had grown up with or had visited in the Pacific, but just like the Lutherans he had known in Parkers Prairie, they were simply people. And like all people around the world, they enjoyed a good celebration. At all stops along the route to Cairo, people of different tongues and ideologies spread banquets before the crew and passengers of the C-54, betraying a hospitality that transcended even war. But the meal in Maiduguri, in the dark of a night beyond which duty spread secretly before him, proved Sture's most memorable feast.

Sture in Giza, 1943. Sigfred collection.

While in Cairo, as meetings were conducted in the still, hot shadows of ancient halls, Sture and his crew were assigned to fly wounded soldiers for medical care to Khartoum, a thousand miles down the Nile in the Anglo-Egyptian area of Sudan. All of their flights occurred at night. During the day, Sture and his crew remained on standby for their VIP passengers. Because the Germans held Crete, only 300 miles away, emergency evacuation might prove necessary at any time. The first flight for Khartoum left each evening immediately after dark. The crew made two flights between Cairo and Khartoum each night, and arrived, exhausted but safe, from their second flight well before daylight.

Though security was tight at all stops, and Sture was on call throughout the day and night, he was able on one afternoon to visit the pyramids at Giza. Like a normal tourist during a peacetime vacation, he rode camels through the dusty streets and explored the dark and dank passages of the ancient pyramids. While riding through the streets of Giza, he picked up a broken piece of stone from one of the pyramids. He paid an old stone carver in Cairo to carve the fragment of the ancient burial site into the shape of one of the great pyramids. The old man engraved in Egyptian along the base of the miniature pyramid "Peace as Everlasting as the Pyramids." In English, as Sture requested, he engraved "Joanna Kathleen Sigfred, November 22, 1943, Captain Sigfred passing from Washington D.C. to Cairo, Egypt."

DC-4 in Miami, 1943. Sigfred collection.

When the conference was complete, Sture and his crew departed Cairo on December 10, 1943, following the same route they had taken on their initial trip. After reaching Washington, they made a side trip to New York, and after leaving New York, they flew to Miami, arriving on December 17, 1943, forty years after the Wright brother's first flight and thirty-five years after Sture had left Parkers Prairie. Although he carried thirty VIP passengers, the only passenger he had the opportunity to grow acquainted with was James Landis, former Dean of the Harvard Law School and a key figure in national defense, primarily in aviation. Landis coordinated the construction of airports in foreign countries, and he and Sture quickly discovered their common passion for aviation. On the return trip from Cairo, as a favor to Landis, Sture flew off course over Lake Chad to allow him to see from the cockpit the thousands of animals that frequented the area's largest water source. Sture later enjoyed Landis' company on a deadhead flight along the coast of South America to Miami. On that trip, they shared a bottle of Scotch and discussed Landis' recent trip to Buenos Aires where he had negotiated for airport facilities with the infamous Juan Peron.

While hopes after the Cairo Conference were high that the war might soon end, it ground on with a ferocity and tenacity unknown in modern history. The tide of war in the Pacific had turned toward the Allies, but no reasonable person expected a quick victory. And despite setbacks in Europe, the Axis forces fought on, often finding renewed strength in desperation and loss. The Allied forces were just as tenacious, and as one year of war faded into the next, they refused to weaken, certain that both might and right were on their side. Like his countrymen and allies, Sture faced the war stoically, serving his country without regret and praying that God would protect his family in his absence.

On September 3, 1944, as daylight waned on the Gulf of Guinea, Sture departed Accra enroute to Khartoum in a C-54. For two hours and twenty minutes, he flew over the African plain when he noticed severe weather over the Niger River. For ten minutes, he flew through the storm, his plane bucking and twisting below him, when he determined that the storm, unlike any other he had seen, was unflyable. He turned around and returned in darkness to Accra. The following day, rather than flying straight east to Khartoum, he flew north to Maiduguri and then east to Khartoum, keeping well away from the area of the Niger. At Maiduguri, where he landed for fuel, he learned that two B-25's had departed the previous day and were forced to fly through the same storm that had turned him back to Accra. One of the planes had returned after several hours, its fuselage and wings a hulk of barely-flyable, twisted metal. There had been no word of the other plane. It was presumed lost.

DC-4 / C-54, 1940s. Sigfred collection.

On October 6, 1944, less than a month after the storm over the Niger River, Sture flew his C-54 for from the Azores to Bermuda. Onboard his plane were fifty passengers, most of whom were pilots who had completed their military missions and were returning home, some to see their newborn children for the first time. Sture's son Sture Jr. "Butch" had been born only four months before, on July 12, and Sture was sensitive to the hopes of the men onboard. The plane departed the Azores at approximately 6:30 PM. Approximately 500 miles west of the Azores, the plane encountered a weak front. One of the lieutenants onboard asked to sit in the cockpit during the plane's ride through the squall, to see what it was like to ride in rough weather. In less than an hour, the plane had passed the front and was flying through light rain. The lieutenant rose from his seat. As he walked aft toward the cabin, he nodded toward Sture.

"That wasn't so bad," he said, saluting and returning to his seat.

Sture smiled and continued flying toward the west. As the day stretched into night, he noticed a gradual increase in turbulence and in the falling rain. By sunset, when darkness enveloped the plane, the turbulence had become so bad that Sture could barely control it. Rain pelted against the hull like rocks on a tin roof, and the winds buffeted the plane up and down like a child's toy. Severe updrafts pushed the plane upward in excess of 6000 feet only to release it to downdrafts that forced it toward the surface of the ocean that, even in the absence of moon and stars, even in the pelting rain, Sture could swear he saw. The swatting of the plane in the winds continued as the storm grew more intense. When Sture was sure the storm could grow no worse, it did.

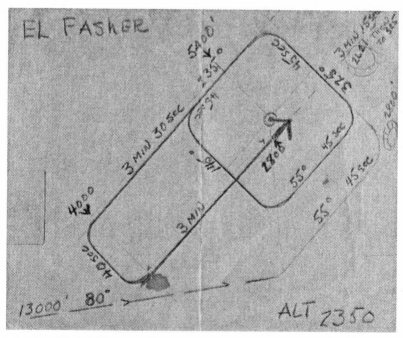

Sketch Sture used for approach to landing field. 1943.
Sigfred collection.

The rain fell so heavily that the skies seemed only a solid wall of water outside the cockpit window. The plane's ventilators took on water, and soon the air outlets within the cabin were emitting a fine mist that seemed to Sture like a weak summer shower.

Despite the takeover by experienced personnel of the Air Transport Command, the war had begun to drain the supply of pilots. The airline was forced to place into service young men with little experience in the air. The young man who accompanied Sture on this flight was an example. Intelligent and quick learning, the man had proven himself a capable copilot in all normal situations. This,

Cover of 1944 Pan Am Annual Report. PAA.

however, was not a normal situation. Sture glanced out of the corner of his eyes at the young man who had only recently learned the purposes of all of the levers and controls that lined the front panel of the cockpit. Though he, too, seemed nervous, he also seemed capable of performing his duties.

"Take the wheel," Sture snapped.

The young man looked at Sture, his eyes wide and dark.

"What," he asked.

"Take the wheel," Sture repeated.

Gingerly, as though for the first time, the young man reached toward the wheel and firmly took hold. Only when he noticed his copilot's body bucking with the torrent that battered his plane did Sture release his own grasp on the controls.

Almost immediately, he grabbed the wheel again and called to his copilot, "That's all."

The copilot, with a befuddled glance, released the wheel and wiped his forehead. Then he began to mechanically survey the instrument panel as he had before Sture ordered him to take control of the plane. For two hours and fifteen minutes, the plane flew blind in the darkness, impotent in the storm over the Atlantic Ocean. With only their instruments to keep them from tumbling into the sea, Sture cajoled the plane through the dangerous night. After approximately an hour of heavy turbulence, he dispatched his engineer to the cabin to reassure the passengers that the situation was under control. The engineer returned after approximately fifteen minutes. Strapping himself into his seat, he called to Sture: "They're pilots, Sig. They know what's happening. Every last one of them says he would rather face an enemy than face a flight like this."

Sture gripped the wheel more tightly.

When the plane finally exited the storm, the navigator took two star sights and determined that the plane had been forced 300 miles north of its projected path. As he tried to regain his normal course, Sture had the crew inspect the plane. To their amazement, she seemed intact. Though he had flown through three other hurricanes, this had been the strongest storm he had ever seen, and he considered it a miracle that the plane had survived the beating it had

Sture on ATC uniform, Miami, 1943. Sigfred collection.

taken for the previous three and a half hours. In Bermuda, he instructed the ground crew to inspect the wing fittings particularly closely, since they had been especially battered by the storm. To his surprise, the C-54 remained in service, apparently having suffered no significant damage from the storm.

Though the storm had not been forecast when he left the Azores, Sture was sure he had flown through and survived one of the strongest hurricanes of his career. He discovered after landing in Bermuda that he was right.

At the ATC facilities in Bermuda, Sture and his copilot shared the same room. The young man seemed especially quiet as Sture told him of the inspection results and the nature of the storm.

"You seem to have something to say," Sture said to him from across the room. "What is it?"

The young man looked away. As though rehearsing his words, he turned back and stared for several seconds. After a long sigh, he lowered his shoulders and spoke.

"I'd like to know why you asked me to take the wheel during the height of the storm."

Sture was silent. Then he laughed quietly. He lowered his head and ran his hand through his thin blond hair. Raising his head, he looked apologetically at the young copilot.

"As a child, I learned to pray in Swedish. The important thing is that I learned to pray with my hands folded. The prayer was '*Käre Gud Hjälp mig*, dear God help me.' It only took a minute, but I couldn't hold the wheel and fold my hands at the same time. I needed your hands too."

The young man stared quietly at Sture. After several seconds, he stood and walked toward the window. Pulling the thick, dark curtain aside, he stared into the night. Though lit by the glow of a waxing moon, the night seemed darker than it actually was, the island black against a hateful war. While the hurricane they had survived swirled somewhere in the ocean miles away from where they sat, a few stars glittered in the sky, and the night seemed strangely calm. Sture thought that if he closed his eyes, he could pretend there was no war, could imagine that he was back home in Miami, with Mildred and Joanna and Sture Jr.. He looked at the young man silhouetted against the window.

"You complied very well," he whispered.

His copilot turned, his hand still on the curtain. In the dim light filtering through the window, Sture could tell he was smiling. The young man pulled his hand from the curtain and it fell back into place, leaving both men in the absolute darkness of night.

Sture's Captain's wings from Pan Am (above) and the Air Transport Command (below). Sigfred collection.

Eugene M. McAvoy and Sture V. Sigfred Sr.

Part III: The Later Years

Sture piloting DC-4, approximately 1947.
Sigfred collection.

Eugene M. McAvoy and Sture V. Sigfred Sr.

Final Flights

1945 - 1985

When World War II ended, Sture was serving in the Africa-Orient Division of the Air Transport Command, making five or six flights between Natal and Africa or India, then returning to Miami for a two-week respite before starting the cycle again. After the surrender of the Axis powers and more than ninety trips across the Atlantic, he returned to his role of Captain on passenger planes with Pan Am. For the next six years, he split his time between his family and flying between Miami and Pan Am's airfields in South America, retracing the path that had originally brought him to his position as a pilot.

Joey, Mildred and Butch, 1949.
Miami. Sigfred collection.

While Sture was happy at last to fly his routes in relative safety, Mildred was even happier that the war lay behind them. With two young children to raise, she welcomed the opportunity to spend more time with her husband and for him to spend more time with the children. For his part, Sture tried to focus the energy he had spent during the war on his family, but always the lure of the skies called him and tore him between the security of his family and the sanctity of the skies. Though he worked as hard at being a good father as he had worked at being a good pilot, he forever deferred praise to his wife. "I do the flying. She takes care of the family," he told anyone who asked.[24]

---

[24] For Christmas in 1997, Sture presented Mildred with a check for services rendered over their more than 50 years together. The check, incorrectly or perhaps

As he flew over the Caribbean and Gulf of Mexico, on his way toward the dense jungles and muddy waters of the Amazon, Mildred joined the growing number of women seeking work outside the home. With the experience she gained from the family's ten acres of South Miami property populated with seventy-five mango trees, 137 avocado trees, and almost 800 lime trees, she went to work as a secretary for the University of Miami at an experimental farm. There, she learned time-tested methods and the latest technological advances for maximizing the production of the family's orchards and helped the staff turn their notes into publishable articles. Sture and Mildred and the children quickly settled into the comfortable life that marked the era between the post war recession and the Korean conflict.

Sture Jr. "Butch," Mildred, Joey and Sture, Miami, 1945.
Sigfred collection.

Throughout his life, despite his success as a pilot, Sture remained painfully aware that he had completed only the eighth grade and that his lack of formal education had delayed, if not in fact limited, his ability to advance with Pan Am. Mildred, too, though she had been

---

correctly dated for 1999 and made out for the sum of ten trillion dollars, has never been cashed.

one of the first two girls in her parish to graduate from high school, was familiar with the limitations that a lack of a formal education offered. She remembered all too clearly her father's question, "Why should you go to high school when all you are going to do is marry someone and become a housewife?" She and Sture ensured that their children appreciated the importance of an education. They did everything in their power to encourage the children to learn.

Their efforts were rewarded when both Joanna and Sture Jr. became model citizens, winning recognition, scholarships and fellowships throughout their high school, college and post-graduate studies. Joanna graduated with honors from college and was accepted for Ph.D. studies at the University of Colorado in Boulder. Sture Jr. completed high school in three years, completed his pre-med studies in three years, and earned his MD by the time he was only twenty-four.

The Sigfreds, though, also realized that learning did not end with books. Sture ensured that Butch knew how to repair engines and how to hunt. Mildred convinced Joanna that if she made her own clothes she could have twice as many, and taught her to sew before she went to college. Mildred and Sture taught both of the children to drive and to cook so that they would always be able to care for themselves regardless of the economic conditions the world might offer. Having seen harder times, they appreciated the relative bounty of the late 1940s, though they understood that at any moment their fortunes might change. Life for the moment was good. But only for the moment.

Sture Jr., Joanna and Mildred, Kendall, Florida, 1953. Sigfred collection.

Between two flights to Brazil in December of 1949, Sture caught a bad cold. He reported to the Pan Am doctor for a routine pre-flight physical, and complained of the cold and pressure in his ears. The doctor, unaware that Sture was allergic to it, gave him a shot of the penicillin and assigned him to flight status. During the flight, Sture experienced difficulty moving his legs and extreme pain while making his descent into Belem. When he returned to Miami, his cold was no better, and he went back to Pan Am's doctor. The doctor could determine no reason for the trouble Sture experienced with his legs during the flight. Once again, he prescribed penicillin. And once again, the ear infection failed to respond. When Sture's hands swelled as large as potatoes, the doctor stopped the penicillin treatments, but not in time. His previous difficulty moving his legs and the swelling in his hands were diagnosed as an allergic reaction to penicillin.

Sture discussed this with the Chief Pilot in Miami and mentioned obtaining medical treatment from his own doctor, but was advised against it. By this time the Pan Am doctor had been fired, and the Chief Pilot expected that Sture would receive better care from the new doctor, Dr. Mansfield. During another physical, Mansfield observed that Sture's ears were blocked and diagnosed his condition as moderately severe airotitis. He prescribed two weeks in bed and air pressure treatments to clear Sture's eustachian tubes. When his ears became unblocked in early February, 1950, Dr. Mansfield ordered him back to flight duty to determine whether his cure was satisfactory. The ear troubles continued. On February 14, 1950, on his first trip to Belem since the treatments ended, the pain in his ears during a descent into Puerto Rico was so intense that he had to be relieved. Dr. Mansfield prescribed radium treatments for his ear problems. The radium proved ineffective, and in April the doctor discontinued the regime. He ordered that all of Sture's teeth be pulled in an attempt to correct any pain that an irregular bite might cause. In May, all of Sture's teeth were pulled as the doctor had ordered, but the ear problems continued.

After almost a year of no improvement, Sture began to feel that his condition could affect the safety of his passengers. During a night landing in San Juan, he had had to delay his descent because the pressure his ears at low altitudes caused him too much pain. Though he successfully landed the plane later that night, the Pan Am clinic in Miami later discovered that his ears were blocked and returned him to Dr. Mansfield.

On this visit, Dr. Mansfield told Sture that he defied any doctor to find anything wrong with Sture's ears and accused him of "laying down on the job." The doctor told him that if he was not able to fly like everyone else, he should resign. He also told Sture that if he did not return to a normal flight schedule, the company would take away his retirement benefits. Mansfield returned him to

Joanna and Sture Jr. in the miniature car Sture built for his son, Kendall. 1955. Sigfred collection.

flight status. On his next flight, three days later, Sture yet again experienced severe pain. A nurse discovered a blood clot in his right eardrum and removed him from the flight list. Pan Am finally referred the case to an ear specialist, but the doctor, Dr. Oliver, could find no problem with Sture's ears and returned him to flight status. The duet between Sture and his doctors continued until September 24, 1950, when Sture again experienced pain and dizziness upon landing.

With the company's permission, he sought private medical advice from Dr. McKenzie, an ear specialist. Dr. McKenzie found severely restricted eardrums and blocked tubes. He initiated treatments to unblock Sture's ears that proved relatively successful until January of 1951 when, as a passenger on a Pan Am trial flight to determine the success of his treatments, Sture again experienced sever pain and vertigo. Dr. McKenzie advised Pan Am that Sture's eustachian tubes were no longer able to adapt to altitude changes, and that it was not safe for him to fly. Pan Am called in additional doctors who found Sture's eustachian tubes open, but because of his history of dizziness, recommended that he not be allowed to fly.

In March of 1951, with no further consideration of his loyalty or his well-demonstrated competence as a pilot, mechanic, and manager, just months after receiving a letter signed by Juan Trippe congratulating him on twenty years of faithful service to Pan Am, he was summarily terminated. The letter terminating his years of service stated that he was not qualified for any other position with the company, despite the countless positions he had held on three different continents over twenty years. At the time of his termination, he was the nineteenth most senior pilot on the Pan Am seniority list and had amassed over 15,000 hours of flight.

Sture tried to joke his way out of the depression that struck him. For years, Pan Am's pilots had claimed that the best things in life were salary, sex and seniority, and of the three, seniority was the best. Telling himself he would now have more time for the only remaining item on the list, he could not forget that he was now absent both a salary and his seniority.

Though he knew that he was doing what was best for his passengers, he could not escape the feeling that his career had been cut short, that he could somehow have gone just a little further, a little higher, a little longer. He knew he could easily serve as a chief mechanic or shop superintendent, perhaps take charge of the company's overhaul program, but Pan Am refused to listen to his claims. He had been terminated, and that, to the company, was that.

After exhausting all recourse with the company and with the union, Sture filed suit against Pan Am. For the next four years, he and his lawyers, John. H. Wahl Jr. and Laurence A. Schroeder, fought the company and its law firm of Smathers, Thompson, Maxwell and Dyer, whose senior partner was Florida Senator George Smathers. In a flurry of conflicting decisions, the case ultimately wound its way to the United States Supreme Court who refused to hear arguments during its October 1955 session. Sture, like virtually everyone else who had fallen before the Pan Am machine, was left in the cold, with nothing to show for his life in aviation.

Sture would admit in later years that his termination had at first enraged him; he would admit that he felt robbed of the retirement he had earned, used like a workhorse and then set out to pasture. He would find it more difficult, however, to admit that more than anything, he had been hurt by the company's treatment of him. He had struggled for almost half his life to realize his dream of becoming a pilot, had spent more than twenty years giving everything of himself to the company, and when he finally achieved his dream, his body and Pan Am conspired to snatch the dream away. It was an ache from which, for many years, he thought he would never recover. While he seldom discussed it and never took out his anger and his hurt on his family, the knowledge of his betrayal and its effect on his understanding of who he was permeated their lives. But even as

Joanna and Sture Jr., University of South Florida, 1961.
Sigfred collection.

Sture's life neared what he knew would be its end, he was hesitant to discuss the resentment that had eaten at him for more than thirty years. Even his family avoided the topic, a period in their lives that Sture Jr. admitted had consumed his childhood and had often sapped the strength and resolve of his father. The topic was for a while taboo, and after that pointless. Life gives, and it takes away, and to mourn the loss excessively is also to forget the joy of the gift. Sture chose to remember the gift.

In 1949, the year before Sture's medical problems arose, he and Mildred had purchased land and a general store in Dora Lake, Minnesota. Distraught at no longer being able to fly and unsure about what to do with the rest of his life, Sture moved the family to Dora Lake in the far northern reaches of Minnesota. There, in the solitude of the woods, he worked himself to exhaustion and tried to plot a course for his life that would deliver him and his family to safety and security. As he and Mildred tended the run-down store, making

323

improvements where they could, Joanna and Sture Jr., with fourteen other local children, attended a one-room school. Though there were few children and only one teacher at the school, Mildred and Sture believed that some of the best lessons their children would ever learn occurred in the small school house, and that there they developed the habits that would guarantee their success in later years. The family lived in Minnesota for part of 1950 and 1951, but once again Sture's ears proved to be a problem. Unable to bear the extreme cold of the northern winters, he moved his family back to Florida.

With the money he had saved from his years with Pan Am, he bought several pieces of heavy equipment and subcontracted work from the Mackle Brothers Home Builders on a new planned community being built on the Charlotte Harbor in Florida. Here too, frequent attacks of vertigo interfered with his work, and after only a short time on the job, he was compelled to sell his equipment. For $28,000, he bought a house on the water across the Peace River from Punta Gorda, and settled into a comfortable life without aviation. Mildred went to work-full time for the local high school and part-time at the hospital. After two years, she quit her job at the high school, but continued to work for the hospital for the next twelve years. After only a short time on the job, she was promoted to executive secretary, and even after resigning from the hospital staff, she remained two more years on its Civic Advisory Council.

Sture with his Rolls Royce Silver Cloud, the last car he bought in is life. Gloucester, Virginia, approximately 1980. Sigfred collection.

The Sigfreds remained in Florida until 1978, long enough to watch their children grow into responsible adults. Then, as though the parenting phase of their lives were complete and should be annotated with physical as well as emotional borders, they moved to Gloucester, Virginia. They also wanted to be closer to their son. After graduating from medical school, Sture Jr. had chosen Newport News, Virginia for his internship. Though he denied it at first, Butch fulfilled his father's prophecy that if he moved to Virginia - what Sture called the "garden spot" of all of the places he had ever lived - he would never return to Florida. After completing his internship and a tour of duty in the Air Force, Sture Jr. settled in Virginia and established a successful practice in radiology.[25] Joanna completed her Ph.D. in Boulder, Colorado, and, after studying in England, moved to New York where she worked at the Brookhaven National Laboratory.[26] Still a young woman, she studied the medical use of radioisotopes and was rapidly making a name for herself in the highly competitive research world of nuclear medicine.

Wanting to have his parents near him so he could keep an eye on them as they aged, Sture Jr. encouraged Sture and Mildred to move to Virginia. Wanting to be near at least one of their children as they neared their eighties, they agreed, and in 1978 followed him to the Virginia Peninsula. They built a new home on forty-five acres of wetlands that Sture Jr. had bought for them near the mouth of the Ware River. To surprise them, Sture Jr., who while driving through Hampton noticed that the building where his father had rented in the 1920s the first apartment in the city was being torn down, bought all

---

[25] Dr. Sture "Butch" Sigfred Jr. became one of the most respected Radiologists in Hampton Roads, Virginia, and a former President of Medical Center Radiologists. In addition to his medical practice and his work as a commercial real estate developer, he is also an active volunteer in numerous community service projects, and an esteemed volunteer faculty member at Eastern Virginia Medical School.

[26] Dr. Joanna S. Fowler has received numerous awards for her groundbreaking research into the nature of addiction. In 1998, she received the Ernest O. Lawrence Award from the U.S. Department of Energy for her "pioneering contributions to Positron Emission Tomography, including the development of flourine-18-fluorodeoxygluocose, a radiotracer used worldwide for measuring brain function and for diagnosing cancer; and for the development of tracers for monoamine oxidase found to be reduced in the brains of smokers.

of the doors from the razed building and installed them in the new house.

Despite a lingering ache from the loss of his career, Sture and Mildred were happy beyond their greatest hopes with their children, their home and their lives. As Sture looked forward to his eighty-fifth year, he could not imagine anything that would make his life better.

A Clipper Again

1985

In early October 1985, Sture received a phone call from his nephew, Paul Ryden. A check flight engineer with Pan Am's fleet of 747's, Ryden had read in September that the company was planning a special trip to commemorate the fiftieth anniversary of the company's and the world's first transpacific flight. As Pan Am sank deeper each day into a morass of debt, the trip promised to briefly rescue the company from the cold realities of global economics and the increased competition that had resulted from airline deregulation, and to restore it for a moment to its days of glory. To help them celebrate, company executives were trying to select which "old-time" pilots should accompany them on the *China Clipper II* as she retraced the path of the original *China Clipper* from San Francisco to Manila. Thinking immediately of his uncle and the dashing figure he had cut

```
UD HUMHMPH DDHEJPH
.NYCDGPA 052104                                        INFO

EMPLOYEE NEWSWIRE
1/THE CHINA CLIPPER WILL FLY AGAIN.....PAN AM WILL CELEBRATE FIFTY
YEARS OF SERVICE ACROSS THE PACIFIC WITH THE REENACTMENT OF THE
HISTORIC FLIGHT OF THE LEGENDARY CHINA CLIPPER FROM SAN FRANCISCO TO
MANILA.  THE SPECIAL FIFTIETH ANNIVERSARY FLIGHT OF THE HISTORIC
PACIFIC CROSSING WILL BE ABOARD A PAN AM 747 LEAVING  SAN FRANCISCO
ON NOVEMBER 22.  TRUE TO THE ORIGINAL ROUTING...CHINA CLIPPER TWO
WILL LAND IN HONOLULU...MIDWAY AND WAKE ISLANDS...AND GUAM...BEFORE
HEADING TO MANILA.  THOSE PASSENGERS WHO FLEW ON THE HISTORIC
ROUND/THE/WORLD FLIGHTS ON CLIPPER LIBERTY BELL AND CLIPPER NEW
HORIZONS ARE BEING OFFERED THE FIRST OPPORTUNITY TO BOOK SEATS FOR
THE NOSTALGIC FLIGHT.  FIRST CLASS TRAVEL...WHICH WILL ALSO INCLUDE
GROUND COSTS...EXCURSIONS...HOTELS...AND GALA CELEBRATIONS IN HNL
AND MNL...WILL BE USD 5,500.  CLIPPER CLASS PARTICIPANTS WILL PAY
USD 4400.  CABIN CLASS TRAVEL WILL BE USD 2900.  THE FLIGHT OF THE
CHINA CLIPPER COVERED THE 8210 MILE DISTANCE IN 1935 IN 59 HOURS AND
48 MINUTES FLYING TIME OVER A PERIOD OF SIX DAYS.  THE REENACTMENT
FLIGHT WILL COVER THE SAME DISTANCE IN 40 HOURS AND 55
MINUTES...INCLUDING THE OVERNIGHT STOP IN HNL AND THE BRIEF
CEREMONIAL STOPOVERS AT MIDWAY...WAKE...AND GUAM.  THE CHINA CLIPPER
TWO WILL DEPART SFO AT 0900 ON NOVEMBER 22 AND ARRIVE IN MANILA AT
1755 LOCAL TIME ON NOVEMBER 24.
```

Pan Am memo announcing the 50th anniversary of the flight of the China Clipper. Sigfred collection.

in his blue serge uniform and captain's wings, remembering the stories he had told on his many visits home, vivid tales of exotic locations and brushes with disaster, Ryden asked his uncle if he would like to be one of the company's guests.

With static humming along the telephone wires that connected the two generations of men, Sture was silent. He remembered having been forced from the company in 1950, tasted again the bitterness and sadness that for thirty-five years had mingled in his memories of Pan Am. Just as quickly, he recalled the exhilaration of his first flight as the captain of his own plane, of the camaraderie he had enjoyed with the pilots and mechanics who had nurtured and grown Pan Am from an upstart company to the world's largest airline, and of the incomparable sense of meaning he had experienced as he transported cargo and troops across the Atlantic Ocean at the height of World War II.

He spoke loudly into the phone. "It would be heaven."

On the morning of Wednesday, November 20, 1985, Sture rose earlier than normal. As the sun appeared above the horizon, stretching a pale shroud of pink around the trees on the shore opposite his home, he draped his legs over the side of his bed and pushed himself up straight. Stroking his face with long, slender fingers, he glanced toward his sleeping wife. Moving as quietly as he could, so he would not wake her, he rose from the bed and made his way into the bathroom where he splashed cold water onto his face. By the time the sun had broken above the tree line, shattering the surface of the river into a million beads of silver, he emerged from the bathroom, dressed and bristling with anticipation. Pacing across the floor, he poked his head into each room of the house to ensure that he was, in fact, ready for his trip. Finally, after verifying that each room was in its own state of readiness, he hurried to the front door and threw it open to the cool, crisp morning.

Stepping from the warmth provided by his wood-burning stove, he surveyed the three-and-a-half acre clearing that surrounded his house. To the west, 1100 loblolly pines swayed in a breeze passing through what had been nothing more than a dusty cornfield when he first moved to Gloucester. Though only five years old, the trees had grown to about ten feet tall, and from the clearing, the former cornfield seemed already a forest, untouched by human hands. Just north of the house, martins frolicked in their birdhouse, and a pair of common sparrows flitted about an azalea bush near the door to the house. In the center of a pond just northwest of the house, the osprey perch remained vacant. Overhead, a flock of geese passed in a dark and silent phalanx above the trees, while a pair of tundra swans swam on the river beside the near shore as though they had no intention of leaving.

As Sture stood outside, awestruck by the day that stretched before him and by a journey for which he could barely contain his excitement, Mildred rose from bed in a ritual surprisingly similar to her husband's. Sure that her husband stood safely on the lawn below, as he normally did on cool autumn mornings, she padded softly to the bathroom and bathed her face in cold water. Then she wrapped a housecoat around a body still acclimating itself to consciousness and walked to the kitchen where she prepared a light breakfast.

While Mildred tidied the kitchen, Sture hiked 700 feet down to the beach, a 1600-foot stretch of white sand emerging from marsh at the eastern bank of the Ware River. Peering downstream, he could barely make out a fishing boat where the mouth of the river poured into Mobjack Bay. He smiled, thinking this would be a perfect day for fishing. When his son Sture Jr. had bought this land, the neighbors informed Sture that the best trout fishing in Gloucester County lay just off this property, a claim he had proven true time and time again since moving to the area. Sniffing the river before him, he knew the fishermen in their gangly boat would enjoy a plentiful catch. Though he knew her crew could not see him, he raised his hand in a two-finger wave toward the boat and wished them a great day.

Sture's stretch of waterfront, like the fertile wetlands in which it sat, teemed with marine, plant and animal life. It claimed one of the most productive oyster beds along this stretch of the river, and every day menhaden fishing boats traversed the river as far upstream as they dared without running aground. The river was approximately one and half miles wide at his beach, and peering across, he could see fish jumping toward its surface for food in the unseasonably warm autumn. Turning from the beach, he started back toward the house. Glancing at his watch, he calculated the number of hours before he would be on his way to San Francisco to join the *China Clipper II* on her 50th Anniversary Flight to the Orient. The sound of waves lapping the shore behind him and the distant splash of fish jumping for their food soothed him as he stopped and closed his eyes. With the house and the river and the marsh and the woods just beyond his sight and reach, he thought of how long it had been since he had last flown a plane and of all that had happened since. Shaking his head as though to ward off an idea he did not wish to ponder, he opened his eyes and trudged back toward the house.

Stepping lightly upon the path, he passed a salt marsh on his left and a fresh water pond to his right. In the distance, a nine-foot tall azalea stood beside the front door of his home, a welcoming splash of color on the palette of autumn. For a moment, struck by an understanding that he had lived in the best of all possible worlds - a comfortable retirement on land that gave and forgave like a selfless lover; a forty-five year marriage to the woman of his dreams; the chance to have flown and to fly again today back to the source of his dearest memories - he forgot what had troubled him at the water's edge. Feeling that something remained undone, that the sky and the water and he must come together one last time, he smiled again and thought of finishing the chapter of his life that had defined it.

His untamed land was the last remaining place where he still felt like the pioneer he had longed to be as a child: his forty-five acres claimed from the marsh of the Virginia peninsula. Hidden from the county road by a twisting approach to the house, the land was isolated from the bustle of the city, a hearkening back to another century except for the modern split-level that overlooked the river. Each winter, he and Mildred cut their own wood. Each summer they grew and canned their own fruit, and harvested the wild asparagus that grew along the beach. They fed the wild turkeys that flocked each morning to their driveway and watched in silence as deer roamed through the woods and across the clearing that surrounded the house. Even now, with the winter solstice only a month away, the land glistened in the crisp air.

Sture inhaled and stepped back into the house. Mildred, a pencil and checklist clenched in her small hands, had finished packing and was performing a final walk-through of each room, as Sture had done only an hour before. Though several hours remained before they needed to leave for the airport, she seemed impatient to finish her work, and more excited than she admitted to join her husband on the historic flight of the *China Clipper II.* As she pressed her pencil to the paper she gripped in her palm, checking one final item off her list, its graphite tip broke off. She looked at Sture, bewildered it seemed, for a moment. Finally she laughed, her face in that brief span of time seeming younger, like that of the girl he had married forty-five years before.

With airline tickets tucked into the breast pocket of his camel-colored coat, Sture and Mildred loaded their luggage into the Lincoln. Driving across the two-lane bridge at Gloucester Point, they left their small waterfront community behind and aimed for more sprawling areas of southeastern Virginia and the adventures beyond. That evening, to ensure nothing would prevent them from making the trip, they stayed at the Norfolk Airport Hilton. The following morning, they departed on United Airlines for Chicago.

The flight on United seemed both bittersweet and ironic to Sture. In April, United had bought for $750 million Pan Am's Pacific Division, and its loss, even in 1985, seemed to Sture a death-knoll for the company. But as never before in his life, he was treated like royalty. United Airlines' hospitality rivaled what Pan Am had offered its passengers in the 1930s, and the passengers and crew of his flight to Chicago treated him with even greater respect than he had enjoyed as a pilot of the Clippers. The captain of the airplane invited him into the cockpit and announced over the plane's loudspeaker that one of the pioneers of aviation was onboard. When he returned to his seat, a stewardess served him and Mildred complimentary champagne. The passengers listened without distraction as he recalled his early years in aviation. He almost believed for those few hours that what he had once been a part of could be considered heroism, and even he was awed that he had seen it.

When the plane finally landed in Chicago, before they could reach the terminal and while Sture accepted congratulations from the rest of the crew, the pilot of the plane grasped Mildred's arm and guided her away from the crowd around her husband.

"Most people don't understand what those men did for us back then," he said, his eyes shining, his voice insistent. "We do. And we appreciate their contribution. What they did enabled us to fly now. You take care of him, okay?"

Mildred promised that she would. Then resting her hand in the crook of Sture's elbow, she pulled her hero from the crowd and led him off the plane.

During their short layover at O'Hare International Airport, Sture reminisced briefly about having been the first man to land a plane on her fields when it had been the Chicago Flying Club's field, discovered and rented by Sture and the Club's president in 1925. With fellow passengers zipping about the concourse, they caught their connecting flight to San Francisco and were on their way.

In San Francisco, the City by the Bay, Mildred's enthusiasm began to match her husband's, and both shared reminiscence and wonder at the changes that had transformed the city since they had lived there in the early 1940s. Where once had stretched open fields, now stood hotels and fast food outlets. Entire neighborhoods - in the forties, home to dozens of different ethnic groups - had been razed and were replaced with parking lots and apartment complexes, remarkable only in their similarity and lack of personality. Despite the changes, however, the city had not lost its charm. This was where they had met, where they had fallen in love, and for that reason alone, time could never change the San Francisco they had known.

They took a taxi from the airport to the Mark Hopkins Hotel, where they spent the night. So exhausted were they from their flight, not even nostalgia and the lingering hint of romance could keep them awake. They shared a club sandwich from room service and fell into bed.

The following morning, they awoke before sunrise to get an early start. The departure ceremony for the "Flight to the Orient" began at 8:00, and the coaches that would take them from the hotel to the airport were scheduled to depart between 6:30 and 7:00. Though neither could recall ever having been late in their lives, they rushed around their room and hurriedly checked that their luggage was still intact. Then, without eating breakfast, they quick-stepped to the elevator where Sture pressed and repressed the call button. When they finally stepped from the doors of the hotel into the San Francisco fog, they discovered that they had to wait for the coach.

Celebration

November 22, 1985

On the morning of November 22, 1985, San Francisco International Airport buzzed with activity. As on most mornings in one of the nation's busiest airports, scores of passengers darted across the cold concourse to catch their flights, to retrieve their luggage, or to steal a final embrace from departing loved ones. Dozens more stood at arrival gates, peering over the heads of debarking passengers for glimpses of their friends and families. But on this morning, exactly fifty years after Pan American World Airways' *China Clipper* made her inaugural flight across the Pacific, one hundred and fifty

Flight crew of the *China Clipper II* 50th Anniversary Flight. San Francisco, 1985. Sigfred collection.

years after the famous Clipper Ships of the nineteenth century first sailed into San Francisco Bay, the terminal hummed with an excitement that everyday air travel could not explain.

Few in the crowd, however, could doubt the cause of excitement. At Departure Gate 57, a small stage, draped in bunting of Pan Am's signature blue and white, stood empty among a mosaic of faces. Above the stage, a banner proclaiming "Bon Voyage *China Clipper II*" hung limp above the crowd. More than two hundred people lingered expectantly near the stage and shouldered their way to the front of the pack, but no one mounted the dais. At the foot of the stage, toddlers and stoop-backed men turned their anxious faces toward a lectern perched atop the stage. Behind them, men and women of all ages and colors jostled for position, trying to situate themselves in the best location from which to view the opening ceremonies of the Fiftieth Anniversary Flight of the *China Clipper*. On the periphery of the crowd, Sture and Mildred stood quietly, not yet a part of the celebration.

A young woman from Pictorial Histories Productions in Missoula, Montana, contracted by Pan Am to record the celebration on videotape, meandered through the crowd, apprising in a glance each person she passed. A man with a video camera balanced on his shoulder followed closely behind. The woman slowed as she passed Sture, but before she could speak, a small group gathered near a distinguished looking gentleman at the opposite corner of the terminal. Latching onto the elbow of her assistant, the woman scurried toward their circle.

For almost an hour, the woman led her cameraman through the crowd, stopping frequently at the side of Pan Am executives or older gentlemen she seemed to suspect might have been involved with the original Clippers. Thrusting a microphone into their faces, she asked each, with a well-rehearsed voice, for his impression of the events. From each, she received an equally well-rehearsed reply.

A relief pilot on the original *China Clipper* flight, Max Weber stared into the camera and recalled the flight as having been difficult for him. He had been required, he explained, to relieve each of the crewmembers when they grew tired. By the time the flight ended, he had stood each of the watches and had grown more tired and less alert than any of the other crewmen. He smiled and patiently explained the importance of his contribution to Pan Am's conquering the Pacific. Thanking him, the woman nodded and marched away.

Harry Canaday, a junior officer on the first Clipper test flight over the eastern United States and navigator of Pan Am's first U.S.-New Zealand flight, was her next subject. Unlike Weber, Canaday held only a tangential claim to the *China Clipper's* first Pacific crossing. Almost sadly, he remembered being pulled from the flight to navigate the *Philippine Clipper*, scheduled to depart for the Orient several days after the *China*. Fate had wrested from him that moment of fame, but he strove to reclaim it as the video camera whirred before him.

Not to be outdone by Pan Am's former aviators, novelist James Michener staked his own claim to the lore of the Pacific and the celebration of the *China Clipper*'s first flight. And less patiently than those who had spoken before, former Pan Am Vice President of Engineering John G. Borger, who had spearheaded the monumental design and preparation of Pan Am's string of island bases, explained the significance of the company's delivery of the first Trans-Pacific payload in aviation history.

While Sture watched and listened in, each man in turn, though merely a part of the team that had made Pan Am's first commercial Pacific crossing a success, seemed to try and trump the man before, to wring an individual moment of brilliance from the twilight of Pan Am's greatness. Remembering the antics and one-upmanship he had shared with his fellow pilots, Sture had to smile. Cumulatively, the lives and accomplishments of these men were impressive, their names a veritable *Who's Who* of the pioneers who had once defied nature and logic, who had seared into history with little more than dreams and determination a list of firsts unmatched by any other airline in American history. Yet individually, they seemed somewhat less than the sum of their talents.

Sture, perhaps more than most in the room, understood that behind the egos, behind all of the accomplishments, and behind the fame that few could rightfully claim, an armada of anonymous workers was truly responsible for what had once been Pan Am's greatness. And all the men gathered for this celebration were, at their best, merely a part of that armada. In their individuality, he found these men more vibrant, more passionate, and more real than the brushstroke of history would claim, for he was one of them, one of the many. But it was the sum of their *individual* stories, he knew, that comprised the legend of Pan Am, an accumulation of anecdotes and data and history and lives that did little to put a face on their experiences. If they exaggerated their roles during what has become known as the Golden Age of Aviation, it was perhaps understandable. It had been many years since they or Pan Am had found cause for celebration.

It might, from all appearances, be many more.

In addition to Weber and Canaday and Borger, the camera also recorded the thoughts of John B. Cooke, station manager at Wake Island on the morning of December 7, 1941, and Cornelius Whitney, the first Chairman of Pan American's Board of Directors. Despite history's claim to the contrary, Whitney surprisingly announced that *he* had recruited Juan Trippe and Charles Lindbergh to the then-struggling airline. He, Whitney claimed, more than Trippe or Lindbergh or the legendary André Priester, was responsible for the vision that made Pan Am, however briefly, America's "chosen instrument" of foreign policy. The woman and cameraman remained silent, refusing to judge the claims of this or any other hero in the hall full of heroes. This was, after all, a celebration, and each of the men, as much as the event that led to their gathering, deserved celebration.

Still, the man of the hour and day, basking in the brilliance of a bygone era despite his reign over the destruction and disassembly of the company, was C. Edward Acker. Pan Am's Chief Executive Officer, a stout man originally from Texas, spoke slowly and carefully into the woman's microphone, choosing his words as purposefully as he pronounced them. Framed by tortoiseshell glasses, his dark eyes darted from side to side and peered at the ground. An almost humble smile playing across his lips, he regaled the camera and the audience around him with the story of the first flight of the *China Clipper* and repeated the company's familiar refrain that fifty years before, it had single handedly conquered the Pacific and shrunk the globe.

Most of his audience already knew the story, had in fact *lived* the story, so Acker needed only to mention the events that led to the flight, and heads nodded around him. Smiles erupted on the faces of his listeners. Men shook hands and slapped each other on the back.

Unacknowledged for the moment were the company's financial difficulties and the fact that Pan Am had only the previous April announced the sale of its Pacific Division, the jewel in its corporate crown, to United Airlines. Seemingly forgotten were the facts that little remained of America's former chosen instrument and her future looked bleak. Acker did not mention these matters. No one reminded the crowd that in a matter of months, the route they were about to fly would no longer belong to Pan Am. Instead, Acker and his guests looked backward, not forward. Behind them was greatness. Before them, a celebration and little more.

But beneath the din of celebration, Sture sensed resignation in the hall, an invisible haze that settled on the celebrants; he suspected that the revelry surrounding him was little more than a last hurrah for the struggling company. Though he could not guess how its story would end or what would survive to remind the world of its former brilliance, he knew that Pan Am would never again return to the greatness it had once known, would never again exercise the power it had once possessed, would never again stretch the arm of American might to all corners of the world. Believing that the celebration before him was a last gasp of denial, he faced his impending journey with skepticism. As the sun climbed higher into the morning sky, struggling to break through the clouds over San Francisco, the day evolved for him into equal parts wake and celebration, but he too remained silent, complicit in his avoidance of discussing the cold hard facts of American business, unwilling to dampen the joy of his fellow revelers.

At 8:00, the woman with the microphone ended her interviews and shrank to the back of the crowd. Her videographer turned his camera toward the stage, and the concourse erupted in applause. John Krinskey, Pan Am's Senior Vice President for Marketing, mounted the small stage and stood proudly at the podium. Asking for the crowd's attention, he officially commenced the *China Clipper II*'s departure ceremony and read Mayor Diane Feinstein's proclamation of November 22, 1985 as *China Clipper II* Day. Mrs. Mary Brown, San Francisco's postmaster and the highest-ranking woman in the U.S. Postal Service, extended the best wishes of the Postal Service to the passengers and crew of the flight, and Mr. Acker ascended the podium.

In a speech he would repeat throughout this and the following day, Acker again offered a brief history of the flight of the original *China Clipper* and introduced each of the dignitaries participating in the flight. Finally, after almost a half-hour of speeches and declarations and congratulations, Acker presented the crew of the *China Clipper II*, some of the most senior and successful pilots in the company.

Captain Donald Pritchett, Pan Am's Vice-President for Flight Operations, commanded the flight. Regional Chief Pilot-Pacific, Captain William G. Frisbie served as the copilot, and Captain

Christopher H. Wharton, a 747 Check Captain, served as the back-up pilot. Richard E. Killer, a Pan Am Standards Flight Engineer was the flight engineer, and Paul M. Ryden, Sture's nephew, the man who had grown up worshipping his uncle and dreaming of following in his footsteps, was the backup flight engineer.

Finally, in a reenactment of receiving the original station reports, Acker called the role of Pan Am's Pacific bases strung like buoys across the Pacific. Though the bases had responded in 1935 over telegraph lines while a translator read their messages aloud, the bases this time responded with real-time voice communications. When the Honolulu, Midway, Wake, Guam, and Philippine stations had completed their readiness reports, Acker turned to Captain Pritchett and directed him to depart in accordance with his written orders.

"Aye, aye, sir," Pritchett responded, crisply saluting his CEO. Followed by his crew, he began the long walk out of the terminal, but after only a few yards, Acker leaned into the microphone, smiled and stopped him.

"This time, fly over the bridge."

Pritchett and the audience laughed, recalling one of the most frightening moments of the first Clipper flight. Captain Edwin Musick, unable to gain sufficient power from his Martin M-130 to fly over the Golden Gate Bridge, had flown between guy wires on the span. The fighters escorting him over the bay followed suit.

Acknowledging Acker's order, Pritchett and his crew left the terminal, and the passengers lined up anxiously to board the plane.

After years of use, Sture's copy of the video that chronicles the flight of the *China Clipper II* flickers and refuses to track. Its audio track cannot keep pace with its images. It is an imperfect document. It reveals imperfections, normal people with eyes that refuse to look directly into the camera, liver spots, stutters and lisps. But it records a story, the true story of a single day in the history of Pan American

Flight crew of the *China Clipper II* in Honolulu. Sture's nephew, Paul Ryden, stands at the far right. 1985. Sigfred collection.

World Airways, the United States, and aviation, when despite the curse that seemed to be descending on the company, some still hoped that Pan Am could regain her stature in aviation. Tucked between the officially sanctioned speeches of executives and the clips of scratched newsreels that once carried the company's propaganda to darkened theatres around the world, the videotape offers bits and pieces of stories that reveal a tenacious belief on the part of many that Pan Am would survive. Though Juan Trippe and Andre Priester, luminaries in the history of aviation, men who carried the company through disasters far worse than economic hard times, were gone, the glorious past trumpeted by C. Edward Acker and the other Pan Am executives seemed to embody and embolden the hopes of thousands of workers, that somehow, someone could rescue the company so quickly losing altitude.

History, however, has proven their hope ill fated.

On December 4, 1991, just six years after the anniversary flight of the *China Clipper II*, the *Clipper Goodwill*, a Boeing 727, flew the last flight for Pan American World Airways. Burdened by debt and corporate mismanagement, cursed by a federal government that refused it domestic service, unable to recover from the publicity surrounding the explosion and crash over Lockerbie, Scotland of flight 103, and betrayed by Delta Airlines that only days before had bought the last of its remaining routes, Pan Am faced its only destiny. With a low pass over the runway before landing, a salute from airport workers, and the blast of a water canon across her bow, the *Clipper Goodwill* came to stop and killed her engines. With tears in their eyes, her crew departed the plane and headed toward their homes. As the sun set brilliantly over Miami, Pan American World Airways officially exhaled her last breath.

But the once great Pan Am had been choking for a very long time. It was, in fact, already little more than a memory and a trademark - even on that blustery November morning in 1985 when the past caught up with the company that had for so long represented the future.

The words on the nose of the *China Clipper II* looked familiar: the same color and curve of the letters that had decorated the hulls of the Clippers Sture had flown fewer than fifty years before. Even the sleek line of the 747's fuselage reminded him of the planes he had guided across the Pacific, though the curve of the hull was smoother, more aerodynamic, and, he had to admit, somehow more beautiful. Still, the plane that loomed around him, that seemed to envelop him in a skin of aluminum and steel, felt alien. The passenger compartment vibrated with the hum of electrical current. Beneath the hum, the murmur of hundreds of private conversations bounced like radar from the insulated bulkheads separating the air-conditioned passenger hold from the expanse of all that lay outside the artificial environment of the plane. A breeze blew noisily from air ducts lining the underside of the luggage bins. And beneath panels of plastic polished to a gleam, hundreds of miles of copper wiring and hydraulic lines, the nerves and arteries of the ship, groped their way to the most remote appendages of the plane. It seemed that the plane's builders had attempted to disguise, quite effectively, he thought, the fact that the passengers were trapped on a vessel not of this world, and only three generations before, not of the dreams of this world.

Built by Boeing in Everett, Washington, in what was at the time the world's largest building, the Jumbo Jet was almost 230 feet long with a wingspan just short of 212 feet. Its length was greater than the entire distance flown by the Wright brothers in their famous first flight eighty-two years before. With four RB211-524G turbofan engines, the plane could carry up to 400 passengers and 45,000 gallons of fuel. At 545,000 pounds, it weighed more than most of the planes Sture had flown in his life put together. It was, he knew, a work of art, a technological wonder, but the computer controls he glimpsed through the cockpit door and the flickering lights that lined the aisle, rather than inviting him into a sense of wonder, estranged him from the symbiosis he had always enjoyed with his own planes. He could not escape a sense of longing for the old Clippers, for the bumpy ride they offered in heavy weather, for the water they sent rooster-tailing from their floats during takeoff, for the creaking of their aluminum hulls as they skimmed over angry waves. Though the seaplanes had long since been replaced at the pinnacle of craftsmanship and technology, he missed the quirks that had made each an individual, almost possessing its own personality, always reminding him that, though they dared break the selfish grip of gravity, they were always of and one with the earth.

340

The *China Clipper II* in San Francisco. 1985.
Sigfred collection.

As the light above his head prompted him, Sture fastened his seatbelt. He glanced to his left. Across the aisle, through one of the small portholes in the bulkhead, he watched a strange-looking vehicle, something of a cross between a golf cart and a tractor, pull to the front of the plane. With a slight jolt of the mammoth plane, the vehicle made contact with the plane's front wheel. Sture watched the landscape drift backwards past him.

The *China Clipper II* joined the queue at the head of the runway, and the roar of jets pierced the hull as Captain Pritchett put the plane through her last minute checks. The brakes groaned, struggling to hold back the engines that fought to thrust the plane forward. When the captain announced that he had received authorization to take off, Sture inhaled. Almost climactically, the brakes released, the jets unwound, and the plane lumbered down the runway, quickly gathering speed. Still bound to the earth, the 747 accelerated, its G-force pressing Sture and Mildred into the backs of their seats, the plane bouncing as its wheels sped over small bumps in the asphalt. Finally, after what seemed long and torturous minutes, the Clipper's nose rose slightly into the air, the bouncing disappeared, and the bow of the plane climbed higher. Without glancing out the window, Sture knew that the plane was airborne.

San Francisco from the air, 1985. Sigfred collection.

He closed his eyes and enjoyed the sensation of heaviness that pushed him down and back in the seat, a sensation that he knew would be replaced with a momentary sense of weightlessness when the plane leveled off. With the noise of the jets now distant and the voices of passengers rising in pitch and excitement, he allowed himself to relax, to fully believe that he was here, in the moment, on this plane. As though in a dream, he peered into the recesses of his memory and prodded the past that had carried him to this day. While the plane sped west, away from the sun, he allowed himself to believe, just for the moment, that he was also speeding away from time.

Back Across the Pacific

1985

From thirty thousand feet, Sture glanced out the window of the 747. Miles below, between scattered patches of clouds, the Pacific Ocean passed isolated and undisturbed. He thought of the millions of gallons of water in that ocean and in all of the other oceans of the world. Though the oceans had once been the bane of flying boats, they had also been vital to the growth of aviation in the years before planes could survive the crushing forces of landing on the ground. Though water had been a threat, an omnipotent presence that promised death from one slight misjudgment or miscalculation, it had also provided the planes with a relatively soft landing cushion and maneuverability that allowed technology to catch up with aviators' dreams.

As the *China Clipper II* sped toward Honolulu, it seemed that the water below him was time itself, and that he was once again staring time in the face. The plane continued its graceful trek to the west, opposite the earth's rotation, at once running away from and toward the sun, running away from and catching up with time. Sunlight danced on the waves of the Pacific and cast shards of light through the sky toward the small window through which Sture

Mrs. Paul Ryden, wife of Sture's nephew, and Cornelius Whitney, founder and former executive of Pan Am, during the 50th Anniversary celebrations. Sigfred collection.

watched. At five hundred miles per hour, this was the fastest he had ever flown, the closest to the speed of light he had ever approached. Though the laws of physics would deny its possibility, he believed for those few hours that time had slowed. He aged at a slower pace, and his past, his memories were closer than they had ever been.

Within five hours, the Hawaiian Islands appeared on the western horizon, cones of green rising from the ocean floor. The *China Clipper II* began a slow descent toward the spots growing larger in the window. The "No Smoking" light flashed in the overhead. The

China Clipper II in Hawaii, 1985. Sigfred collection.

"Fasten Seat Belt" light flickered. Stewardesses walked up and down the aisle, smiling as they bent toward their passengers, collecting the remnants of meals and drinks, tightening the seat belts of children, and laughing at jokes they had heard hundreds of times before. An announcement crackled over the plane's intercom: sunny skies, warm weather. Sture sat up straight in his seat. He looked at Mildred and smiled. The sun shone brilliantly through a starboard window. Honolulu grew closer, and the past was all at once with him. He lived it again as the Boeing 747 landed safely within sight of the beach.

The *China Clipper II* touched down on the runway, a puff of smoke from her tires against the hot pavement announcing her arrival. At 9:00 AM Pacific time, the flight had departed San Francisco. It arrived in Honolulu, 2,397 miles to the southwest, at 12:15 PM local time. It had taken the original Clippers, propeller driven and clumsy in comparison to the Boeing 747, between eighteen and thirty hours to make the same flight, always at night so that the crew could land in daylight. As when Sture had flown Pan Am's seaplanes, the sun loomed brightly over the Hawaiian coast. The jet rapidly decelerated when the pilot reversed thrust and pulled to a stop at the gate designated for her welcoming ceremony. The passengers and crew, stiff from the long flight, anxiously departed the plane and entered the air-conditioned terminal where a line of hula dancers placed leis around their necks and welcomed them to the islands.

There was little time for merriment, however, upon their arrival. Within minutes of their entering the terminal, the governor of Hawaii officially welcomed Pan Am and its guests in a short and surprisingly reserved speech. Following the governor, C. Edward Acker presented him with a scale model of the original *China Clipper* and, with almost the same speech he had used in San Francisco, recalled Pan Am's importance in developing international mail service and travel, and in helping maintain the national defense. The audience applauded politely, though not enthusiastically, when the half-hour ceremony ended.

Immediately upon completion of the ceremony, the Pan Am dignitaries and their guests departed for Pearl Harbor where, beneath a brilliant blue sky, they witnessed the commemoration of a memorial plaque honoring Pan Am's fifty years of air service across the Pacific. As Sture listened to the speeches that already sounded trite and overused, he looked out upon the sparkling water and the remnants of the concrete ramp where he and other Clipper captains had tied up their planes for maintenance. Within sight of the gathering was the scene of the infamous Japanese bombing of December 7, 1941. Sprinkled throughout the crowds that passed in boats and busses and on foot were several Japanese tourists, incongruous in the midst of this most holy of American shrines. The crowd was quiet and respectful throughout the commemorative ceremony, as much it seemed for the war memorial as for the memories of Pan Am's glory days.

Crew departing the China Clipper II in Honolulu. 1985. Sigfred collection.

At 2:00, busses transferred the guests back to Honolulu's Royal Hawaiian Hotel where they spent the night. Sture and Mildred passed the rest of the afternoon settling into their room and admiring their view of Waikiki Beach. At 6:00 PM, 11:00 PM back in Virginia and well past their normal bedtime, they attended a reception on the hotel's Ocean Lawn, followed by a testimonial dinner at the hotel. Though the energy of the crowd was somewhat higher than it had been earlier in the afternoon, a haze of distraction fell upon the room when, again, the same stories of Pan Am's historic importance as the United States' chosen instrument were recited from the podium.

Finally, after more than sixteen hours of flight and activities, Sture and Mildred found themselves gratefully alone in their room, free until the next morning's departure. Though both were draped in memories and nagged by the desire for conversation, neither had the energy to speak. As soon as they changed clothes and lay upon the king-sized bed, both fell fast asleep.

Quickly shaking off the cloud of sleep, they awoke early the following morning, refreshed and feeling younger than they had felt in years. The previous day's exhaustion had been replaced in the night with vigor and excitement. Mildred spoke with animation about their upcoming flight to Midway, and Sture hummed on his way into the bathroom. After showering and dressing, Sture told Mildred that he had dreamed of an old friend. "The airman I saw on the day I left Parkers Prairie, I dreamed about him, about running into him several years later when I was a pilot. He wasn't surprised."

They left with their fellow travelers for the airport at about 6:30 AM, November 23, 1985. And after still another ceremony similar to those of the previous day, they boarded the *China Clipper II*. The passengers buckled themselves into their seats as the plane departed for Midway Island. Above the vintage music playing softly in the cabin background, there was, of course, conversation, lively and animated. As they made the short, 1300-mile, jaunt from Honolulu to Midway, old-timers from Pan Am's more glorious days reconstructed the story of how they personally and collectively developed a network of communications and supply bases that supported transpacific travel. The woman who had recorded the memories of many of the pilots over the past two days, stood beside Sture and asked him if he would speak for the video she was recording.

He took the small microphone and held it close to his lips. More quickly than any other speaker, he smiled broadly and spoke into the microphone. "I'm Sture Sigfred, and I am eighty-five years old." He laughed, his eyes sparkling. "I was a pilot on the Clippers." Though Pan Am had at one time fought to keep Sture from his rightful legacy as a Clipper Ship Captain, this moment, broadcast later on national TV, seemed for him to make up for all that he had lost.

Sture and his nephew Paul Ryden in Honolulu. Sigfred collection.

Slightly less than three hours after taking off from Honolulu, the *China Clipper II* approached Midway Airport, an asphalt strip across the small island, still little more than a military outpost. After a short ceremony, another model of the original *China Clipper* was presented to the local military commander. Before reboarding the plane, the passengers were allowed to stroll through the island's gardens, littered still with hundreds of gooney birds. With little more fanfare, the *China Clipper II* departed for her two hour and forty minute, 1182 mile flight to Wake Island. Sture noted as the pilot powered up the jets, roaring loudly even through the insulated hull, that a military pickup truck raced down the airstrip ahead of the plane to frighten the gooney birds away. Little, it seemed, had changed since the early 1940s.

At approximately 12:35 local time on November 24, 1985, having flown over the International Date Line in mid flight, the plane landed on Wake Island. As he had done before and as he would in Guam and Manila, Acker made a short speech about Pan American Airways, the *China Clipper* and the pioneering spirit that had secured Pan Am's place in history. Like all of his speeches, this was modified somewhat to reflect the contribution or activities of the specific location, but the information remained essentially the same. Still, Acker could not end his speech without a reference to the role Wake had played in winning World War II, and when he mentioned the famous and costly battle that had been essential to the Allied victory in the Pacific, the guests were reverent and respectful of the nameless dead.

Faced with another 3100 miles to fly that day, the passengers were not allowed to linger over their memories. As soon as Acker finished speaking and delivering his thanks to the contingent of military personnel on Wake, the guests were herded back onto the *China Clipper II* for the 1503-mile, three-hour flight to Guam. Walking back to the plane on Wake, Sture was approached by a young sailor who asked him for his autograph. Sture happily obliged.

Sture at Guam. 1985.
Sigfred collection.

Without glancing at the autograph, the sailor took the paper from Sture and nodded. "I have read all of your books, Mr. Michener."

Sture smiled and turned to the plane.

Located eight hundred miles north of the equator at thirteen degrees north latitude and one hundred and forty-four degrees east longitude, the island of Guam lies at the southern end of the Marianas Islands chain in the Western Pacific Ocean. Its time zone twelve hours ahead of the California coast, Guam prides itself as the place "Where America's Day Really Begins." The island, about thirty miles long and four to eight miles wide, covers approximately two hundred and twelve square miles. These facts clicked through Sture's mind as the Boeing 747 banked to starboard on her approach to Apra Harbor glistening like a sapphire below the plane. Though he could see only the haze of hills along the southern horizon, Sture knew that volcanic hills soared 1,300 feet into the air on the southern portion of the island. Below him, the highlands descended toward a limestone plateau that formed the central and northern portions of the island. In the distance, shear cliffs dropped steeply to a narrow coastal shelf. Even from this altitude, he could make out coconut palms lining the coral beaches like a natural stockade that held at bay the island's encroaching jungle.

Sture remembered with laughter that the company had forgotten to account for the International Date Line when they planned the original *China Clipper's* arrival in Manila, forcing the crew to lay over an extra day in Guam lest they ruin the festivities. He remembered also that the ocean trenches surrounding Guam and extending southwest toward New Zealand held the graves of many of his friends. Shaking off a sadness he was surprised to feel after almost half a century, he looked toward the coast of the lush, green island emerging from the endless sea.

The ceremonies in Guam proved uneventful. The same speeches traded lips. The same gifts traded hands. Sture listened politely to the banter, applauded in all of the right places, laughed at all of the right points, but was unable to shake off the haunting reminders of those who had died in the waters of all the islands he visited.

Sture and Mildred, his wife of almost sixty years, on Midway, 1985. Sigfred collection.

For years he had told his friends and relatives grand stories of his days in aviation. Most of the stories he peppered with brave exploits and ridiculous occurrences. Some betrayed a lingering resentment toward "America's Chosen Instrument," a resentment he hoped would diminish with this trip. All of his stories encouraged the belief that at eighty-five, still young by his family's standards, he had lived a full and exciting life, had lived the American Dream. He had accomplished what too few in the world were ever able to do: to spend a portion of his life doing exactly what he chose. These things, he admitted, were true. He had few regrets, and was thankful for what he had been given. But mingling with his memories of more vibrant days were the death knolls of friends, family and coworkers he had lost.

Aviation, illness, two world wars, and old age had defeated them, as the jungles of South America and the oceans of the world had not defeated him. Sture was one of the few to survive, one of the few to have welcomed the automobile and the airplane and the computer and an endless list of other miracles. Through it all, with the grip of a man clinging to the brace wire on the exposed wing of a plane, he had clung to the fragile cloth of life. But in the air between Guam and Manila, the man who claimed to feel forever young suddenly felt the weight of his eighty-five years. In the blink of an eye, the glint of the sun upon a wave, he pondered his mortality.

Increased pressure on his ears informed him that the *China Clipper II* had commenced her descent toward Manila. Sitting upright, he noticed that his hands were white from gripping the arms of his seat. Looking around, he saw that no one noticed, and again leaned back.

The descent continued. The engines roared. And still, he clung.

After the 1597 mile flight from Guam to Manila, the passengers and crew of the *China Clipper II* faced still more celebration. They had spent over twelve hours in flight and had traveled almost six

View of Manila from the Sigfred's room in the Manila Hotel, 1985.
Sigfred collection.

thousand miles since rising that morning, but their day was almost finished. After attending a reception at the Manila Hotel where the mayor of Manila presented Acker with the key to the city, they were invited to retire for the evening. Both Sture and Mildred fell into bed, more exhausted than they could remember having been for several years.

November 25, 1985 rose sleepily, as did Sture and Mildred. With the poverty for which Manila had grown famous hidden from the weary eyes of Pan Am's pioneers, the city glistened brilliantly beneath the November sun. They took a tour of the city, and that afternoon enjoyed the first stretch of leisure they had enjoyed in several days. That evening they attended a gala dinner and show at the Manila Restaurant in the Manila Hotel he remembered from so many years before. Sture in a white jacket tuxedo and Mildred in a black floor-length floral print gown enjoyed a formal dinner of exotic, local dishes. Sated from their meal, they sat back in their chairs to watch a show featuring traditional songs and dances of the various tribes of the islands comprising the Philippine Republic. The highlight of the entertainment was a serenade by the Philippine First Lady Imelda Marcos. As the night stretched into morning, Sture shared a dance with the gracious and graceful woman who within a few years would face revolution and fall under the scrutiny of the American press. Years later he would boast of having danced with Mrs. Marcos and would tell of the shoes she wore. He would laugh, remembering a joke he had whispered that evening to Imelda, as he would forever call her after their dance.

The story he seldom told, however, for it was perhaps too dear to share with anyone who might not understand, was the brilliance of his wife's beauty as he guided her across the parquet floor of a ballroom in the Philippines. That memory was his alone, not a part of Philippine mythology or aviation culture, just a quiet moment, between a man and his wife as the Pacific sky bathed what they imagined was the entire world in a warm and comforting darkness.

Above: the streets of Manila, 1985.

Left: Sture dancing with Imelda Marcos at the Manila Hotel, 1985. Sigfred collection.

Tuesday, November 26, 1985, was filled with tours of Tagaytay, Pagsanjan Falls and Corregidor, followed by a sunset cruise on Luzon Bay. When Sture and Mildred returned to their room after a busy but relaxing day, they quietly celebrated Mildred's birthday. The next day, they departed on the return flight to San Francisco, once again celebrating Mildred's birthday when they crossed the International Date Line in the opposite direction. At San Francisco they boarded a United Airlines flight to Norfolk, via Dallas, Texas, where they were delayed for an hour by poor weather. Finally, the Sigfreds returned to their Gloucester cottage, the trip and an era finally and truly over.

Epilogue: Time and the Midday Sky

Midway Island, 1985

The afternoon sun bore down upon the island, little changed since 1941. True, sand and the sea had reclaimed the ramp where the Clipper ships had once tied up, and more grass grew in the fine coral sands of the island. True, the Pan Am Hotel was only a memory, long ago destroyed by Japanese bombs and replaced by uninteresting but utile blocks of military buildings. True, the runways were longer and smoother than they had been before the Japanese attack. The land had recovered from and repaired the scars of that Sunday morning and the battle just off the island's shores that had marked a turning point in the Pacific theater during World War II.

But in a sense, a sense that had little to do with the appearance of a new, modern terminal at the head of the airfield, or the statue of a gooney bird, or a memorial to the Battle of Midway, the island seemed very much the same. Gooney birds still lazed and frolicked in the sand. A breeze still blew calmly across the lagoon that separated Sand and Eastern Islands. And the Pacific still glistened deep blue and seemingly endless. Neither war nor time had eroded the beauty of the islands. The sun seemed to shine for Sture alone as he prepared to execute his plan.

In the shade of the terminal, the passengers and crew of the *China Clipper II* gathered and mingled with Navy personnel detached to the island. A simple wooden podium equipped with a microphone and speaker stood before a large painting showing two gooney birds supporting the island's insignia. "Welcome to the Naval Air Facility, Midway Island" the sign announced. Like the statue of a gooney bird in the island's small park, the sign dominated the exterior of the hangar that formed the terminal. At the podium stood Sture in brown slacks and camel hair jacket, his white shirt open at the collar. In his left hand he held his hat, the red feather of a fishing lure still tucked into the band. In his right, he held a clear glass float, slightly green, and no larger than his palm. To his left stood C. Edward Acker, and to his right stood the military commander of the island.

"This is a glass float I picked up forty-eight years ago, on the beach here." Sture held the bulb above his shoulder and showed it to the audience. "I think it's about time I return it to its rightful owner."

He turned to his left and handed the float to Acker, who in turn gave the float to the Navy commander. The commander nodded and thanked Sture for the float. Then Acker launched into yet another speech as Sture walked back to his seat.

The moment passed quickly, with less fanfare and pomp than had the other speeches and presentations of the last two days. But as Sture strolled past the expectant but tired faces in the audience, some of whom he remembered, most of whom he had never seen and would never see again, he was struck by the importance of his gesture. The Japanese float had washed ashore forty-eight years before, even as the Japanese had planned their attack on the Pacific Islands. The Battle of Midway had marked the point at which the Allied Powers took the upper hand in the Pacific theater and in the war overall. Though there would be setbacks after the battle, the die had already been cast.

Sture presenting a model of the China Clipper after returning the float to Midway. November, 1985. Sigfred collection.

Sture had clung to that float during the ensuing years, a symbol of the world that had been and that would follow. It was reminder - of everything it symbolized, he could not be sure - but he knew it was a reminder, at least, of something deeply important, something that had to do with a more innocent, perhaps more ignorant world in which men, like small floats of glass, could find their way safely ashore. It had to do with changes and turning points, the small quiet moments in life, that mark those changes. By giving it up, by taking his first jet flight only days before, by facing the past only miles from where the past and future mingled, he accepted what had been and what would come without question. He accepted whatever it was that the float was meant to remind him of as just a part of life, a long life well lived and enjoyed, a life of which he was deeply proud. Most important, he knew, by giving it up, he had released the cancer of his resentment for the company. Time had passed *her* judgment; he could give up the task.

Sture and Mildred strolled into the lush green park where the memorial to the Battle of Midway and the giant statue of a gooney bird towered over a lawn on which the birds still rested. Sture stopped in the grass and stared toward the sea. Squinting into the glare of sun upon water, he imagined for a moment that he could see the *China*

Clipper at anchor in the lagoon, her nose pointing toward the sky as she bobbed silently on her seawings.

Standing with his face to the sea, the wind ruffling his thin white hair, he smiled to himself, remembering a chick he had watched the day he found the float. Prodded by its mother into learning to fly, the chick had tumbled over itself before digging a hole in the sand and falling to sleep. While watching that chick, Sture had noticed the glint of the float in the waves and had retrieved the small piece of glass. Tucking it into his pocket, he had walked back to the hotel with the sun descending toward the western horizon. But there had been something else he had seen that evening. Just as he reached the tree line, with the music from the hotel drifting toward him and the sound of the surf drifting away, he turned back toward the beach and saw the chick raise its head.

Perhaps thinking itself alone at last, the chick climbed back to the top of a dune and turned into the wind. Stretching its wings out to its side, it began to run down the dune, waddling on too-short legs toward the water. As before, it tripped and tumbled across the sand, but as it neared the bottom of the dune, something miraculous occurred. The chick regained its footing, flapped its wings several times, and lifted clumsily into the air. Turning into the wind, it gained altitude, and dipping a wing it turned into the setting sun. There, in the middle of the ocean, caught between day and night, the chick flew across the sky. It soared across the sun and landed gracefully in the sand. Again, it dug a hole and curled into the sand to sleep.

And all that remained important to Sture, after forty-eight years away from this God-kissed gem on the sea, after a lifetime of hope and disappointment, a lifetime of challenge and love, all that remained important was that before sleeping, the chick had finally flown.

355

The Final Approach

1998

Near 5:00 AM on the morning of Saturday, August 8, 1998, as the eastern horizon still rested in darkness, Sture turned slowly another time in bed, trying to find a comfortable position.

"Maybe you would be more comfortable in your chair," Mildred suggested.

Sture nodded, and Mildred helped him walk across the room. He sat in his favorite recliner and stared out the window into the morning darkness, beyond which lights twinkled on the surface of the Elizabeth River like stars in nighttime flight.

Mildred retrieved a blanket from the linen closet and draped it carefully from his shoulders to his toes.

Turning his head away from the window, Sture looked up at Mildred.

"Thank you, Mom," he said simply, "for everything." His voice rose scarcely above a whisper. Then he shut his eyes as though to dream.

Appendix: Documents

Figure 1: Letter to Sture from Lt. Ralph Davison, his commanding officer on the Flight Up the Mississippi shortly after Sture left the Navy in 1923. Sigfred

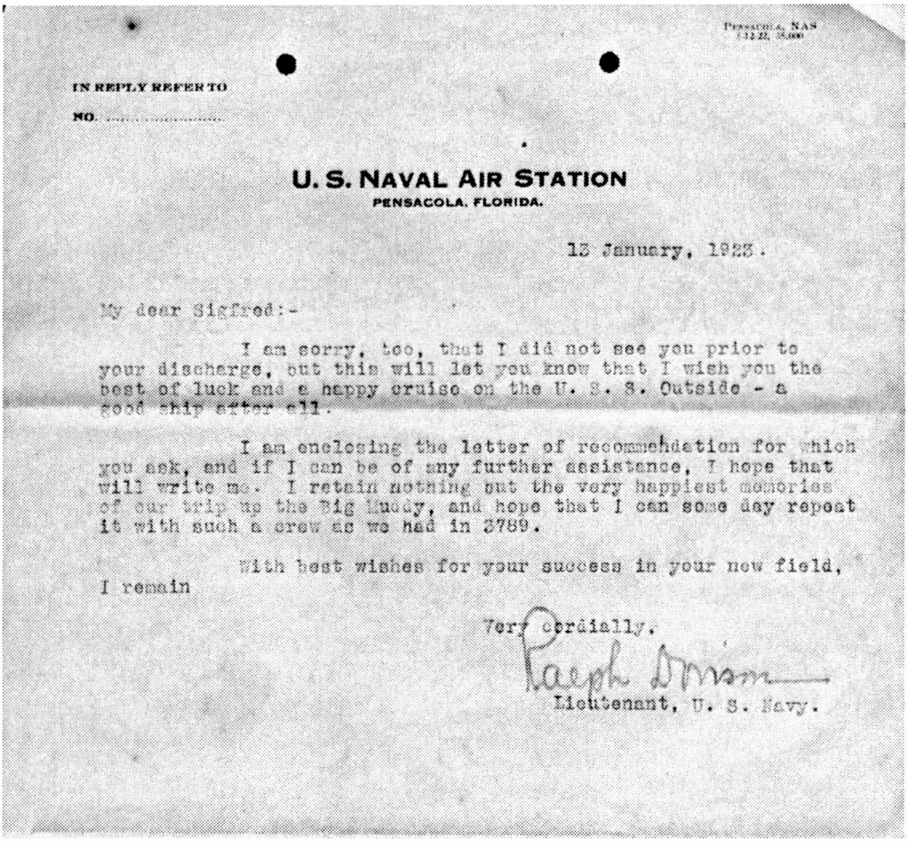

U. S. NAVAL AIR STATION
PENSACOLA, FLORIDA.

13 January, 1923.

My dear Sigfred:-

I am sorry, too, that I did not see you prior to your discharge, but this will let you know that I wish you the best of luck and a happy cruise on the U. S. S. Outside - a good ship after all.

I am enclosing the letter of recommendation for which you ask, and if I can be of any further assistance, I hope that will write me. I retain nothing but the very happiest memories of our trip up the Big Muddy, and hope that I can some day repeat it with such a crew as we had in 3789.

With best wishes for your success in your new field, I remain

Very cordially,

Ralph Davison
Lieutenant, U. S. Navy.

Figure 2: 1931 orders to assume position of Chief Mechanic at the Rio Maintenance Base. Sigfred collection.

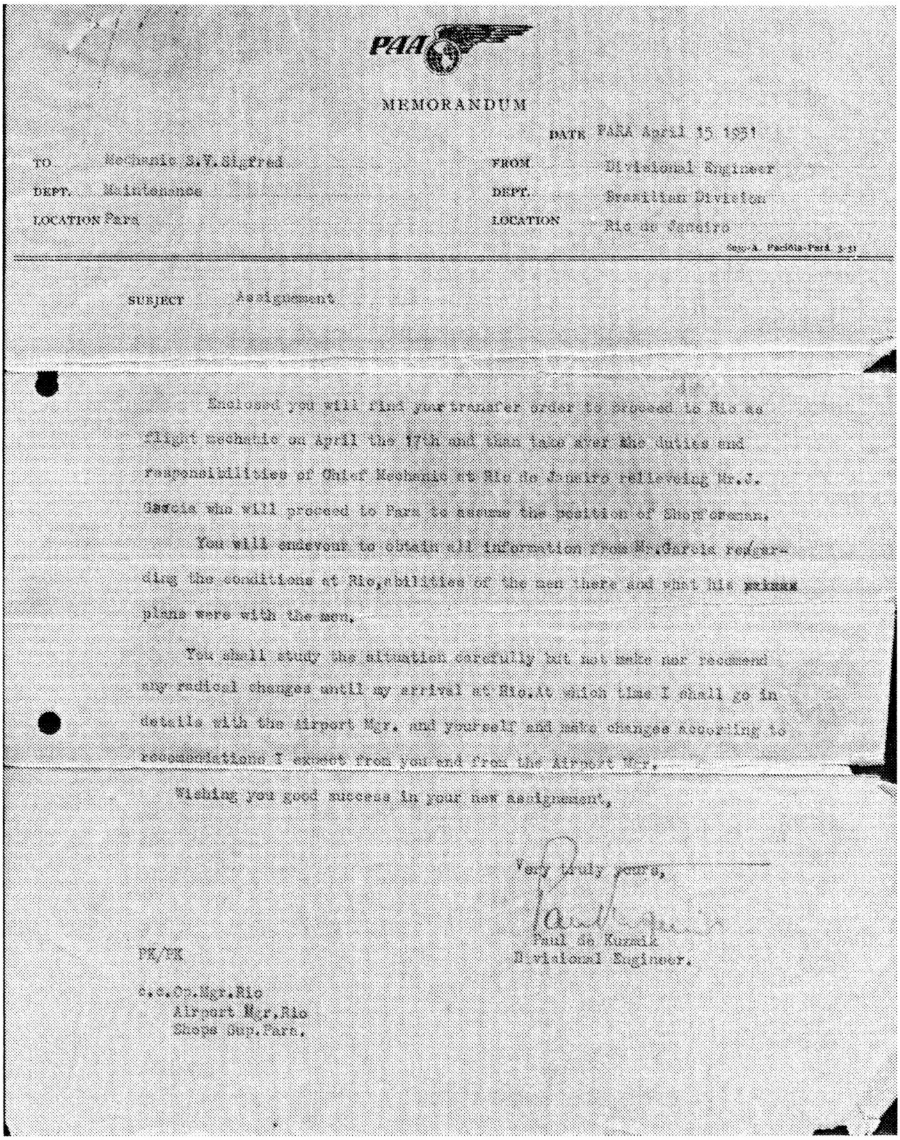

PAA

MEMORANDUM

DATE PARA April 15 1931

TO Mechanic S.V.Sigfred

DEPT. Maintenance

LOCATION Para

FROM Divisional Engineer

DEPT. Brazilian Division

LOCATION Rio de Janeiro

SUBJECT Assignement

Enclosed you will find your transfer order to proceed to Rio as flight mechanic on April the 17th and than take over the duties and responsibilities of Chief Mechanic at Rio de Janeiro relieveing Mr.J. Garcia who will proceed to Para to assume the position of Shop Foreman.

You will endevour to obtain all information from Mr.Garcia regarding the conditions at Rio,abilities of the men there and what his plans were with the men.

You shall study the situation carefully but not make nor recommend any radical changes until my arrival at Rio.At which time I shall go in details with the Airport Mgr. and yourself and make changes according to recommendations I expect from you and from the Airport Mgr.

Wishing you good success in your new assignement,

Very truly yours,

Paul de Kuzmik
Divisional Engineer.

PK/PK

c.c.Op.Mgr.Rio
Airport Mgr.Rio
Shops Sup.Para.

Figure 3: 1932 orders to Reserve Flight Mechanic, allowing Sture to serve as copilot. Sigfred collection.

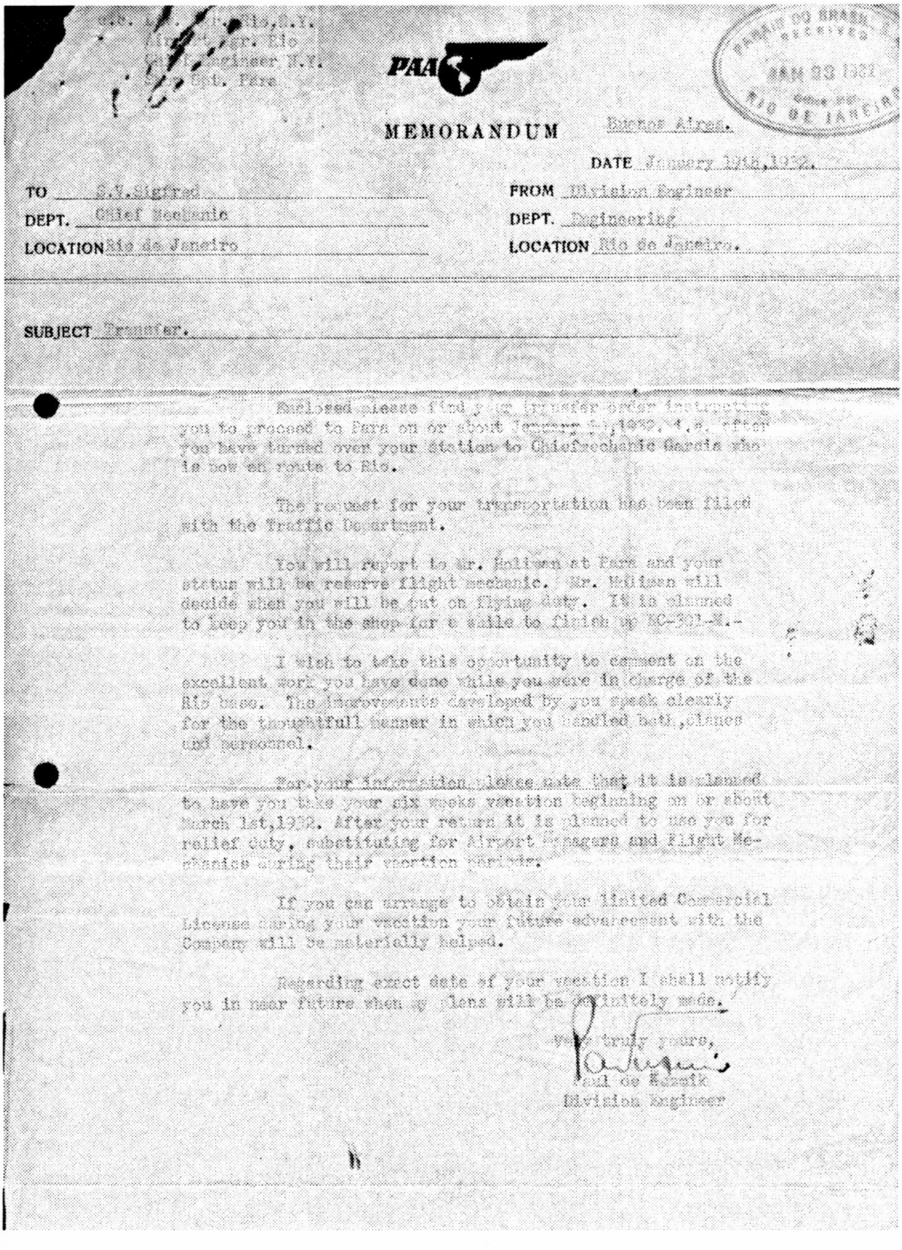

PAA

MEMORANDUM Buenos Aires.

DATE January 19th,1932.

TO S.V.Sigfred

DEPT. Chief Mechanic

LOCATION Rio de Janeiro

FROM Division Engineer

DEPT. Engineering

LOCATION Rio de Janeiro.

SUBJECT Transfer.

Enclosed please find your transfer order instructing you to proceed to Para on or about January [illegible],1932, i.e. after you have turned over your station to Chief Mechanic Garcia who is now en route to Rio.

The request for your transportation has been filed with the Traffic Department.

You will report to Mr. Holtsen at Para and your status will be reserve flight mechanic. Mr. Holtsen will decide when you will be put on flying duty. It is planned to keep you in the shop for a while to finish up NC-[illegible]-M.-

I wish to take this opportunity to comment on the excellent work you have done while you were in charge of the Rio base. The improvements developed by you speak clearly for the thoughtfull manner in which you handled both,planes and personnel.

For your information please note that it is planned to have you take your six weeks vacation beginning on or about March 1st,1932. After your return it is planned to use you for relief duty, substituting for Airport Managers and Flight Mechanics during their vacation periods.

If you can arrange to obtain your limited Commercial License during your vacation your future advancement with the Company will be materially helped.

Regarding exact date of your vacation I shall notify you in near future when my plans will be definitely made.

Very truly yours,

Paul de Ñeznik
Division Engineer

Figure 4: 1937 orders to Pacific Division. Sigfred collection.

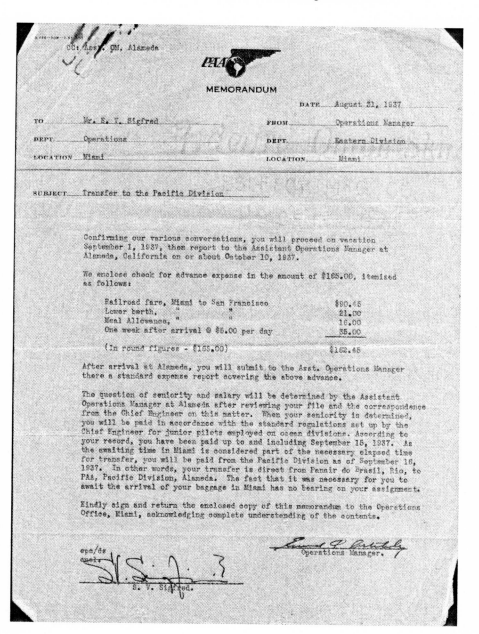

Figure 5: 1942 orders to Eastern Division. Sigfred collection.

MEMORANDUM

FOR USE BY ADDRESSEE

SEND ORIGINAL BY

DATE June 18, 1942

TO Mr. S. V. Sigfred

FROM Operations Manager

DEPT. OR DIV. Operations

DEPT. OR DIV. Transpacific Division

LOCATION Treasure Island

LOCATION Treasure Island

SUBJECT: TRANSFER ORDERS

REFERENCE:

You are hereby directed to proceed from San Francisco to Miami and to report at Miami on or about June 25, 1942. On your arrival please report to the Operations Manager, Eastern Division for assignment to duty.

We are enclosing our check for $300.00 to cover necessary expenses incidental to your transfer. Such expenses are itemized below:

Two Adult First Class Pullman fares $248.86
(San Francisco - Miami)
Per diem allowances en route for travel expenditures 40.00
Miscellaneous 11.14
TOTAL $300.00

Please obtain receipts for such expenditures as made from this advance and submit your travel expense report to the Operations Manager, Miami.

In accordance with your request, you may travel in your private automobile from San Francisco to Miami covering the cost of same with the funds as advanced above.

Your effective date of transfer will be June 15, 1942, and you will be paid salary by this Division up to and including that date. The Eastern Division will take you on their payroll as of June 16, 1942.

Please take your uniform in your hand baggage with you so as to have it available upon your arrival at Miami.

According to our records you have thirty days vacation due you.

We sincerely regret losing your services in this Division and wish you to know that you have been greatly appreciated here. We hope that your new assignment will be both enjoyable and advantageous to you.

for W J Barrows
J. H. Tilton

Enclosure

I have read and understood the above transfer orders and accept them as a satisfactory basis for this assignment in the Eastern Division.

cc:Division Manager - Eastern, Transpacific
Operations Manager - Eastern
Division Accountant - Eastern, Transpacific
Chief Pilot - Eastern, Transpacific
Flight Surgeon - Transpacific
Chief, Stores & Purchasing - Eastern, Transpacific

SHOW COPIES IN ABOVE SPACE, GIVING NAME OR TITLE, LOCATION, AND MAILING INSTRUCTIONS

Figure 6: 1943 orders to Africa-Orient Division. Sigfred collection.

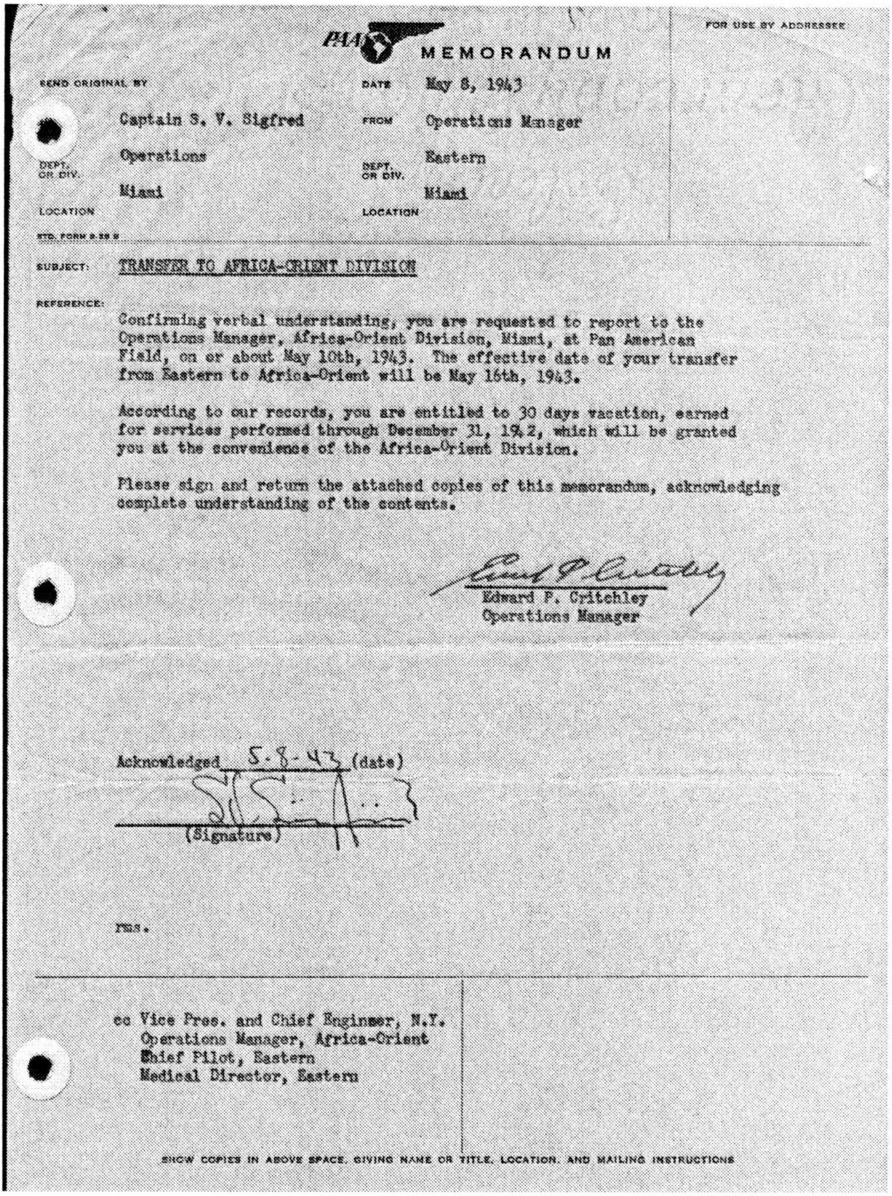

PAA MEMORANDUM

FOR USE BY ADDRESSEE

SEND ORIGINAL BY

DATE: May 8, 1943

Captain S. V. Sigfred

FROM: Operations Manager

DEPT. OR DIV.: Operations

DEPT. OR DIV.: Eastern

LOCATION: Miami

LOCATION: Miami

STD. FORM P-29-9

SUBJECT: TRANSFER TO AFRICA-ORIENT DIVISION

REFERENCE:

Confirming verbal understanding, you are requested to report to the Operations Manager, Africa-Orient Division, Miami, at Pan American Field, on or about May 10th, 1943. The effective date of your transfer from Eastern to Africa-Orient will be May 16th, 1943.

According to our records, you are entitled to 30 days vacation, earned for services performed through December 31, 1942, which will be granted you at the convenience of the Africa-Orient Division.

Please sign and return the attached copies of this memorandum, acknowledging complete understanding of the contents.

Edward P. Critchley
Operations Manager

Acknowledged 5-8-43 (date)

(Signature)

rms.

cc Vice Pres. and Chief Engineer, N.Y.
Operations Manager, Africa-Orient
Chief Pilot, Eastern
Medical Director, Eastern

SHOW COPIES IN ABOVE SPACE, GIVING NAME OR TITLE, LOCATION, AND MAILING INSTRUCTIONS

Figure 7: 1943 ATC Liberty Pass. Sigfred collection.

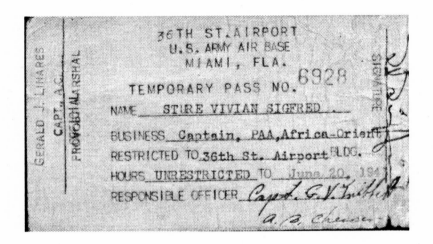

Figure 8: 1938 Department of Commerce temporary ID corresponding to Transport License. Sigfred collection.

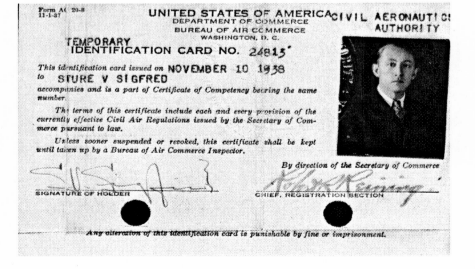

Figure 9: 1943 draft card. Sigfred collection.

NOTICE OF CLASSIFICATION

Registrant _____ Sture V. Sigfred _____ Order No. __T10059__

has been classified in Class __2B__ (Until __6/2/43__ , 19____)
by ☐ Local Board   (Insert Date for Class II-A and II-B only)
    ☐ Board of Appeal (by vote of _____ to _____)
    ☐ President

      B · W · TOMPKINS

__12/3/42__ , 19____
(Date of mailing)   *Member of Local Board.*

NOTICE OF RIGHT TO APPEAL

Appeal from classification by local board or board of appeal must be made by signing appeal form on back of questionnaire at office of local board, or by filing written notice of appeal, within ten days after the mailing of this notice. Before appeal, a registrant may file a written request for appearance within the same ten-day period; and, if he does so, the local board will fix a day and notify him to appear personally before the local board; if this is done, the time to appeal is extended to ten days beyond the day set by the local board for such appearance.

There is a right in certain dependency cases, of appeal from appeal board decision to the President; see Selective Service Regulations.

The law requires you—To keep in touch with your local board. To notify it of any change of address. To notify it of any fact which might change classification.
D. S. S. Form 57 (Rev. 4-13-42)   16—10071-1   U. S. GOVERNMENT PRINTING OFFICE

Figure 10: World War II instructions from mail censors.
Sigfred collection.

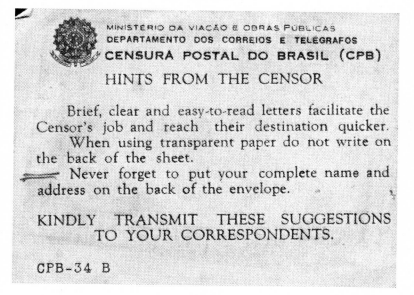

MINISTÉRIO DA VIAÇÃO E OBRAS PÚBLICAS
DEPARTAMENTO DOS CORREIOS E TELÉGRAFOS
CENSURA POSTAL DO BRASIL (CPB)

HINTS FROM THE CENSOR

Brief, clear and easy-to-read letters facilitate the Censor's job and reach their destination quicker.

When using transparent paper do not write on the back of the sheet.

Never forget to put your complete name and address on the back of the envelope.

KINDLY TRANSMIT THESE SUGGESTIONS TO YOUR CORRESPONDENTS.

CPB-34 B

Figure 11: Letter of Congratulations from Juan Trippe for fifteen years of service. 1945. Sigfred collection.

PAN AMERICAN AIRWAYS SYSTEM

GENERAL OFFICES, CHRYSLER BUILDING, 135 EAST 42ND STREET, NEW YORK 17, N.Y.

OFFICE OF THE
PRESIDENT

September 14, 1945

Mr. Sture V. Sigfred
Pan American Airways System
Miami

Dear Mr. Sigfred:

You have completed fifteen years of service with this Company and have earned the insigne which has been especially designed to indicate your years of association with us. I therefore send you this emblem—the gold lapel insigne with three five-year stars impressed on the ring.

With this letter, I also send you my personal appreciation of your loyalty to the Company it has been our privilege to serve and to express the hope that this association may continue with the forward progress of the System in years to come.

Sincerely,

Figure 12: Letter of Congratulations from Juan Trippe for twenty years of service. 1950. Sigfred collection.

PAN AMERICAN WORLD AIRWAYS SYSTEM

CHRYSLER BUILDING, 135 EAST 42ND STREET, NEW YORK 17, N. Y.

OFFICE OF THE
PRESIDENT

October 16, 1950

Captain Sture V. Sigfred
Pan American World Airways System
Miami, Florida

Dear Captain Sigfred:

Upon completion of your twentieth year of service with Pan American World Airways I am sure you feel, as I do, the deep significance of a period so long, dedicated to work so progressive, and resulting in the great achievement which is our present System.

To symbolize the Company's gratitude for your steadfast and devoted service during these twenty years, I am sending you this emblem — the gold lapel insigne especially designed for that small group who have pioneered our growth during the last fifth of a century.

With it are sent my warmest personal thanks for your loyalty, my hearty congratulations, and the strong hope that this anniversary will be for you only the latest milestone in continued progress with the Company we serve.

Sincerely,

[signature]

==

Primary Sources

Ryden, Paul M. Correspondence. June 1999: Careers of Paul M. Ryden and Captain Sture V. Sigfred.

Schroeder, Laurence A. *Petition for Writ of Certiorari to the United States Court of Appeals for the Fifth Circuit.* Sture V. Sigfred, Petitioner, vs. Pan American World Airways, Inc., Respondent. October 1955.

- - - Correspondence. 1951 - 1960: Sture V. Sigfred vs. Pan American World Airways.

Sigfred, Captain Sture V. Interviews. July 1994 – August 1998: Lifetime in aviation, especially at Pan Am.

Sigfred, Mildred. Interviews. August 1998 - June 2002: Career of Captain Sture V. Sigfred.

Secondary Sources

Anderson, Frank. *Orders of Magnitude: A History of NACA and NASA, 1915-1976*. NASA History Press: Washington D.C. 1976.

Cohen, Stan. *Pan American Clipper Planes 1935 to 1945: Wings to the Orient*. Pictorial Histories: Missoula. 1985.

Daley, Robert. *An American Saga: Juan Trippe and His Pan Am Empire*. Rand House: New York. 1980.

Davies, R.E.G. *Pan Am: An Airline and Its Aircraft*. Orion Books: New York. 1987.

Diamond Jubilee. Parkers Prairie Commercial Club: Parkers Prairie. 1978.

Gandt, Robert. L. *China Clipper*. Naval Institute Press: Annapolis. 1991.

Kenney, General George C. *The Saga of Pappy Gunn*. Duell, Sloan and Pearce: New York. 1959.

Klaás, M.D. *Last of the Flying Clippers: The Boeing B-314 Story*. Schiffer Military/Aviation History: Atglen. 1997.

Knott, Richard C. *A Heritage of Wings: An Illustrated History of Navy Aviation*. Naval Institute Press: Annapolis. 1997.

Krupnick, John E. *Pan American's Pacific Pioneers: A Pictorial History of Pan Am's Pacific First Flights 1935-1946*. Pictorial Histories: Missoula. 1997.

Levering, Robert. *The Clipper Heritage*. Inter-Collegiate Press. No city or date provided.

National Aeronautics and Space Administration. *Fifty Years of Aeronautical Research*. NASA: Washington, D.C. 1967.

O'Neill, Ralph. *A Dream of Eagles*. Houghton Mifflin: Boston. 1973.

Spenser, Jay P. *Aeronca C-2: The Story of the Flying Bathtub*. Smithsonian Institution Press: Washington D.C. 1978.

Stephens, Lynn. "From Sopwiths to Space, Sig Knows the Industry." *Miami Herald*. March 24, 1968.

About the Author

Captain Sture Sigfred Sr. was Pan American's nineteenth most senior pilot when he retired in 1950. One of the nation's "Pioneers of Aviation," Captain Sigfred amassed more than 15,000 hours of flight on five continents during his thirty-one year career. From the Navy's fledgling fleet of seaplanes to Pan Am's famous fleet of *Clippers*, his career paralleled the "Golden Age of Aviation" and serves as a testament to the power of dreams.

Eugene McAvoy holds an MFA in Creative Writing from Old Dominion University. His fiction, nonfiction and poetry have appeared in several publications, including *Rebel Yell II, HGMFQ*, and the *Virginian-Pilot*. He teaches at Old Dominion University, and lives in Virginia, where he is working on his first novel.

Printed in the United States
27260LVS00001B/2

9 781403 387363